Clothing in 17th-Century Provincial England

Clothing in 17th-Century Provincial England

Danae Tankard

BLOOMSBURY ACADEMIC
LONDON • NEW YORK • OXFORD • NEW DELHI • SYDNEY

BLOOMSBURY VISUAL ARTS
Bloomsbury Publishing Plc
50 Bedford Square, London, WC1B 3DP, UK
1385 Broadway, New York, NY 10018, USA
29 Earlsfort Terrace, Dublin 2, Ireland

BLOOMSBURY, BLOOMSBURY VISUAL ARTS and the Diana logo are trademarks of
Bloomsbury Publishing Plc

First published in Great Britain 2020
This paperback edition published in 2021

Copyright © Danae Tankard, 2020

Danae Tankard has asserted her right under the Copyright, Designs and Patents Act, 1988, to be identified as Author of this work.

For legal purposes the Acknowledgements on pp. ix-x constitute an extension of this copyright page.

Cover design: Charlotte Daniels
Cover image: Portrait of Arthur, 3rd Viscount Irwin, 1700 (oil on canvas), by Leonard Knyff (1650–1721). (© Leeds Museums and Art Galleries, Temple Newsam House, UK/Bridgeman Images)

All rights reserved. No part of this publication may be reproduced or transmitted in any form or by any means, electronic or mechanical, including photocopying, recording, or any information storage or retrieval system, without prior permission in writing from the publishers.

Bloomsbury Publishing Plc does not have any control over, or responsibility for, any third-party websites referred to or in this book. All internet addresses given in this book were correct at the time of going to press. The author and publisher regret any inconvenience caused if addresses have changed or sites have ceased to exist, but can accept no responsibility for any such changes.

A catalogue record for this book is available from the British Library.

A catalog record for this book is available from the Library of Congress.

ISBN: HB: 978-1-350-09840-4
       PB: 978-1-350-22758-3
       ePDF: 978-1-350-09842-8
       eBook: 978-1-350-09841-1

Typeset by RefineCatch Limited, Bungay, Suffolk

To find out more about our authors and books visit www.bloomsbury.com and sign up for our newsletters.

Contents

List of Illustrations	vi
Acknowledgements	ix
List of Abbreviations	xi
1 Introduction	1
2 Literary Constructions of Clothing, the Individual and Society	23
3 Clothing and Textile Production, Distribution and Acquisition	47
4 London and the Provincial Consumer	73
5 The Clothing of Provincial Gentlemen	99
6 The Clothing of Provincial Gentlewomen	129
7 The Clothing of the Poor	157
Conclusion	181
Notes	189
Bibliography	237
Index	257

List of Illustrations

1.1	Map of southern England, showing location of Sussex and its principal towns.	3
1.2	Map of Sussex, showing location of market towns and places of residence of men and women featuring in case studies.	19
1.3	John Speed's map of Chichester, 1610.	20
2.1	Wenceslaus Hollar, Adam ploughing from 'The Dance of Death', 1651.	24
2.2	London-made silver snuff box with 'bawdy' picture, c. 1680.	32
2.3	Marcellus Laroon, London courtesan from his series 'The Cries of the City of London', 1688.	33
2.4	Woodcut of a country man from 'Downright Dick of the West', 1685–8.	44
3.1	Trade token of Edward Waters of Horsted Keynes, tailor, 1668.	52
3.2	Extract from probate inventory of Michael Woodgate of Horsham, mercer, 1679.	59
3.3	Trade token of Edmund Middleton of Lewes, haberdasher, 1666.	62
3.4	Pedlar with his pack from 'Sorrowful Lamentation of the Pedlars and Petty Chapmen for the Hardness of the Times and the Decay of Trade', 1685–8.	64
3.5	Marcellus Laroon, second-hand clothes seller from his series 'The Cries of the City of London', 1688.	66
3.6	Extract from probate inventory of Edward Napper of Chichester, cordwainer, 1623.	70
4.1	Print of Mercers' Hall, showing row of shops on the ground floor, 1680.	77
4.2	Wenceslaus Hollar, Interior View of the Royal Exchange, 1647.	78
4.3	Trade card of Thomas Jacomb, glove seller, c. 1700.	80
4.4	Page from Giles Moore's account book, showing entries for 1656–9.	86
4.5	Wenceslaus Hollar, The Winter Habit of an English Gentlewoman, 1644.	89
4.6	Letter sent by James Gresham to Judith Morley, January 1641.	92

List of Illustrations vii

5.1	Short doublet and petticoat breeches made in England or France, 1660.	102
5.2	Brown worsted coat and breeches, *c.* 1680, shown with brown worsted cloak, *c.* 1670.	105
5.3	Jean Dieu de Saint Jean, 'Homme de Qualité en Habit d'Hiver', 1678.	106
5.4	Leonard Knyff, Portrait of Arthur Ingram, 3rd Viscount Irwin, 1700.	108
5.5	Unknown artist, Edward Sparke (d. 1693), vicar of Tottenham and chaplain to Charles II, wearing skull cap, bands and gown, 1666.	111
5.6	Silver tobacco box engraved with coat of arms, made in London possibly by Caleb Westbrooke, 1691–2.	115
5.7	'Lord Clapham', one of a pair of fashion dolls, *c.* 1690.	117
5.8	Letter from James Wightman to Samuel Jeake, undated, probably April 1681.	121
5.9	Pages from Richard Stapley's memorandum book, 1684–5.	123
5.10	Calendar watch made by Benjamin Hill, 1650–1660.	125
6.1	Ivory satin bodice trimmed with bobbin lace with parchment and coloured silk, stiffened with whalebone, 1660–9.	131
6.2	'Lady Clapham', one of a pair of fashion dolls, *c.* 1690.	133
6.3	Tin-glazed earthenware dish, 'The À-la-mode Dress or the Maiden's Mode Admired and Continued by the Ape, Owl and Mistress Puss', 1688.	134
6.4	Cornelius Johnson, Portrait of Lady Coventry, *c.* 1635.	141
6.5	Wenceslaus Hollar, Still life with muffs, gloves, fans, mask and kerchiefs, 1647.	142
6.6	Wenceslaus Hollar, Portrait of a young woman, showing the fashionable hairstyle of the 1640s, 1642.	143
6.7	Peter Lely, Portrait of a young woman, *c.* 1662–3.	148
6.8	Nicolas Arnoult, 'The Iron Age' from his series 'The Four Ages of Man', *c.* 1690.	151
6.9	Letter from Samuel Jeake to Elizabeth Jeake, 1699.	153
7.1	Jacques Callot, Beggars, 1630.	158
7.2	Jacques Callot, Marching gypsies, 1621–31.	161
7.3	Charles Beale, Portrait of an elderly woman, possibly a household servant, 1680.	164
7.4	Randle Holme's original drawings of working men for his *Academy of Armory* (Chester, 1688).	166

7.5 Cowfold overseers' account for the cost of clothing Jonathan Mote, 1642. 172
7.6 Edward Barlow's drawing of himself leaving home aged fourteen, 1673. 174

Acknowledgements

I would like to thank the staff at the West Sussex Record Office, the Surrey History Centre and the East Sussex Record Office where the majority of the research for this book was undertaken. Especial thanks are due to Christopher Whittick, County Archivist at the East Sussex Record Office, for answering many of my queries about early modern records and Sussex people. I would also like to thank Sarah Cooper and Linden Thomas at the Rye Castle Museum for giving me access to the museum's extensive Jeake archive. Robin Eagles, Editor of the House of Lords section (1660–1832) at the History of Parliament Trust, offered useful advice on parliamentary procedure in relation to my discussion of sumptuary legislation in Chapter Two. Vanessa Harding, Professor of London History at Birkbeck, University of London, kindly read and commented on a draft of Chapter Four. Sir George White Bt, Consultant Keeper of the Clockmakers' Museum, and Laura Turner, Curator of Horological Collections at the British Museum, provided advice on seventeenth-century watches and watchmakers, James Wightman and Benjamin Hill. Thanks also to Kim Sloan, Curator of British Drawings and Watercolours at the British Museum, and Diana Dethloff, Senior Teaching Fellow at University College London, for advice on the dating of the Peter Lely drawing used in Chapter Six. My colleague at the University of Chichester, Dan Carline, kindly prepared the maps used in Chapter One. I am extremely grateful to Valerie Cumming, dress historian and editor of *Costume*, for reading through and commenting on Chapters Four and Five and for helping me with a number of queries relating to seventeenth-century clothing. Valerie also provided invaluable advice about the portrait of Lady Elizabeth Coventry and the Peter Lely drawing of a young woman, both used in Chapter Six. Others who have provided information or advice during the course of my research or whilst preparing the book for publication include David Cleverly, Tim McCann, Barbara Painter and Jonathan Spangler. I am grateful for the financial contribution made by the University of Chichester towards the costs of buying images and to the Sussex Archaeological Society for giving me a Margary Research Grant to pay for the book's index. I would also like to thank the editors and publishers of the following journals for permission to re-use some of the content of articles previously published with them: *Costume* (Edinburgh University Press), *Rural*

History (Cambridge University Press), *Cultural and Social History* and *Textile History* (Taylor and Francis Group). Last but not least, I would like to thank my partner, Hugo Frey, Professor of Cultural and Visual History and Director of the Institute of Arts and Humanities at the University of Chichester, for his constant support and encouragement.

List of Abbreviations

BL	The British Library
Diary	Michael Hunter and Annabel Gregory (eds.), *An Astrological Diary of the Seventeenth Century: Samuel Jeake of Rye 1652–1699* (Oxford: Clarendon Press, 1988)
ESRO	East Sussex Record Office
'Journal'	Ruth Bird (ed.), 'The Journal of Giles Moore', *Sussex Record Society* 68 (1971)
MC	Magdalene College, Cambridge
NLS	National Library of Scotland
RCM	Rye Castle Museum
SAC	Sussex Archaeological Collections
SHC	Surrey History Centre
SRS	Sussex Record Society
TNA	The National Archives
WSRO	West Sussex Record Office

1

Introduction

In 1646 Mary Watts was indicted in the court of quarter sessions sitting at Petworth in Sussex for the alleged theft of a silver bowl. Giving evidence against her, Henry Cox of Worth told the court that when he had seen her two weeks before at the Warnham iron furnace she had been 'in very mean clothes' but that now she was 'in a habit not fit for a woman of her quality to wear'.[1] Cox presented Mary's sartorial transformation to the court as clear evidence of her guilt: she was wearing clothes that she could not have afforded by any honest means. But his succinct statement also contained within it a value judgement about what a woman of her status ought to be wearing. 'Very mean clothes' were appropriate to her status; those she had been wearing on his last encounter with her were not, reflecting a widely held view that clothing should reflect the social status of its wearer. In her statement to the court Mary denied the theft but made no reference to her clothing. However, if we take Cox's statement as true it suggests that clothing was important to her; she did not want to wear 'mean' clothes and as soon as she had the chance she exchanged them for some that were better. The disparity between her appearance and her social status was no doubt less important to her than the way her new clothes made her feel.

This case serves as a useful introduction to a book that sets out to examine in broad terms the clothing culture of seventeenth-century Sussex. Like Mary Watts, many of those who appear in subsequent chapters were poor, part of that large and diverse group that contemporaries described as the 'poorer' or the 'meaner' sort.[2] Their role in this narrative of clothing is usually brief, short walk-on parts, reflecting their brief appearance in contemporary records. More substantial roles are provided for a small number of individuals belonging to the 'middle' or the 'better' sort, including a clergyman and his niece, an urban merchant and his wife and an established middle gentry family, who have left behind them more extensive archives.[3] Collectively, these archival legacies have been used to explore a number of interrelated subjects: local clothing markets and individuals' involvement with them as producers and consumers; the role of

London as a centre of consumption and its significance to the provincial consumer; what more affluent men and women were wearing and how their sartorial choices reflected contemporary fashion trends; and the clothing of the poor and the challenges they faced in maintaining socially acceptable standards of sartorial decency. In addition, this book addresses more complex and nebulous questions about the relationship between the individual and his or her clothes and how these reflected, or were shaped by, his or her social and material milieu. Here broader contemporary cultural understandings are important, and these have been surveyed using a wide range of literary sources. Central to contemporary ideas about clothing was the belief that it should reinforce established and stable social hierarchies. Allied to this were a range of well-articulated views about clothing, gender, age and marital status. Seventeenth-century English society also had an uncomfortable and often ambivalent relationship with consumption; excessive consumption, particularly of foreign goods, was viewed as corrupting to the individual and damaging to the nation's economic wellbeing.[4] Clothing, therefore, carried with it entrenched societal values, some positive, many that were negative, which undoubtedly shaped men's and women's relationship with their own clothing and provided the cultural spectrum through which they viewed that of others. As significant, or possibly more significant, however, were the personal circumstances and character of the wearer; male or female, young or old, urban or rural, rich or poor, conservative or progressive, fashion-conscious or fashion-averse, thrifty or spendthrift. These factors are considered here through a series of case studies that analyse men's and women's sartorial behaviour in the context of their individual biographies.

Inevitably a book that examines individuals' sartorial choices is also about consumer behaviour.[5] Reference has already been made to ambivalent contemporary attitudes to consumption. A close reading of a range of seventeenth-century literature also reveals a surprisingly complex set of ideas about the collective and individual drivers of consumer behaviour. Many of these were based around ideas of emulation – a desire by the 'meaner' sort to ape their betters.[6] But contemporary writers, like today's historians of consumption, also offered a range of other explanations for why men and women consumed as they did.[7] Consumer choice is of course contingent on the individual having the financial means and personal freedom to exercise it. The poorest and the youngest members of seventeenth-century society had little or no consumer choice at all; they were, in the words of John Styles, 'involuntary consumers', dependent on others for their clothes.[8] Nevertheless,

Figure 1.1 Map of southern England, showing location of Sussex and its principal towns.

whilst opportunities for sartorial display amongst the poor may have been highly circumscribed, this did not mean that they were indifferent to their appearance, as the case of Mary Watts suggests. Women's dependent status and narrower spheres of activity could also place significant constraints on their consumer choice.

The exercise of consumer choice is also reliant on there being a range of consumer goods to choose from in the first place. This volume, therefore, is intended as a contribution to the study of early modern shopping. Historians of consumption have differentiated the activity of 'shopping' from the activity of 'purchasing' – the former being defined as a 'social and leisure activity, largely of rich women, in which the actual buying of goods was not of primary importance'; the latter an entirely functional transaction.[9] 'Shopping' is associated with the purchase of non-essential and luxury goods; 'purchasing' with the purchase of essential and utilitarian goods. Until recently historians had argued that shopping was a development of the eighteenth century, associated with the so-called consumer revolution and the advent of the glass-fronted, well-lit 'modern' shop. Before that time, it was thought, retail circuits and outlets were simply too poorly developed to allow for anything other than purchasing. However, Nancy Cox, Karin Dannehl, Claire Walsh and Linda Levy Peck have all presented evidence for shopping in seventeenth-century England and have highlighted the increased range of goods that were available to buy.[10] Moreover, a collection of essays about retail circuits and practices in medieval and early modern Europe demonstrates that shopping was a familiar activity in Europe well before this time.[11]

In part, the relative neglect of the experience of shopping in the seventeenth century is down to lack of coherent evidence. As Cox and Dannehl point out, there is little pictorial evidence of seventeenth-century shopping streets and whilst evidence of shop stock is available from shopkeepers' probate inventories, we know very little about what shop interiors looked like.[12] However, it is also a limitation of the definition itself which has viewed shopping as an activity that can only take place in a shop. In fact, as Cox and Dannehl have argued, shopping could take place in a variety of locations. Moreover, many men shopped with as much energy and enthusiasm as women, challenging the somewhat pejorative historical view that shopping was largely a female activity.[13]

Studying seventeenth-century clothing

Until recently little attention has been paid to the clothing of the non-elite in seventeenth-century England, reflecting what was perceived to be a lack of source material, whether archival, pictorial, or in the form of surviving garments. This perception no doubt explains why the only substantial studies of seventeenth-century clothing had been of the elite for whom source material is relatively plentiful.[14] One study that does address the non-elite clothing market and to an extent what ordinary men and women were wearing in the seventeenth century is Margaret Spufford's *The Great Reclothing of Rural England*, although its primary focus is the role of itinerant traders.[15] The eighteenth century, by contrast, is better served. Nearly forty years ago Anne Buck included a chapter on the clothing of 'the common people' in *Dress in Eighteenth-Century England*, and more recently John Styles examined the clothing of 'plebeian' men and women in *The Dress of the People: Everyday Fashion in Eighteenth-century England*.[16] A significant attempt to fill the void for the seventeenth century has been made by the late Margaret Spufford and Susan Mee in their recently published study, *The Clothing of the Common Sort 1570–1700*, which draws on a substantial database of clothing and textile references found in probate and overseers' accounts to look at what children and young adults of the 'common sort' were wearing. Using these and a range of other sources the authors also explore the production, distribution and acquisition of clothing during this period.[17]

As Spufford and Mee have proved, it is possible to reconstruct the clothing culture of the non-elite for the seventeenth century. Whilst the limitations on the availability of pictorial and artefactual material are undisputed, there is in reality a vast body of documentary material available.[18] One especially rich source for this study has been the records of the Sussex courts of quarter sessions. Sussex was unique in having separate quarter sessions for the eastern and western divisions, which effectively acted as two independent benches. This meant that it had seven rather than four annual meetings. The county is also unusual (although not unique) in having an almost complete survival of seventeenth-century material, including depositions taken from alleged perpetrators, victims and witnesses that are included in the session rolls.[19] Evidence relating to cases of clothing and textile thefts recorded in some of these depositions reveal complex and often conflicting narratives about clothing, including its appearance, ownership and provenance. The overwhelming majority of those appearing in the session rolls as victims and perpetrators were poor; some were completely destitute, others were poor but economically independent husbandmen and craftsmen.[20] There is also some good, and underexploited, evidence for clothing amongst the records of coroners' inquests into felonious suicide; the goods and chattels of those judged to have committed self-murder or *felo de se* were forfeited to the crown and therefore had to be inventoried by local officials.[21] Another underused source is church court depositions, although evidence relating to clothing in them is sparse and where it does occur it is typically piecemeal and anecdotal.[22]

The usefulness of probate material – wills, inventories and accounts – to a study of non-elite clothing, its production and acquisition is better known. Each type of probate document, however, comes with its own limitations.[23] As Margaret Spufford noted, wills are 'slow to mine': vast numbers survive but relatively few contain clothing bequests.[24] Moreover, clothing bequests are more common in the wills of women (usually widows) than in those of men; whilst women sometimes bequeathed male clothing it was mostly their own clothing that was recorded.[25] Seventeenth-century probate inventories can be extremely informative about those involved in clothing and textile production and distribution: weavers, tailors, shoemakers and mercers for example. However, they seldom record clothing in any detail; anyone who has used them as a source will be familiar with the standard opening line, '*Imprimis* his wearing apparel and money in his purse', or variations of the same.[26] Probate accounts, which have been used extensively by Margaret Spufford and Susan Mee, list all disbursements out of the deceased's estate, including the cost of maintaining minor children, during a period specified by the probate court after the grant of probate had been made.[27] The obvious limitation in using these accounts to study clothing culture more broadly is that they only include clothing provided to dependent children. Moreover, the age of the children is seldom recorded in the accounts and it can be difficult to identify which child a purchase had been made for or when the purchase was made.[28]

Overseers' accounts detailing expenditure on the parish poor have been used to examine the clothing of the rural and urban poor in the eighteenth and early nineteenth centuries, but there have been few equivalent studies for the seventeenth century.[29] In his magisterial study of the operation of the poor law in rural England, *On the Parish*, Steve Hindle offered only one paragraph on the provision of pauper clothing.[30] Overseers' accounts can of course be problematic: there is patchy survival for the seventeenth century and where they do survive they are often incomplete and scrappy. Moreover, as Hindle notes, 'the inconsistencies of accounting practices, sometimes identifying specified items of clothing to be provided for a particular named claimant, sometimes subsuming expenditure on clothing under quarterly bills paid to tradesmen, make it extremely difficult to calculate how much clothing an individual might receive from the overseers either as occasional relief or during a pension career.'[31] But, where coherent sets of accounts survive, they record the cloth, clothing and accessories provided to individual paupers in considerable detail and reveal the overseers' clothing policies and often their production and supply networks.[32]

Collectively these sources provide considerable evidence about what poor and middling men, women and children living in provincial England were wearing in the seventeenth century as well as revealing much about how clothing and textiles were produced, distributed and acquired. Moving up the social scale to wealthy provincial merchants and the lesser and middle gentry, other sources present themselves, including personal correspondence, household and personal accounts, diaries and memorandum books. The discussion that follows in subsequent chapters relies heavily on a number of detailed case studies of men and women living in Sussex in the seventeenth century for whom some of these sources survive. The subjects of these case studies, and the sources they have left behind, are introduced below.

Case studies

Judith Morley (1583–1660)

Amongst the Gresham family archive are approximately fifty letters sent by James Gresham from London to his mother, Judith Morley, who from 1639 to around 1643 was living in Chichester. In these, James responds to his mother's shopping requests, many of which were for items of clothing and clothing accessories.[33] There are also two tailors' or mercers' bills for clothing and other items supplied to Judith during this period.[34] From these sources it has been possible to investigate what Judith was wearing and the challenges James faced as her proxy shopper. With one exception, Judith's letters to James do not survive.[35] Judith was the daughter of Sir William Garrard of Dorney in Buckinghamshire (d. 1607) and his wife, Elizabeth.[36] She married Thomas Gresham in 1605 with whom she had two sons, John Gresham (1610–1643) and James Gresham (c. 1617–1689). At the time of his death in July 1620 Thomas Gresham owned two properties and about 600 acres of land in Lincolnshire, and a house and about twenty-seven acres of land in Fulham, Middlesex. Under the terms of his will Judith was appointed sole executrix and legal guardian to nine-year-old John, Gresham's principal heir.[37] The Lincolnshire properties were leased out and it was the rents from these leases that provided the majority of the family's income. However, legal disputes with the various tenants embroiled them in extensive, and expensive, court cases which reduced their income. Added to these problems were ongoing difficulties in securing rent payments when they became due. As a result, the Gresham income was erratic and unstable.[38]

After her husband's death Judith was courted by other men, including Thomas Fitch who in an undated letter declared himself to be 'overwhelmingly in love' with her.[39] However, she turned them down and remained a widow until 1639. In April of that year she married a Chichester resident, William Morley, in the parish of St Giles in the Fields in London. She travelled down to Chichester in the summer and took up residence at a 'Mr William's House', which may have been in West Street.[40] Morley, who had already buried two wives, was the younger brother of Sir John Morley (1572–1622) of Halnaker, MP for New Shoreham and Chichester, and the uncle of Sir John Morley (d. 1654), one of the leaders of the Royalist faction that took control of the city in November 1642 shortly after the start of the English Civil War.[41] From the outset the marriage was a disaster. In August 1639 James wrote to his mother seeking news of her new husband and hoping that he might have amended his behaviour.[42] However, in November after an unsuccessful meeting with him James wrote to Judith telling her that his new stepfather's intentions were dishonest. Not only was he already seeking to break the terms of her first husband's will but as yet he had not settled the £500 on her that he had promised at the time of their marriage.[43] In her sole surviving letter to him, dated 18 December 1639, Judith wrote to James referring to her husband obliquely as 'him that is always more welcome away than present' and implying that she was living in fear of his 'strange combustions'. Moreover, he had given her no money and she had been forced to borrow some to pay for her letters.[44] Morley's death the following year no doubt came as a great relief to Judith and her immediate family; in September 1641 her brother, George Garrard, wrote to her saying that he had heard that she was much happier now she was rid of her 'Great Gundy Husband'.[45] Unsurprisingly, she never remarried. She continued to live in Chichester for the next few years and was there when the city was besieged by Parliamentary forces for seven days in December 1642.[46] By 1646 she was living in Compton in Surrey, possibly with James, and had reverted to her former married name of Gresham.[47]

Judith had a close and affectionate relationship with her younger son, James. In contrast, her relationship with her elder son appears to have been strained. Although retaining legal possession of the family's estates during her lifetime, once he had reached his majority their management largely fell to John. Both mother and younger son thought that he did a poor job and blamed him for their impecuniousness; James in particular seems to have had ongoing difficulties securing the £40 annuity payable to him under the terms of his father's will. In her letter of 18 December 1639 Judith complained to James that John had 'undone' them both. Her animosity towards him may also have been related to his lifestyle; in the same letter she said that there was little point challenging him about his behaviour because 'God is gone from him'.[48] James too appears to have disliked his brother and clearly thought he was a poor parent to his two motherless children, Thomas and Judith. In a letter to his mother dated 17 October 1640 he told her that his nephew and niece were in good health but 'they only lack a good father that would spend his money so idly and let his children lack not only breeding but clothes on their back'.[49] He also wrote a vitriolic assessment of his brother's new 'mistress', Katherine Williams, in January 1641, describing her (amongst other things) as little better than a whore and having a 'horse-like' face and poor standards of personal hygiene.[50] John died of smallpox in May 1643.[51]

There is no evidence of Judith's political views but she is likely to have been a committed Royalist like her son. She was also, like James, an Anglican.[52] Her surviving letter to him and her two wills show her to be a pious and moralistic woman.[53] In 1641 James married Ann More, daughter of Sir Robert More of Loseley in Surrey, with whom he had three daughters, Anne, Fines and Elizabeth. By 1650 he was living in Haslemere where he remained for the rest of his life. Here he was involved with 'dubious' electioneering activities; his election to the Haslemere seat in 1661 was overturned after three days; in 1679 he was elected again but lost his seat a few months later. He had an extensive library of books, both printed and manuscript, and was, according to the antiquarian John Aubrey, 'a lover of antiquities'.[54]

Giles Moore (1617–1679)

A major source in this monograph is the household and personal account book or 'journal' of Giles Moore which covers the period 1656 to 1679 when he was rector of the mid-Sussex parish of Horsted Keynes.[55] The manuscript in which the account book is included contains 475 pages of which 377 were used. It is divided into two parts: part one is a detailed record of tithe accounts; part two records household and personal expenditure, including his own clothing and that of his niece, Martha. These accounts are organised by types of expenditure, for example, 'Linen', 'Dairy', 'Servants' wages', 'Books', 'Hats', 'Stockings', 'Gardener', 'Taxes', rather than chronologically; entries under individual headings are, however, recorded chronologically. The first seven pages of part one and the whole of part two were edited by Ruth Bird and published by the Sussex Record Society in 1971 under the title 'The Journal of Giles Moore'.[56]

Moore, the eldest son of a minor Suffolk gentleman, was a graduate of Caius College, Cambridge. He was ordained in 1641 and may have served as a chaplain in the Royalist army during the civil war.[57] He became rector of Horsted Keynes in 1656 where he remained until his death in 1679.[58] Moore's wife, Susan, was an affluent widow with two adult sons.[59] Their marriage may not have been a happy one: a note in his book written in Latin in June 1656 records that there can be 'no peace at home with such a wife' and compares her 'domination' to that of the 'despot' Oliver Cromwell.[60] Susan must have accounted for her own personal expenditure since it is not included in Moore's book.[61] They had no children of their own, but in 1667 they took into their house Giles's young niece, Martha (c. 1655–1727), the daughter of his sister, Susan Mayhew, of Beyton in Suffolk. She stayed with the Moores until 1673 when she married John Citizen, rector of

Streat. Moore meticulously records his expenditure on Martha during the six years and three months she lived with him. Susan died around 20 September 1679 and Giles died around 1 October 1679, the proximity of their deaths suggesting that they may have been caused by some kind of virulent infection like typhus or smallpox.[62]

Moore's status in society was determined by his clerical profession and by his membership of the lesser gentry. As the incumbent of Horsted Keynes he derived his income from a combination of tithe (worth about £130 a year), his fifty-acre glebe land and fees for Easter offerings, baptisms, marriages and burials.[63] On its own, this would have given Moore a modest but comfortable income of perhaps £200 a year. However, Susan also had an annuity from her dead husband's estate and there may have been other sources of income that Moore's book does not disclose.[64] In 1673, shortly after the marriage of Martha to John Citizen, Moore recorded in his book that he was 'worth not above £840 in monies, besides my library and household stuff and the stock in and without doors'.[65] The money legacies in his will (made in 1673 and not altered before his death) amounted to £816 and his probate inventory, dated 14 October 1679, recorded the total value of his moveable estate as £1678 15s.[66] Within his parish he would undoubtedly have been regarded as one of the 'better' or 'best' sort; within the county of Sussex as a whole with its substantial gentry and aristocratic families he would perhaps have been more 'middling'.

Moore reveals much about himself through the expenditure he details as well as through the occasional comment he makes about it. As we shall see in Chapters Three and Four, he was an enthusiastic shopper with a penchant for shopping in London. An avid reader, part of London's appeal for him may have been the opportunity to visit the bookshops around St Paul's Cathedral. Most of the books he purchased were works on theology or church governance; amongst other book purchases were martyrologies on the life and death of Charles I and conduct books including Henry Peacham's bestseller, *The Complete Gentleman*, first published in 1622, and *The Ladies Calling* (1673), attributed to Richard Allestree.[67] Moore was interested in the wider world, purchasing books on the history of Portugal and New England and a number of maps.[68] He appears to have had no taste for popular literature and his purchase of Thomas Shadwell's new comedy, *Epsom Wells*, in 1673 stands out as something of an oddity.[69]

At the front and the back of the manuscript are a number of Latin passages which reveal Moore's Royalist sympathies and his hatred for the Cromwellian regime.[70] For example, in October 1656 he observed, 'I can scarcely believe that this regime will be long lasting for God is just and does not allow evil men to keep for long what they obtained by force and by deceit … What is acquired by foul means by foul means will pass out of the hands of those who acquired it'.⁷¹ We have already seen that he compared the domestic rule of his wife to the tyrannical rule of Cromwell. These, together with occasional comments interspersed through his accounts, also suggest a man with an austere temperament who judged himself as harshly as he judged others. In a Latin passage written at the end of the manuscript he compared his assiduous financial accounting with what he saw as a failure to carry out a similarly rigorous moral accounting, lamenting: 'Oh, if I had kept such a strict daily record of my sins as I have of my continual outgoings and expenses, or [if I had recorded] the free and generous gifts of [my] gracious God to me as much as the trifles which others have given me sparingly!'.⁷² A careful analysis of Moore's book in its entirety reveals him to have been a conservative, moral and highly erudite man, cautious with money but also enjoying the finer things in life, with an efficient and business-like approach to managing his parish.

Samuel Jeake (1652–1699) and Elizabeth Jeake (1667–1736)

Samuel Jeake the younger was born in Rye in 1652. His mother, Frances (b. 1630), died of smallpox in 1654, a week after giving birth to Jeake's sister, Frances, born alive but dead the same day. His younger brother, Thomas, born in 1653, died in 1656. Thereafter he lived alone with his father, Samuel Jeake the elder (1623–1690), a prominent Rye nonconformist, town clerk and lawyer, until 1680 when both men moved into the house of his future mother-in-law, Barbara Hartshorne (1630–1708) and fiancée, Elizabeth, in Middle Street.⁷³ Jeake the younger died on 22 November 1699, survived by his wife and three children, Elizabeth (b. 1684), Barbara (b. 1695) and Samuel (b. 1697). A fourth child, Francis, was born five months after his death.⁷⁴ His widow Elizabeth married Rye gentleman, Joseph Tucker, in 1703 and went on to have a further two children, Philadelphia and Joseph.⁷⁵

To the extent that Samuel Jeake is known at all, it is through his astrological diary, which was edited by Michael Hunter and Annabel Gregory and published in 1988.⁷⁶ Jeake records that he 'began first to set down memorandums of my life in a diary' on 18 July 1666 but the diary was in fact compiled from disparate sources (his 'memorandums') at a specific time, between 12 July and 19 November 1694. As Hunter described in the introduction, the diary is a 'conscious artefact': he clearly intended it to be read by others and, in the sense that it was written retrospectively over a relatively short period of time, it is perhaps closer to an autobiography in intent. One of Jeake's main motives in compiling the diary was to subject the events of his life to astrological analysis, which he saw as entirely compatible with a strongly providential worldview.[77] The diary also details Jeake's extensive reading, his frequent illnesses and their treatment, his activities as a merchant and, to a lesser extent, aspects of his family and social life. In addition to the diary there is an extensive collection of manuscript material associated with Jeake and his circle, including business and personal correspondence, a single business ledger and a set of Jeake's personal expenditure accounts.[78] The correspondence is predominantly about Jeake's business interests but many of the letters also contain references to current affairs, family matters and shopping requests.[79]

Like his father and his business partner, Thomas Miller, Jeake was a nonconformist, enduring intermittent periods of persecution in the late 1670s and 1680s, which disturbed his family life and damaged his business interests. It is not clear what congregation the Rye nonconformists belonged to; most likely they were Independents although as John Spurr has shown it can be difficult to demarcate one nonconformist group from another.[80] Whatever the precise complexion of Jeake's religious beliefs they clearly did not interfere with his business interests or, indeed, with his material concerns as expressed in his diary and in his letters. Hunter notes that religion is not a particularly prominent theme in the diary, which has 'an overwhelmingly worldly air'.[81] Moreover, whilst providence is constantly invoked in the diary it is invariably benevolent and Jeake appears to have seen little conflict between his worldly self-interest and God's purpose for him.[82]

Jeake's complex business interests are explored by Hunter and revealed in his diary and correspondence; they are described only in summary here. Financed by his father, Jeake entered into trade in 1674 in partnership with his friend, the established merchant, Thomas Miller, who was eight years his senior, initially importing coarse linens from northern France.[83] When French imports were banned in 1678 Jeake had to find other commodities to trade in; in 1680 he began dealing in wool, which he bought from producers in East Sussex and Kent and exported to other English ports.[84] He also began to lend money out at interest, either by bond or mortgage, and to negotiate bills of exchange. In the mid-1680s Jeake's trading and exchanging activities were seriously disrupted by religious persecution, which obliged him to absent himself from Rye for extended periods of time. However, by 1686 he was trading again; in addition to importing linen and exporting wool, he was also dealing in hops, which he exported to London and to the West Country. The outbreak of the Nine Years War in 1689 once more disrupted Jeake's business activities and the following years saw him looking around for new investment opportunities. In 1694 he invested in new government schemes for raising war funds, buying ten tickets in the Million Adventure and becoming one of the first subscribers to the newly-established Bank of England.[85]

Whilst Jeake's business career may have been turbulent, it did bring him considerable financial rewards. What really set Jeake up as a man of substance, however, was the £1000 marriage portion he received in 1681, along with his mother-in-law's house, which he described as 'one of the best in the town'.[86] Although wealthy enough to form part of the Rye urban elite, Jeake's nonconformity meant that his membership of that group was not a conventional one. Until the Toleration Act of 1689 he was denied the rights of a freeman to which his birth should have entitled him and so he could have no formal role in the town's government. But he seems to have had little interest in civic government in any case; he rarely attended the town's assembly after his election as freeman in 1690 and in 1694 he paid the corporation £60 on condition that he was excused future office-holding.[87] However, both Jeake and his wife participated in conspicuous and fashionable consumption – in the clothes they wore, the exotic foods they bought and the household objects they surrounded themselves with – something which has been seen as an identifying characteristic of the so-called 'urban gentry'.[88] They were also both highly educated. Under his father's supervision Jeake learned (amongst other subjects) Latin, Greek and Hebrew, natural philosophy, mathematics and geometry, cosmography, astronomy and astrology, poetry and history.[89] Less is known about Elizabeth's education. The daughter of Rye schoolmaster Richard Hartshorne (1628–1680), she was sufficiently competent in Latin to instruct their daughter Elizabeth (Betty) during one of Jeake's prolonged absences in London and she seems to have held her own on a visit to Gresham College in 1701 where she met a fellow from the Royal Society, telling her mother that she had been 'styled a philosopher for my learned talk'.[90] Elizabeth also managed Jeake's business affairs whilst he was away in London, guided by advice and instructions that he sent to her by letter.[91]

Samuel Jeake the elder owned a considerable library of some 2,100 items which came with him when he took up residence in his son's marital home in August 1680.[92] This included a large number of radical religious and political books from the 1640s and 1650s alongside a wide selection of books on English and continental theology, an extensive range of English literature and works on history, law, mathematics, science and magic.[93] Amongst the works that do not fit comfortably into any of these categories are volume two of Pietro Bertelli's *Diversarum Nationum Habitus* (1594), Henry Peacham's *The Complete Gentleman* (1622 and later editions) and Hugh Plat's *Delights for Ladies* (1602 and later editions), the latter possibly owned by his wife, Frances.[94]

The Roberts men and Edward May

The Roberts were a middle gentry family who had been resident on the manor of Boarzell in Ticehurst in north-east Sussex since the fifteenth century.[95] Boarzell comprised 140 acres of land lying in Ticehurst and Etchingham; in addition the family owned 160 acres of land at Dalehill in Ticehurst and 140 acres of land at Stonehouse in Warbleton, together with smaller parcels of land in Ticehurst and elsewhere.[96] Their income derived from rents and their farming activities; a probate inventory surviving for John Roberts (d. 1639) taken in June 1639 records thirty-two acres of wheat, thirty-five acres of peas, seven acres of oats and seven acres of hops 'on the ground' and 120 heaps of wheat and 160 heaps of oats 'in the barns', valued at £202, and cattle and sheep valued at £186.[97] Ticehurst was unusual in having three other resident gentry families, the Mays of Pashley, the Courthopes of Whiligh and the Apsleys of Wardsbrook.[98] These families were all more prominent than the Roberts family both socially and politically. For example, George Courthope (1616–1685) became MP for Sussex in 1656 and for East Grinstead in 1659, 1660 and 1661 and was knighted in 1661; he also served as a Sussex JP along with Anthony Apsley; Anthony May (d. 1636) was High Sheriff of Sussex in 1629. In contrast, the Roberts men do not appear to have held any political or public offices in the seventeenth century.[99]

Whilst there is an extensive archive for the Roberts family, there is limited information within it about their clothing or their wider personal expenditure.[100] Evidence for clothing expenditure is mainly restricted to a series of 'vouchers to account' or suppliers' bills. The most coherent set are those sent by London mercer or tailor, John Heath, to Walter Roberts (1635–1690) for payment: ten bills survive covering the period from 1677 to 1687. In 1677 the Roberts family consisted of widower, Walter Roberts senior, and his two sons, Walter Roberts junior (1655–1700) and John Roberts (1662–1728).[101] In 1674 Walter senior had become guardian to 10-year-old Edward May (1664–1685) of Pashley after the death of May's elder brother, Thomas.[102] Heath supplied clothing to all of them. As will be discussed in Chapters Four and Five, there are also a number of bills from other tradesmen such as Ticehurst mercer, Thomas Nash, who was supplying Walter senior with clothing in the 1670s and another London mercer or tailor, Samuel Jones, who was supplying Walter junior with clothing in the 1690s.

Most of Walter's familial connections were with other members of the Sussex gentry; his sister, Elizabeth, was married to John Everenden of Sedlescombe, his wife, Mary (d. 1666), was the daughter of John Busbridge of Haremere in Etchingham and his sister-in-law, Anna (d. 1705), was married to Peter Farnden of Sedlescombe (d. 1681).[103] Walter was also connected to London trade through his brother-in-law, Thomas Busbridge, who became a citizen and wax chandler of London in 1676 although his surviving business ledger shows that he dealt almost exclusively in silk.[104] Walter's younger son, John, was apprenticed to Busbridge in 1677 but seems not to have entered trade himself since he was living at Boarzell again by 1684.[105] However, as we shall see in Chapter Four, there is little evidence that Walter exploited his London connections and none to indicate that he spent any significant time there. There is no evidence at all that Walter or his sons had any intellectual interests and evidence for their religious and political affiliations is slim.[106] Between 1671 and 1674 John Roberts was at school in nearby Burwash.[107] The schoolmaster, Thomas Goldham, had been ejected from his living in Burwash in 1662 for nonconformity which may suggest Walter Roberts was sympathetic to puritanism. However, his choice of school may also have been influenced by the fact the son of Sir John Pelham (1623–1703), 3rd baronet of Halland and one of the wealthiest men in Sussex, was attending there.[108]

Richard Stapley (1657–1724)

Richard Stapley of Hickstead Place in Twineham was the son of Anthony Stapley (1620–1667) and younger brother to Anthony Stapley (1654–1733) who inherited Hickstead Place and the manor of Twineham under the terms of his father's will.[109] Although a middle-gentry family, the Stapley's familial connections were quite mixed: they were linked by marriage to a number of other local gentry families, including the Luxfords of Hurstpierpoint, the Boardes of Lindfield and the Spences of South Malling, but also to the Burts of Cuckfield, a family of wealthy tanners and butchers.[110] Richard did not marry but lived with his mother, Jane, at Hickstead Place until her death in 1699 and from 1713 with his brother, Anthony, until his own death in 1724. The evidence used in this book for his clothing and accessories is taken from his memorandum book, a printed almanac for the years 1682 to 1687 into which he made notes of financial transactions, including clothing purchases, and recorded local events – most of them relatively banal such as the giant trout found in November 1692 or the pollarding of a 'great yew tree' in the churchyard at Bolney in January 1700, others more notable such as the 'terrible tempest' of August 1703 in which a man drowned.[111] The entries, which continue until January 1724, do not follow each other in date order and appear to have been squeezed in wherever there was room. The use of printed almanacs to record significant events, personal expenditure and daily activities was common in the seventeenth century and Adam Smyth has argued that they constitute a form of 'life writing' like diaries and autobiographies.[112] Whilst there are no introspective reflections in Stapley's book his apparently haphazard recording does offer the reader a kind of piecemeal life narrative, which can be made fuller when combined with other surviving sources.

The evidence from Stapley's book suggests that he seldom ventured out of his locality. There is one reference to him being in London but on the whole he seems to have stayed in Twineham and the adjoining parishes of Hurstpierpoint and Cuckfield.[113] It is notable that many of the financial transactions that Stapley records, including payment for clothing and accessories, took place in his own house. The entries in Stapley's book also suggest that he preferred male company to that of women. One of his closest associates was William Sheward, curate of Twineham from *c.* 1691 and subsequently rector from 1704 until his death in 1715.[114]

Stapley suffered from a debilitating condition, which may explain why he led such a geographically circumscribed life. In 1719 Anthony noted in his own memorandum book that 'my brother, Richard's, infirmities are growing so fast upon him, that he is now unable to transact the business he has heretofore been accustomed to do. I have therefore begun this year to receive his rents for him and to look to all household matters'.[115] By 1723 Richard had become paralysed and, according to his brother, he was no longer able to do anything for himself.[116] He died intestate but an inventory made by his brother after his death showed that he had few personal possessions of his own, valued at a modest £42 14s: his clothing (valued at £10 together with his 'pocket'), his bed and bedding, a chest of drawers, 'tables and boxes', books and plate, presumably all things that he kept in his own room.[117] Some of these items are referred to in his memorandum book. In 1686 he paid 19s for a new bedstead and table and a further 36s for bed curtains, curtain rods and a valance.[118] Book purchases recorded in his memorandum book included *The Works of the Author of 'The Whole Duty of Man'* (1684) usually attributed to Richard Allestree and Thomas Comber's *Companion to the Temple and the Closet* (1672), both obtained for him by William Sheward.[119] At the time of his death Stapley also had £1650 in money tied up in various investments.[120] After his death his brother, Anthony, described him as a man who had been 'socially and hospitably inclined towards his neighbours' with a 'heart and hand ... ever open to the calls and wants of charity ... as became a man of his rank and station'.[121] A modest and a pious man, he asked his brother to ensure that his funeral be conducted 'in as plain and quiet manner as could well be' and left a large silver flagon and two large patens to his parish church.[122]

Seventeenth-century Sussex

The 'province' that forms the subject of this study is Sussex, a county bordered by approximately 75 miles of coast to the south, by the county of Hampshire to the west and by the counties of Surrey and Kent to the north and north-east. It was divided for administrative purposes into eastern and western parts, each with its own regional capital, Chichester (the diocesan seat) and Lewes. The primary units of civil administration were the six rapes that ran from the north to the south of the county, with the rapes of Lewes, Pevensey and Hastings lying within the eastern division, and those of Chichester, Arundel and Bramber lying within the western division. Rapes were subdivided into hundreds and the hundreds into smaller units called tithings in the west and boroughs in the east.[123]

There were three distinctive economic regions within the county, the Weald, to the north-east, the downland and coastal plain to the south, both straddling eastern and western parts, and the marshland of eastern Sussex. The Weald, with its dense woodland and heavy clay soil, was more suited to cattle ranching than arable farming and much of what farmers grew was used as animal fodder. Hop cultivation had been established by the late sixteenth century and by the 1650s supposedly accounted for about a quarter of the hop acreage of south-eastern England. Rural industries were more significant here than in other parts of Sussex, the largest being iron manufacture, which provided seasonal employment for iron-workers and charcoal makers. The downland and coastal plain area were primarily corn-growing regions, with sheepwalks on the Downs. Rural industries were small-scale and local in their markets, which meant there were few employment opportunities outside of agriculture. The marshland area of eastern Sussex, notoriously unhealthy and sparsely settled, was mainly used for fattening stock, much of which was raised or wintered on home farms in the Weald.[124]

Sussex had approximately twenty market towns in the seventeenth century, which varied considerably in size.[125] The two largest were Chichester in the west and Lewes in the east, with populations of about 2500 and 2000 respectively in around 1625. Mid-sized towns with populations of between 400 and 1000 included Arundel, Midhurst, Petworth and Horsham in the west and Rye, Hastings and Battle in the east. Smaller, but still significant, trading centres included Storrington and Steyning in the west and Cuckfield and Brighton in the east. There were also a number of market 'towns' which were little more than villages, for example Westbourne and Tarring in the west and Ditchling in the east. Market towns were not evenly spread across Sussex, however. Overall, downland areas were better served than those in the Weald, despite the heavier population densities towards the north of the county, because the clayey Wealden roads hindered the movement of goods and people.[126] Writing to her daughter from Etchingham in September 1648, Anna Busbridge reported that 'the ways be so dirty and deep as in winter that I heard no wagons will go to London'.[127] In 1720 Daniel Defoe expressed amazement at seeing 'an ancient lady, and a lady of very good quality' in a parish near Lewes travelling to church in a coach drawn by six oxen because the clay was too 'stiff and deep' for horses.[128]

The difficulties of moving goods around or through Sussex by road were to some extent compensated for by the county's coastal position and the number of navigable rivers.[129] Barge navigation along the Ouse, the Brede, the Rother and the sewers of the Pevensey levels meant that most of eastern Sussex, except its northern fringes, was reasonably accessible to river transport and allowed for the export of most of its natural and manufactured commodities by sea; in western Sussex the Arun and the Adur, navigable inland from the coast for approximately twenty-five miles and eleven miles respectively, fulfilled the same function.[130] There were coastal ports at Rye, Hastings, Newhaven, Shoreham and Chichester with inland ports at Lewes and Arundel on the rivers Ouse and Arun. In the second half of the seventeenth century Rye, which had previously been the leading Sussex port, lost much of its foreign trade as a result of Anglo-French commercial rivalry but the trade in Chichester was increasing fast, chiefly due to the growth of corn exports. Its harbour, about three miles from the city, had its principal landing place at Dell Quay. The import trade at Chichester was never as large as the export trade. The chief foreign imports were wine from France until 1678, then from Spain and Portugal, deals and timber from Norway and cargoes of miscellaneous manufactures from Rotterdam. The most significant coastwise imports were coal from Newcastle and Sunderland. London cargoes included a range of manufactured goods of foreign and English origin, especially wine, tobacco, sugar, textiles, leather, earthenware, glass, metal manufactures, groceries, spirits and oil.[131] For example, in 1678 the cargo of the 'Bergavenny' of London

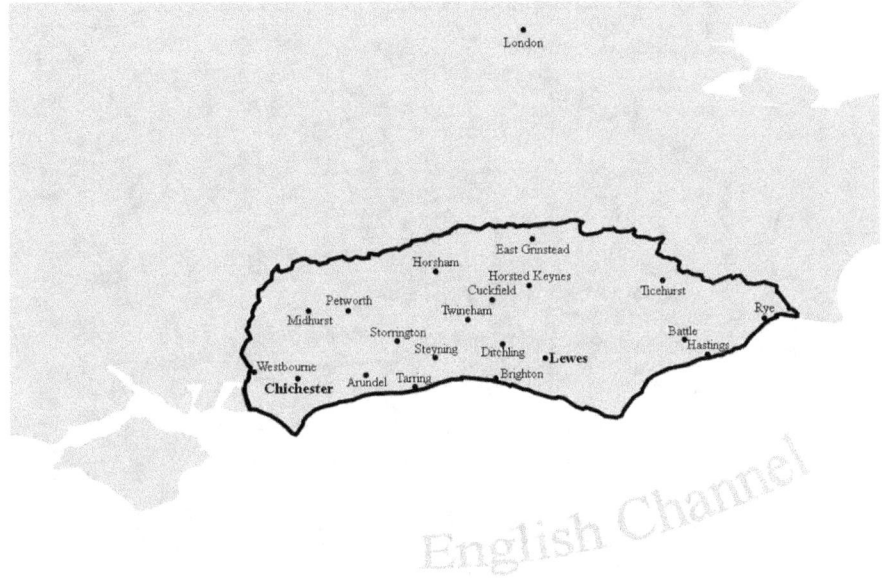

Figure 1.2 Map of Sussex, showing location of market towns and places of residence of men and women featuring in case studies.

included iron pots and glasses, Virginia tobacco, grocery wares, cheese, butter, pitch, beans, two trusses of 'common cloth', herrings, ironmongers' ware, brandy, oil, lees, tar, soap, cork, birdshot, gunpowder, alum and grindstones.[132] This was one of four London shipments to Chichester that year, all carrying mixed cargoes.

Seventeenth-century Chichester, approximately seventy miles from London, was a small walled city divided into four quadrants by its principal streets which radiated out from a central Market Cross. As the seat of the bishop, it was the ecclesiastical centre of Sussex, as well as being an important administrative and trading centre for the western part of the county.[133] Chichester's significance as a trading centre is reflected in the number of merchants operating within it in the seventeenth century. They acted as wholesalers, buying and selling raw and processed commodities and importing and exporting through the port at Dell Quay.[134] Many of them were involved in the malt trade, but the city had a range of other trades and industries besides malt production. In 1616 thirty artisans petitioned the city's Common Council to establish a guild of clothworkers, dyers, weavers and fustian weavers to protect their livelihood from 'diverse foreigners and out-dwellers', suggesting a sizeable textile industry.[135] In the early seventeenth century there was also a substantial needle-making industry based in the suburb

Figure 1.3 John Speed's map of Chichester, 1610. Reproduced with the permission of West Sussex Record Office.

of St Pancras but this was severely disrupted by the destruction of much of the parish by Parliamentary forces in 1642 during the siege of Chichester.[136] The city was well served with shops: there were (amongst others) shoemakers and cordwainers, upholsterers, booksellers and stationers, clockmakers, tobacconists and mercers.[137] A mercers' guild or company with six members was established in 1622 to preclude any but its own members from selling mercers' and grocers' wares from retail premises within the city.[138] The shop stock of mercer, John Godfrey, who died in 1683 was probably fairly typical. He sold a range of woollen cloth including broadcloth, kersey, serge, stuff and mohair as well as silk and linen cloth. He also sold stockings, linen ware and haberdashery, the latter including buttons, ribbons and silver lace.[139] The city's close links to its rural hinterland are reflected in its weekly livestock market held in East Street and North Street.[140]

Although lacking the prestige of diocesan leadership Lewes, approximately sixty miles from London, was an important ecclesiastical and administrative centre; it was where ecclesiastical visitations and church courts for the Archdeaconry of Lewes and the quarter sessions for eastern Sussex were held, ensuring a regular influx of litigants, jurors and clergymen. In 1675 the cartographer, John Ogilby, described the town as 'a place of good antiquity; large, well-built and well inhabited … [with] diverse handsome streets'; it was, said Ogilby, 'esteemed the best town of the county'.[141] Its position at the junction of the Weald and the Downs and at a navigable point of the river Ouse meant that it acted as a centre for goods moving from east to west and from north to south.[142] Ready access to hops, barley and water encouraged malting and commercial brewing in the suburbs of Southover and Cliffe.[143] The High Street was the main trading thoroughfare: here wealthy mercers, haberdashers, drapers, hatters and grocers had their shops.[144] Rector of Horsted Keynes, Giles Moore, was a regular visitor to High Street mercer, William Marshall, whose shop was next to The Star Inn; he also made use of three other High Street mercers, Hercules Courtney, Edmund Middleton and Stephen Snatt as well as apothecary, Thomas Fissenden, whose premises were across the street from Marshall's.[145] The High Street was also where the Sussex magnate, Sir Thomas Pelham (1597–1654), 2nd baronet of Halland, had his town house.[146] At the street's widest point was the market place where a daily provisions market was held; at the centre of the market place was the Sessions House. As well as being a market and a depot for local produce such as wheat and barley, hops, wool and timber, Lewes served as a warehouse for a wide range of merchandise brought up river from the coastal port of Newhaven. Its wharves and warehouses received groceries, wines and textiles from London and from ports in the West Country and the Netherlands, along with increasing cargoes of coal from Tyneside; exports included wheat, hops, malt, Wealden iron and timber.[147] In 1675 the cargo of the 'John and Dorothy' of London included nails, wrought iron, lead, glasses, rub stones, steel, bottles, pots and earthenware, soap, tar, grocery wares, paper, deal, pewter, Spanish and Rhenish wine, 'strong waters', Virginia tobacco, four trusses of linen cloth, hemp and flax and half a load of household goods.[148]

Outsiders' views about Sussex were frequently skewed by their difficult encounters with its muddy and treacherous roads. Most found something positive to say about it, however. Defoe for example commented on the richness of the natural resources in the Weald and the beauty of the South Downs, 'the pleasantest and most delightful of their kind in the nation'.[149] Celia Fiennes, travelling through Sussex around 1695, admired the parkland and newly built house at Uppark and was impressed by Chichester's cathedral.[150] Few were as vitriolic in their assessment as Home Circuit barrister, William Cowper, the future Lord Chancellor. In a letter to his wife written in 1690 he described the county as 'a sink of about fourteen miles broad which receives all the water that falls from two long ranges of hills on both sides'. It was, in his view, a 'melancholy consideration that mankind will inhabit such a heap of dirt for a poor livelihood'.[151] It is the clothing worn by this 'mankind' living in its 'heap of dirt' that is the subject of this study.

2

Literary Constructions of Clothing, the Individual and Society

When Henry Cox described Mary Watts as wearing clothes 'not fit for a woman of her quality to wear' he was drawing on a widely held view that clothing should reflect the social status of its wearer.[1] Seventeenth-century clothing was imbued with a broad range of cultural values that shaped the sartorial behaviour of the individual and mediated the way that his or her clothes were perceived by others. It frequently acted as a nexus for the expression of broader societal concerns about individual and collective behaviour and the nation's social and economic wellbeing. Clothing could also be used in a more light-hearted way to parody the *mores* and pretensions of social groups and to emphasise differences between the 'city' (i.e. London) and the 'country' (i.e. the provinces). This chapter examines these values, concerns and parodies as they are expressed in a diverse selection of contemporary literature, including conduct books, ballads, plays, satirical pamphlets and medical, religious and economic treatises. Despite the eclecticism of the source material, there is a consistency in the ideas that are being expressed, suggesting that they were well established in seventeenth-century society and would have resonated in some form with the men and women who feature in this book.[2] They therefore provide an essential context for many of the themes explored in subsequent chapters.

Clothing and the social order

O how strangely is apparel metamorphosed! We read in Genesis that it was first used to hide our shame but now 'tis worn to show our pride . . .[3]

In Christian tradition, clothing was first used by Adam and Eve after they defied God's orders and ate from the tree of knowledge. With the sudden, shameful, realisation of their nakedness they sewed themselves aprons out of fig leaves and hid themselves from God. On discovering their transgression God made Adam and Eve coats out of animal skins and banished them from the Garden of Eden. With Adam and Eve's original sin, the human body became corrupt, shameful, and mortal. Clothing became necessary not only to hide man's shame but to protect him from the elements from which he had previously been immune. Clothes, in Richard Braithwaite's words, were the 'rags of sin' or the 'robes of shame'; those leading lives of Christian humility should view them only as reminders of their mortality. However, whereas our ancestors had been content to select their clothing on the basis of necessity – to cover their shame and to keep them warm in winter and cool in summer – men and women in the present age driven by pride and vanity had turned the 'use' of clothing into 'abuse', dressing themselves in extravagant, immodest, impractical and frequently *foreign* attire.[4]

However, in the contemporary view clothing had a purpose other than mere necessity and that was to give visual expression to social distinctions: as the author of *Coma Berenices or the Hairy Comet* (1676) reminded his readers, 'by the

Figure 2.1 Wenceslaus Hollar, Adam Ploughing from 'The Dance of Death' (1651), The Metropolitan Museum of Art, 51.501.2114.

ordination of God, as there are distinctions of callings and degrees amongst men, so there ought to be distinctions of habits'.[5] The link between clothing and status had been given legal form through sumptuary legislation that had existed in various guises since the fourteenth century. The repeal of such legislation in 1604 was, according to Negley Harte, the consequence of parliament's failure to reach a consensus on how it should operate rather than its rejection of the principle that the state had the right, and possibly the duty, to regulate the clothing of its citizens.[6] There were regular attempts to reintroduce sumptuary legislation over the course of the seventeenth century but none were successful.[7] Bills introduced into parliament typically had two goals: the restraint of excessive consumption amongst the nation's elite and the protection of its native manufactures, especially its woollen cloth industry. They gave expression to a widely held view that the unrestrained consumption of luxury goods was more than merely a private vice but was economically damaging to the nation as a whole.

Whilst the promoters of these bills showed little interest in the clothing of the majority, contemporary writers frequently commented on the sartorial disorder of the present day. Addressing himself to the nobility, the author *of England's Vanity* (1683) observed, 'the whole Kingdom [is] in masquerade, the distracted mimics of your grandeur, each pitiful fellow cheek-by-jowling it with your lordships and every mechanic's wife aping your high-born ladies'.[8] Such sartorial disorder, which as we shall see was thought to be particularly acute in London, undermined the integrity of the social structure and posed a potential threat to the nation's political and economic stability. As the nation's ruling class, the gentry and the aristocracy were expected to lead by example and show sumptuary restraint. In 1622 a report to the Privy Council's clothing committee putting forward proposals to redress the decline of the woollen cloth industry recommended that 'the nobility and gentry... might be persuaded to the wearing of [woollen] cloth in the winter season *by example* rather than commandment'. In contrast, the committee recommended that 'the meaner sort of people as apprentices, servants and mechanics' should be ordered by proclamation to 'wear of cloth and stuff of wool made in this kingdom'.[9]

This did not mean that the elite should not use clothing to assert their status but that they needed to do so with moderation. Thus a careful balancing act was required between display and restraint. Henry Peacham advised the gentleman to

> Be thrifty... in your apparel and clothing lest you incur the censure of the most grave and wisest censor... Neither on the contrary be so basely parsimonious or frugal... But using that moderate and middle garb which shall rather lessen than make you bigger than you are...[10]

Sumptuary restraint was also about protecting the gentry's assets, in particular their landed estates. In his speech to the House of Commons introducing his second sumptuary bill in 1614, York MP, Christopher Brooke, complained that 'women carry manors and thousands of oak trees about their necks'.[11] A similar accusation was made by Braithwaite in *The English Gentlewoman* (1631), 'Here the remainder of a greater work, the relics of an ancient manor converted into a pearl chain, there the moiety of an ill-husbanded domain reduced to a carcanet [necklace], long trains must sweep away long acres'.[12] Those who bankrupted their estates through their excessive consumption ruined not only themselves but also the many men and women whose economic welfare was inextricably linked with theirs – their tenants who depended on them to be good landlords and the local poor who depended on their largesse. For those who remained solvent it was still the case that money spent on extravagant, fashionable and superfluous clothes could more properly be spent on charitable relief.[13] As will be discussed in more detail later on, what compounded their selfishness was the fact that members of the elite were choosing to spend part of their year in London. Not only did this deprive their rural localities of their custom but it also meant that their country houses were left empty, becoming the 'mock-beggar halls' of popular literature. Christopher Brooke acknowledged the link between sumptuary excess and what he described as the 'want of hospitality' amongst the elite in his speech to the House of Commons introducing his third sumptuary bill in 1621.[14]

The naked Englishman

He that will describe an English man must draw him naked with a pair of tailor's shears in one hand and a piece of cloth on his arm.[15]

Inconstancy in dress was seen as a characteristic of the English in the present time. Authors typically contrasted such sartorial fickleness with the supposed sartorial stability of our own ancestors or with that of other nations, either past or present. Thus for Braithwaite our ancestors had retained a 'simple, honest rusticity' in their clothing; their sartorial constancy was a sign of the respect they held for their own ancestors and they thought it 'ominous to innovate or bring in any new form'.[16] For the author of *New Additions to Youth's Behaviour* (1663), 'in all ages and all places it has been the wisdom of states to suppress innovations, whereof the Turks and Persians are to this day exceedingly jealous and therefore will endure no change of manners or habits'.[17] Some authors also commented on the economic and social benefits that sumptuary laws had brought to past societies. Braithwaite, for example, maintained that the sumptuary laws introduced into ancient Rome by Numa Pompilius had 'in short time' made the state wealthy and reduced vice.[18] Similarly, the author of *New Additions to Youth's Behaviour* commended the '*censores morum*' of ancient Rome whose role had been to 'punish and restrain all excesses and exorbitancies in fashions, habits and behaviours'.[19] When offering exemplars of sartorial stability such authors typically either looked to the distant past or to contemporary societies that were geographically and culturally distant from their own – the Turks, Persians, Russians, Muscovians, Ionians and even 'the barbarous Indian'.[20] Moreover, the continuance of sumptuary laws in other European countries, especially in France, England's greatest sartorial rival, went unremarked.[21] As we shall see, sartorial instability was also seen as a characteristic of the present-day city with the country becoming its counter in its sartorial constancy.

The supposed fickleness of the English in choosing their clothes was of course a well-worn theme.[22] As early as 1542 Andrew Boorde had satirised the Englishman's obsession with fashion by depicting him naked with a pair of shears in his hand because he could not decide what to wear: 'For now I will wear this and now I will wear that/ Now I will wear I cannot tell what/ All new fashions be pleasant to me'.[23] In 1683 the author of *England's Vanity* complained that 'no colour, form nor fashion long contents them. One while we imitate the Spaniard, another while the French, one while the Italian, another while the Dutch. Every nation is a several pattern for us'.[24] Some thought this fickleness had a physiological basis: as an island race, the English were believed to be especially susceptible to the waxing and waning of the moon and the ebb and flow of the tides.[25] The author of *New Additions to Youth's Behaviour* said that he would 'leave it to men of more learning and leisure to sound out the original cause of this giddy humour, whether it be from the changeable complexion of the climate, or the peculiar influence of some fantastical planet'.[26]

According to the author of *England's Vanity* 'in wearing Dutch hats with French feathers, French doublets with collars after the custom of Spain, Turkish coats, Spanish hose, Italian cloaks and Valencian rapiers' the English man had 'likewise stolen the vices and excesses of those countries'.[27] The taste for foreign fashions undermined the nation's moral strength by corrupting its wearers. Moreover, it damaged the nation's economic strength because men and women eschewed the products of its native industries in favour of those of its European rivals. It also, quite simply, made us the laughing stock of Europe.[28]

Whilst the pan-Europeanism of contemporary fashion may have been roundly condemned, it was the nation's slavish devotion to all things French that attracted more ire.[29] According to the author of *A Satire against the French* (1691), 'All the fantastic arts of dress we know/ Did first from France, that impure fountain, flow'.[30] For John Evelyn, a French tailor was like 'the enchantress Circe over the companions of Ulysses', changing his customers into strange and ridiculous shapes.[31] For Francis Boyle, French fashions 'infatuated our minds and debauched our fancies'.[32] Our obsession with French fashions was such that Evelyn claimed that a French shopkeeper had told him that 'the English did so torment her for the mode, still doubting that she brought them not over the newest edition of it' that she was forced to invent new 'French' fashions to pacify them.[33] The author of *The Grand Concern of England Explained* (1673) similarly claimed that the gentry were so reluctant to buy English-manufactured goods that manufacturers used French middle men to sell them 'as French' to shopkeepers who could then charge double for them.[34]

Men and women, youth and age

No time [is] more perilous than the heat of youth or more apt to give fuel to the fire of all inordinate desires . . .[35]

In contemporary medical theory the ages of man each had their own humoral characteristics based on the premise that life was sustained by a combination of an innate 'radical heat' and moisture, the balance of which shifted as the ageing process progressed: whereas the young were hot and moist, the old were cold and dry reflecting the fact that by then the radical heat and moisture of the body had largely been used up.[36] These physiological characteristics of youth and old age determined behavioural characteristics, for example the 'heat of youth' made young men prone to what Braithwaite described as 'inordinate desires'.[37]

In his *Directions for Health* (1626), William Vaughan divided the ages of man into seven.[38] The third age, 'the strippling age', began at age fourteen and continued until the age of twenty two. Governed by the planet Venus, young men at this age were 'prone to prodigality, gluttony, drunkenness, lechery and sundry kinds of vices'.[39] In *Lessons Moral and Christian for Youth and Old Age* (1699), John Strype wrote that the spirits of the young were hot and vigorous, so they are more violently carried out towards external objects, that promise them pleasure in the enjoyment. And they cannot bear any restraint, they must have their desires, however inconvenient or unlawful they be. Their lusts, and their appetites and passions, must be satisfied. And they will break through all bars and impediments whatsoever for the gratification thereof. The pleasures and vanities of the world impetuously assault them and they cannot withstand.[40]

Excess and a lack of restraint were therefore inherent to youth. Sartorially, this translated into a weakness for fashion and external display. For the young themselves the desire to adorn themselves was perfectly natural, a sign of their youthful *joie de vivre* and relative sexual independence. As the female narrator of the ballad 'The London Ladies' Vindication of Top-Knots' (*c*. 1675–1696) sings,

'Tis fit that young women should go fine and gay/ in spite of their bugbears, brave girls, let us wear/ rich towers and top-knots with powdered hair/ Were we to be ruled by some sort of men/ we should go like women of fourscore and ten...[41]

According to the author of *The Ladies Calling* (1673) vanity in dress was more excusable in young women who had not yet 'outworn the relics of their childhood'; it was also essential that those of marriageable age dressed themselves to their best advantage so that they did not make themselves appear 'less amiable' than God had made them.[42]

As a man aged his humoral balance changed from hot and moist to cold and dry, tempering his natural impulses. Moreover, his life experiences were expected to teach him the folly of vanity and the pursuit of material goals. A man in his fourth age (twenty two to thirty four), according to Vaughan, was 'witty, well advised, magnanimous, and coming to know himself'; a man in his fifth age (thirty four to sixty) was 'stout, covetous and worldly'; in his sixth age (sixty to seventy four) he was in his 'flourishing old age', and was equitable, temperate and religious; finally, in his seventh and last age he was melancholic, drooping, decrepit and cold.[43] But were the old any more restrained in their behaviour than the young? Some authors thought not. According to Strype, many old men were slaves to vice and sin, 'the sinful frailties of their youth [turning] into the very habits of their old age'. Men and women in their fortieth, fiftieth or even sixtieth years could still be 'passionate and hasty, covetous and worldly minded, unclean in their desires, blasphemous and vain in their speeches, woefully negligent of God and their souls.'[44]

Whilst sartorial excess was deplorable at any age, it was particularly so when the wearer was past their prime. In *The Folly of Love* (1691), Richard Ames condemned 'old madams ... who one would think stood tottering upon life's extremist brink, those who in spite of nature will be young ... dressed and set off like girls of seventeen'.[45] When worn by the old, therefore, fashionable clothing and, perhaps more damnably, makeup and cosmetic accessories like hair pieces and false teeth became a form of trickery enabling the wearer to maintain an outward illusion of youth. This was something that a hapless 'north country gentleman' in the ballad, 'News from Hyde Park' (*c.* 1682) found out to his cost when he picked up what he thought to be a lovely young lady only to discover when she removed her cosmetic additions that she looked like 'a Lancashire witch of fourscore and ten'.[46] But old men, too, were guilty of using clothing and accessories to try to stave off the appearance of age. The author of *Coma Berenices* criticised 'ancient men' for following the fashion for wearing wigs. Covering their grey hair with a wig was, in his words, 'to forfeit that honour which is due to the hoary head' and to suggest that the wearer was ashamed of 'that which is their glory'. Moreover, 'a flaunting youthful bush of hair does ill become them (as if it were yet but early spring with them) when their faces are wrinkled, their joints tremble and they have December in their bones'.[47]

As the more rational sex, men were expected to show greater restraint in their clothing since women would follow where men led; or, in Thomas Dekker's words, women were men's 'she apes for they will not be behind them the breadth of a tailor's yard', following them in any 'new-fangled, upstart fashion'.[48] For the author of *Coma Berenices* God was willing to show greater tolerance of female vanity since women's adornment made them more desirable to those 'whose helps and individual companions they are ordained to be'.[49] The author of *New Additions to Youth's Behaviour* similarly defended women's vanity since 'whatever embellishment a woman bestows on her own beauty, is to be adjudged but her duty and an effect of the subordinate complacency which she owes to the male whose servant she is by creation'.[50] For these two authors, therefore, women's fashionable attire was acceptable because it was a sign of their sexual subordination to men.

In seventeenth-century ballads criticism of fashionable excess, vanity and pride is levelled fairly evenly at men and women.[51] In 'The Fantastic Age or the Anatomy of England's Vanity in Wearing the Fashions of Several Nations' (*c.* 1633–1669) the author accuses both sexes of being 'chameleon-like' in their adoption of the fashions of other nations and says that he will 'make excuse for neither'. Men, however, should know better than the 'frail female sex'; moreover, their obsession with fashion unmans them. Women he accuses of pestering their husbands, friends and fathers to buy them the latest fashion 'at whatever price it cost'.[52] Some ballads set up fictitious male or female narrators who admonish the opposite sex for their fashion obsession and defend their own sartorial behaviour. For example in 'The Young Men's Advice to Proud Ladies' (1692), the male narrators caution young women against 'the folly of pride', accusing them of constantly seeking out new fashions,

> Pride is a folly which reigns in young women/ see their black patches and powdered hair/ commodes with laces and other rich trimming/ which is their absolute study and care/ how other fashions may still be invented/ or else they will not, or can't be contented.[53]

However, in 'The Virgin's Vindication, or, the Conceited Fashion-mongers Fairly Exposed' (c. 1664–1703), the female narrators criticise young men for accusing them of fashion excesses when they are equally culpable,

> We have been degraded by gallants long ago/ and told of our high toppins [topknots], this of a truth you know/ with our paint and powdered hair, but I think we may declare/ you cannot blame us nor defame us, though the same we wear/ having now followed us in our pride/ with silk a shining gold, nay, and twenty things besides/ now gallants of the game, henceforward never blame/ young maids nor women for their trimming, first yourselves reclaim.[54]

Young women also complain of men's hypocrisy in 'The London Ladies' Vindication of Top-Knots' (c. 1675–1696),

> Some young men may flout us, yet mark what I say/ there's no woman living now prouder than they/ observe but the many knick-knacks which they wear/ more costly than top-knots or powdered hair/Their wig, watch and rapiers we daily behold/ and embroidered waistcoats of silver and gold/ likewise turn-up stockings they constantly wear/ more costly than top-knots or powdered hair.[55]

In the late seventeenth century the stereotype of the fashion-obsessed young man was the 'fop'. According to Mark Dawson, 'fops were, first and foremost, fictive creations' who derived their primary impetus from the theatre and other forms of popular literature. Usually depicted as gentlemen born to landed estates, their natural habitat was the city and in particular its fashionable social spaces like coffee houses, theatres and parks.[56] One of the best-known fictive fops is Sir Novelty Fashion, newly created Lord Foppington, in John Vanbrugh's *The Relapse* of 1696. The first thing he does on coming into his estate is purchase a baronetcy for £10,000'.⁵⁷ Wearing a wig that is so long 'it will serve ... for hat and cloak in all weathers', a fashionable 'steinkirk' cravat and stockings thickened at the calves to make his legs more shapely, Foppington sets off for Town 'to make 'em [i.e. polite society] acquainted with his title'.⁵⁸ The portrayal of Foppington is similar to that of the character of the 'Nice Affected Beau' whom we encounter in *The Character of the Beaux*, published in the same year. As with Foppington, the comic depiction of the Beau rests on his elaborate use of accessories including his 'extravagantly powdered and exactly curled' wig, his rose-scented handkerchief, his precisely-tied cravat, his beauty patches, his scarlet stockings and his snuff box 'as big as an alderman's tobacco box, lined with a bawdy picture'. Their significance rests as much in their skilful deployment as in their possession, so the act of lifting snuff from his snuff box to his nose allows the Beau to show off his slender white fingers and diamond ring. His deportment is not just about these external indicators, however, but his 'mien and air', subtle and intangible qualities that were as essential as his fashionable accoutrements.⁵⁹

Figure 2.2 London-made silver snuff box with 'bawdy' picture (*c*. 1680), Victoria and Albert Museum, 808-1864. The inscription reads 'Arceo sed ardeo' ('I ward off but I burn')/ 'Dulceo est sic decipi' ('Sweet it is to be so enticed'). © Victoria and Albert Museum, London.

The closest to a female equivalent of the fop was the 'town miss'. Like fops, 'town misses' were to be found in London. Their main characteristic was their sexual availability and in popular literature there was often little to distinguish a 'miss' from a prostitute. In *The Character of a Town Miss* (1680) the reader is informed that a 'Miss is a new name, which the civility of the age bestows on one that our unmannerly ancestors called whore and strumpet'.[60] Whilst the character of the 'fop' was intended to be comical – his fashionable clothing and simpering manners the outwards sign of a vacuous mind – literary depictions of the 'miss' were more savage. Her painted face and fashionable clothes were used as tools of seduction and men who were foolish enough to fall for her wiles faced moral, physical and financial ruin. She was, according to *The Character of a Town Miss*, 'a caterpillar that destroys many a hopeful young gentleman in the blossom, a land siren far more dangerous than they in the sea, for he that falls into her hands runs a three-fold hazard of shipwrecking soul, body and estate'.[61] Moreover, the town miss's elegant and fashionable appearance tricked the unwary gentleman into thinking

Figure 2.3 Marcellus Laroon, London courtesan from his series 'The Cries of the City of London' (1688), British Museum 1972,U.370.50. © The Trustees of the British Museum. All rights reserved.

that he was conversing with a lady. In Thomas Crowne's *The Country Wit* (1675) the naïve country gentleman, Sir Mannerly Shallow, arriving in London for the first time, encounters what he thinks are a couple of 'young gentlewomen' dressed in lace and with the reddest cheeks and lips that he had ever seen. Much to his surprise and delight they took him 'about the neck and kissed [him] as if they had been [his] sisters or as if they had known [him] these twenty years'. Not realising that they were prostitutes he began to follow them upstairs when he 'chanced to put [his] hands in [his] pockets and as if the Devil had been there [his] money was all flown out'.[62] As the town miss got older she was forced to rely more heavily on artifice to disguise her age. Amongst the cosmetic enhancements used by the 'young' woman encountered by the north-country gentleman in 'News from Hyde Park' were heavy makeup, a wig and false teeth, a false eye and a false nose – the latter presumably necessary because she had lost her nose to syphilis.[63]

Understanding excessive consumption

> *But not to waste time in calculating the nativity of new fashions, we may resolve it that the mind of man, even as his body, is liable to the constant invasion of new diseases.*[64]

As we have seen, sartorial fickleness was a characteristic of the English, linked to our innately 'giddy humour'; in other words, we were physiologically and psychologically predisposed to run after the latest fashions.[65] For Richard Braithwaite it was a consequence of our fallen natures: 'before we had clothes, we wanted nothing; having clothes, we stand in need of all things'. Our sinful natures had driven our consumption habits to the point where they were now out of control, a sign of our personal vanity and pride and what Braithwaite described as the 'misery and levity of this age'.[66] To the author of *New Additions to Youth's Behaviour*, our proclivity for new fashions was a disease of the mind grown especially virulent in the present age.[67] Nicholas Barbon, who, as we shall see, was an advocate of what we would now term 'conspicuous consumption', also thought that our consumption habits were driven by a kind of mental restlessness,

> Wares, that have their value from supplying the wants of the mind, are all such things that can satisfy desire. Desire implies want; it is the appetite of the soul and is as natural to the soul as hunger to the body. The wants of the mind are infinite ... Amongst the great variety of things to satisfy the wants of the mind

those that adorn man's body and advance the pomp of life have the most general use and in all ages and amongst all sort of mankind have been of value.[68]

Although differing in their views about the merits of unbridled consumerism, each of these authors suggests that the compulsion to spend on new commodities was part of what made us human. Indeed for Barbon, rather than being a sign of our sinfulness, clothing proved our superiority over animals as well as acting as an external marker of society's social divisions: 'the decking of the body does not only distinguish man from beast but is the mark of difference and superiority between man and man'.[69]

Our obsessive need to purchase new clothing was also driven by the desire to emulate others, especially our betters. As we have seen, the author of *England's Vanity* claimed that the whole Kingdom was 'in masquerade', with the 'pitiful fellow' and the 'mechanic's wife' aping the fashions of the nobility.[70] This kind of mimicry was especially prevalent in London. As the author of *Coma Berenices* said,

> ... in cities of great resort and commerce, and where princes keep their royal residence, as men grow wealthy, so they grow proud and wanton, not knowing what they may eat, or what they may drink, or wherewithal they may be clothed ... Pride like the gout harbours chiefly amongst rich people and in great opulent cities ... It is too visible that a great number of citizens take not their measures from their estates or quality, when those of mean occupations vie with great personages of fashionableness and gallantry, as if all London's tradesmen were merchants and all their merchants were princes ...[71]

For Barbon, emulative consumption was also a uniquely urban phenomenon, a consequence of the large number of people living within a confined urban space and the fact that every man was constantly trying to 'out-vie' his neighbour and improve his social and economic condition. Barbon also noted that the air in the city was 'thicker' than that in the country which he argued suppressed physical appetites leaving men greater mental energy to pursue non-essential commodities such as clothing and furnishings: the wants of the body being easily satisfied men turned instead to the wants of the mind. In contrast, in the country where the air was 'sharp' and provoked hunger, 'the great end of all men's labour is to satisfy that craving appetite'. Moreover, the solitude of the countryside meant that there was little desire for emulation for 'if a man be fed and clothed he is a prince to himself for there is nobody by him that is better fed and clothed'.[72]

For authors like Richard Braithwaite the unrestrained consumption of fashionable clothing was a sign of an individual's vanity and pride – both sins in God's eyes. Distracted by the beauty of her outward appearance, the wearer also neglected her soul or, in Braithwaite's words, 'so her skin be sleek [she] cares not if her soul be rough'.[73] However, in the contemporary view excessive consumption was more than just a private vice but threatened the stability of the nation at large. Amongst Braithwaite's targets in *The English Gentlewoman* was our preference for foreign fashions, which drove an overseas trade increasingly dominated by 'fashions, feathers and follies'.[74] As we have seen, one of the main concerns of those who sought to reintroduce sumptuary legislation in the seventeenth century was the need to protect our native industries against the threat of foreign imports. This was linked to a concern that England was operating an unfavourable balance of trade with the value of imports exceeding the value of exports. In introducing his sumptuary bill in 1621 Christopher Brooke argued that reintroducing sumptuary legislation would save the nation £200,000 per annum, presumably by forcing men and women to wear English rather than imported cloth and trimmings.[75] This argument was more fully expounded by Thomas Mun in *England's Treasure by Foreign Trade*, printed in 1664 but possibly written in the 1620s. Mun was not particularly bothered about excessive consumption as long as what was being consumed was of English manufacture. Like Brooke, he called for the reintroduction of sumptuary legislation to require men and women to wear English-produced cloth and clothing.[76]

In Thomas Shadwell's comedy, *Epsom Wells* (1673), the argument about the importance of achieving a balance of trade is put into the mouth of Hugh Clodpate, a Sussex Justice of the Peace with a pronounced aversion to London and all 'scurvy French kickshaws',[77]

> ... if the manufacture or commodity exported be not equal to the commodity imported we must ruin our trade, that's clear demonstration. Now we send them money in specie for foolish superfluities, for currants to make mince pies with.[78]

Clodpate, who only consumed ale, beef and mutton, 'the manufactures of the country', would undoubtedly have agreed with the author of *The Grand Concern*, published in the same year as *Epsom Wells*, who recommended that all foreign manufactures should be banned and that men should be persuaded to wear only clothes 'of our own growth and manufacture'.[79] Whilst arguments about the damaging effects of excessive consumption on the nation's economy continued to rage in the last three decades of the seventeenth century, when expressed by Clodpate, a man who still believed that churchyards were places where 'sprites and dead folks walk', such views were presumably supposed to appear old fashioned, especially to a sophisticated and materialistic London audience.[80]

In the late 1670s two publications appeared, both of which promoted conspicuous consumption as an economic benefit.[81] The first of these, *England's Great Happiness* (1677), was by apothecary and advocate of free trade, John Houghton (1645–1705).[82] Its subtitle was 'a dialogue between content and complaint, wherein is demonstrated that a great part of our complaints are causeless and we have more wealth now than ever we had at any time before the restoration of his sacred Majesty'. Houghton's argument was that imported luxuries and excessive consumption created national wealth. According to Houghton, French imports 'set us all agog' and had allowed the development of English luxury products, the quality of which were on a par with, or exceeded, those of England's European neighbours. If such 'super-necessary trades' were removed England would be reduced to a primitive state of tankard-bearers and plough men and London would 'in short time be like an Irish hut'. Moreover, consumerism was a stimulus to trade across Europe as nations strove to outdo each other in the range and quality of their products.[83] For Houghton, it was the individual's responsibility to balance his expenditure against his resources: 'he that spends more than he is able to pay for, is either a fool or knave, or in great necessity'. Provided a man lived within his means, material success and acquisitiveness should be embraced as signs of God's blessing.[84]

The second work was Nicholas Barbon's *Discourse showing the Great Advantages that New Buildings and the Enlarging of Towns and Cities do Bring to a Nation* (1678). Barbon, one of the most prolific builders of post-Fire London, used this work to defend London's growth against those, like the author of *The Grand Concern*, who argued that its disproportionate size was damaging to the nation's economy.[85] Quite reasonably Barbon argued that the construction of new housing stimulated the building and domestic furnishing trades, whilst the consequent growth in population led to increased spending. This in turn promoted trade and manufacture as suppliers sought to keep up with demand. Alongside Barbon's economic analysis of the relationship between a city's physical growth and consumerism was a psychological one. As we have seen, Barbon thought that the physical proximity and social mix of people in cities led to emulative consumption as neighbours sought to keep up with each other. A physical need like hunger could be satisfied, leading to a temporary cessation of industry: 'as the proverb says, "when the belly is full the bones will be at rest"'. But a psychological need like emulation could never be satisfied: 'emulation provokes a continued industry and will not allow no intervals or be ever satisfied'.[86]

Barbon expanded his ideas about the benefits of conspicuous consumption in his later work, *A Discourse of Trade* (1690). Instead of viewing the sartorial constancy of other nations as a source of moral and economic strength as authors like Richard Braithwaite had done, Barbon argued that it acted as a brake on trade. In contrast the mercurial fashion culture of the French and English stimulated trade because it encouraged the consumer to purchase new clothes before the old ones had worn out:

> It is the spirit and life of trade; it makes a circulation and gives a value by turns to all sorts of commodities; keeps the great body of trade in motion; it is an invention to dress a man, as if he lived in a perpetual spring; he never sees the autumn of his clothes.[87]

According to Barbon, there was no inherent social value in the *style* of clothing; that was given to it by the wearer and the context in which it was being worn or, in his words, 'it is only use and custom by which habits become grave and decent, and not any particular convenience in the shape'.[88] As a man given to risky financial ventures, Barbon was well aware of the social power of clothing. According to Roger North when meeting with his creditors Barbon would deliberately turn up late and then 'make his entry as fine and as richly dressed as a lord of the bedchamber on a birthday'. His creditors, 'that had prepared to give him all the affronts and opposition that their brutal way suggested, truly seeing such a brave man, pulled off their hats and knew not what to think on it'.[89] Like Houghton, Barbon thought that moral responsibility for consumer behaviour lay with the individual: 'prodigality is a vice that is prejudicial to the man but not to trade; it is living a pace, and spending that in a year, that should last all his life'. In contrast, covetousness was damaging both to trade and the individual: 'it starves the man and breaks the trader'.[90]

The city and fashion excess

Pride like the gout harbours chiefly amongst rich people and in great opulent cities.[91]

In much of the literature discussed in this chapter London is depicted as a centre of fashion excess and sartorial instability. Its particular qualities, including its wealth and the size and socio-economic mix of its population, supposedly encouraged emulative or competitive consumption. In the contemporary view,

London's shifting social hierarchies contrasted unfavourably with the fixed and stable social hierarchies of the countryside. Expressed sartorially, whereas country dwellers continued to wear clothing appropriate to their status, in the city this link had broken down, replaced instead by a sartorial free-for-all where tradesmen dressed like merchants and merchants like princes. The fictional London tradesman narrator of 'The Invincible Pride of Women' (c. 1675–1696) complained that his 'proud and imperious wife' used her fashionable clothing to appear 'more great than any merchant's London dame'.[92] To the author of *The Grand Concern* such competitive spending was possible because of the excessive wages paid to London servants and tradesmen; if their wages were dropped then their spending would fall.[93]

London's apprentices and domestic servants were noted to have a particular weakness for fashionable clothing, something that some masters and mistresses encouraged since a finely-dressed servant enhanced their own status.[94] The author of *The Grand Concern* claimed that 'Gentlemen and ladies do fancy greatly to have their servants that are about them so fine and neat that they must be in their silk gowns and petticoats laced, whisks and cuffs, fine shoes and stockings'. In consequence, such servants would not do any 'ordinary' work, meaning that the householder had to employ additional servants to carry out the more menial chores. Tradesmen too took more apprentices than they had formerly, which meant that it was difficult for them to maintain discipline. This new breed of apprentice 'must live high and wear finer clothes than they formerly did' and no longer did the sort of menial work that would have kept them humble.[95]

Many of those leaving the countryside for London were young men and women, looking for work or coming into the city to take up apprenticeships or work as domestic servants.[96] However, for the author of *The Grand Concern* it was not just the young who were abandoning the countryside for London. Any man who could 'get two or three hundred pounds in his pocket' moved to London and took a house, 'furnishing it for lodgers, thereby promising himself a lazy life, free from care' or else set up an ale house or brandy house.[97] Many of the country gentry, 'weary of an honest and commendable country life', also came up to London and squandered their estates on fashionable clothing and high living.[98] The advent of the stage coach had made their access to London considerably easier and more comfortable with the result that 'gentlemen come to London oftener than they need and their ladies either with them, or having the conveniences of these coaches quickly follow them'.[99] Amongst the consequences of these social changes, according to the author of *The Grand*

Concern, were that the countryside was being depopulated, farms were untenanted and the gentry were no longer receiving part-payment of tenants' rents in household provisions but instead taking them all in specie to spend in London.[100]

However, for the country gentry unfamiliar with city ways a visit to London was fraught with danger. In planning for a visit they might usefully have read Henry Peacham's *The Art of Living in London* (1642) which advised 'gentlemen, countrymen and strangers' visiting London how to live there 'in the thriftiest way'.[101] According to Peacham, for the country dweller the city was like 'a vast sea (full of gusts), fearful dangerous shelves and rocks, ready at every storm to sink and cast away, the weak and inexperienced bark … as wanting her compass and her skilful pilot'. Amongst the city's poisons were 'clothes in the fashion, this or that new play, play [i.e. gambling] at ordinaries, tavern feasts and meetings'.[102] Peacham's antidote for these 'several' poisons was to avoid idleness, seeking out 'useful company' or reading improving works; staying sober; avoiding cards, gaming and prostitutes. Caution with money was required and Peacham urged the country man to avoid falling into debt with his tailor in trying to keep up with London fashion.[103]

One of the difficulties for the country gentleman visiting London was understanding its sartorial and behavioural codes. We have already encountered Sir Mannerly Shallow, a character in John Crowne's *The Country Wit* (1675), who is unable to recognise that the heavily made up young women he meets on arriving in London are prostitutes and not ladies. The audience is told at the start of the play that Shallow, a young baronet from Cumberland who is obsessed with his dogs and horses, has never been to London before. In his 'fine country-fashioned suit' and with his 'country breeding' Mannerly is ultimately undone by his inability to understand city ways.[104] A similar theme is explored in *The Character of the Beaux*. On coming into his inheritance the 'Country Beau', 'having been bred up in ignorance and from his infancy led a retired country life', 'has an itch to be rambling'. So, 'having washed his face with milk and water, put on his best leather breeches, tied at the knees with red taffeta, his new blue jacket and his grey coat with buttons no bigger than nutmegs and smugged himself up very handsomely, [he] takes his best nag and gallops up to London'. There he is embraced by the 'Bully Beaux' who show him the sights, take him to plays and, at their own expense, refashion his country appearance to 'teach him a little breeding'. Initially 'amazed at their civility', it takes the country beau several weeks to realise that they are playing him, cheating him at cards and making him pay for all their entertainments. Now seriously in debt, having been forced to sell his best horse and mortgage his estate, and possibly having contracted the pox, he returns home 'repenting of his folly and resolving to do penance for his past luxury'.[105]

The rural gentry, therefore, were best off remaining in the countryside where they belonged and were most likely to find contentment. In the ballad 'The Country Gentleman, or, the Happy Life' (c. 1684–1686), the narrator celebrates his rustic life,

> I am a man of wealth and land/ and gold I have good store/ a good estate I now command/ what can one wish for more?/ I value not an hundred pound/ to tenants I'll be kind/ I'll have my hawk and have my hound/ and such delights will mind.
>
> To London I will not repair/ here sweeter pleasures be/ I live in a more healthy air/ and fairer beauties see/ I love the noise of 'hey-ge-ho'/ the whistling at the plough/ the baaing of the tender ewe/ and lowing of the cow ...[106]

Staying away from the city would also bring the gentry sartorial contentment. According to the author of *The Grand Concern* 'country ladies would be well pleased (provided they be kept from London) as if they had all the rich clothes, modes and fashions, vainly and extravagantly invented and worn in the city'; gentlemen would save the money they would have spent on travelling to London, whilst also being able wear clothes 'as good as need to be worn in the country'. Buying all their clothes from provincial suppliers would also mean that they boosted the local economy instead of starving it by shopping exclusively in London.[107]

Clothing, the 'golden age' and present-day rustic contentment

> In ancient times when as plain dealing/ was most of all in fashion/ there was not then half so much stealing/ nor men so given to passion/ but nowadays truth so decays/ and false knaves there are plenty/ so pride exceeds all worthy deeds/ while mock-beggar hall stands empty.[108]

As we have seen, sartorial excess was viewed as a disease of the present age in contrast to the sartorial stability of former times. According to Richard Braithwaite our ancestors had retained a 'simple, honest rusticity', continuing the sartorial traditions of their own ancestors.[109] The theme of present-day sartorial disorder was often linked to wider themes of social decay, characterised by a breakdown in traditional social hierarchies and the replacement of communal values of 'plain dealing' and mutual respect with a selfish, dishonest and arrogant individualism. For example, in 'A Description of Old England, or a True Declaration of the Times' (*c.* 1674–1679) the social turbulence of 'new' England is contrasted with the stability of 'old' England when people lived within their means, treated each other with honesty and respect and the rich were charitable to the poor. In this ballad 'new fashions' are blamed for the current 'bad times',

> What is become of your old fashioned clothes/ your long-sleeved doublet and your trunk hose/ it is turned to French fashion and other fine shows/ ... For now there's new fashions comes up every day/ with costly attire and sumptuous array/ it is pride in the kingdom does bear all the sway.[110]

The temporal location of the lost 'golden age' varied; in some instances it appeared to be in the long-distant past but it could also be located in the time of the immediately preceding generation. Responsibility for contemporary social ills was to some extent collective: as the author of 'A Cheat in all Trades' argued, 'Most men have forgot to be honest and true/ for to find out a friend when you fall to decay/ you may as well find a needle in a bottle of hay.'[111] However, one target was the gentry who, as we have seen, were accused of abandoning their country estates, their tenants and the local poor for a life of luxurious and self-indulgent living in the nation's capital. The decay in traditional forms of hospitality was given literary form in the motif of 'mock-beggars hall', the empty country house from which the indigent were turned away whilst the householder and his family squandered their wealth in London. In a ballad entitled 'The Map of Mock-beggar's Hall with his Situation in the Spacious Country called Anywhere' (*c.* 1640) the author laments the tendency of young heirs to sell their father's land for cash or to increase their tenants' rents and head off to London to spend their new-gotten wealth on leisure pursuits and fashionable clothing. In this, the present generation are accused of using extravagant and luxurious dress to achieve an aggressive, and aspirational, display of social status in contrast to the modest, sober and socially 'honest' dress of their fathers,

> Their fathers went in homely frieze/ and good plain broadcloth breeches/ their stockings with the same agrees/ sewed on with good strong stitches/ they were not then called gentlemen/ though they had wealth great plenty/ now every gull's grown worshipful/ while mock-beggar hall stands empty/ No gold, nor silver parchment lace/ was worn but by our nobles/ nor would the honest harmless face/ wear ruffs with so many doubles/ our bands were to our shirts sewn then/ yet cloth was full as plenty/ now one band has more cloth than ten/ while mock-beggar hall stands empty.[112]

Once again, the sartorial excesses of the present time are contrasted with the supposed sartorial stability of the past.[113]

Another way of criticising the social instabilities and greed of the present day was to contrast the sartorial instability of the city with the supposed sartorial constancy of the country.[114] In a number of ballads this is achieved either by means of a debate between two stock figures (usually a husbandman and a serving man) or through a direct address to the audience from a country man or woman. In these, the 'voice' of the country always defeats the voice of the city: as the Londoners who take on the countryman in 'Downright Dick of the West' (1685–1688) discover, 'the ploughman in wit is too hard for them all'.[115] One of the ways in which the country proves its superiority is by contrasting the hard-wearing and home-produced clothing of the rural poor with the self-indulgent frippery and luxury of urban fashion. An example of a 'debate' ballad is 'God Speed the Plough, and Bless the Corn Mow' (1684–1686) in which a serving man argues for his superiority over the 'honest' husbandman by drawing attention to his fine clothes:

> At the court you may have/ Your garments fine and brave/ and a cloak with a gold lace laid upon/ A shirt as white as milk/ And wrought with finest silk/ that's pleasure for a serving man.

But the husbandman is not persuaded and responds:

> Such proud and costly gear/ Is not for us to wear/ amongst the briars and brambles many a one/ A good strong russet coat/ And at our need a groat/ that will suffice the husbandman.

The serving man is eventually obliged to concede defeat and admits that the husbandman's calling is the best.[116] A similar debate takes place in 'The Contention between a Countryman and a Citizen for a Beauteous London Lass' (1685–1688) but this time the stakes are higher since they are arguing over the hand of a young woman. To the countryman the citizen's clothes are 'gay and gaudy' suggesting false wealth, unrealistic expectations ('you build castles in the air') and lack of constancy. He tells the citizen 'although you wear fine cloth and beaver/ and I but poor felt and frieze/ leather breeches will not leave her'. In other words, what you see with the countryman is what you get. His integrity and steadfastness win out and the young woman chooses him over the citizen.[117]

In these ballads the husbandman or ploughman appears to be modestly prosperous in the sense of having enough for his needs. But in the ballad world even the truly indigent could express their delight with their lot. In 'A New Song called Jack Dove's Resolution' (c. 1602–1646) Jack Dove declares himself to be

Figure 2.4 Woodcut of a country man from 'Downright Dick of the West' (1685–8), British Library c.20.f.8 (117). © British Library Board.

poor but 'content with what little I have'. This includes his clothing for as he says, 'some men do suppose, to go in brave clothes/ does purchase a great deal of respect/ though I am but poor, I run not on score/ I think myself honestly decked'.[118] A similar theme runs through 'Ragged Torn and True, or the Poor Man's Resolution' (1628–1629) in which the poor man wanting both money and clothes asserts that he nevertheless lives 'wondrous well' and has a 'contented mind'. His cloak is 'threadbare', his doublet 'rent in the sleeves' and his jerkin 'worn and bare' but he remains 'honest and just'. In contrast, he has seen 'a boot of Spanish leather … set fast in the stocks' and gallants wearing their wealth on their backs ride up Holborn in a cart.[119]

Country women are similarly modest in their attire and expectations. In 'The Country Lass' (c. 1628) the female narrator tells her audience:

> Although I am a country lass/ a lofty mind I bear a/ I think myself as good as those/ that gay apparel wear a/ my coat is made of homely grey/ yet is my skin as soft a/ as those that with the chief wines/ do bathe their bodies oft a.

She keeps to 'country fashion' and in her 'country guise' she is 'as pretty as those that every day devise new shapes in Court and City'.[120] Moreover, the country lifestyle keeps country women healthy and sexually wholesome, in contrast to their city sisters whose painted faces and fancy clothes disguise their 'green sickness' and queasy stomachs. Their love of fashion is their undoing: 'dressed up in their knots/ Their jewels and spots/ and 20 knick-knacks beside/ their gallants embrace 'em/ at length they disgrace 'em/ and then they will weep and wail'.[121]

The modesty and thrift of the rural poor, content with their locally produced russet and frieze, allows them to live within their means: as Downright Dick tells his London Don, 'both linen and woollen, whatever we will wear, we have of our own by industrious care'.[122] The serving men and gallants, on the other hand, are forced to borrow money or resort to crime to fund their fashionable attire. Moreover, much of their clothing is made of foreign materials: silk from France, fine linen and lace from the Netherlands, leather from Spain. The adjective that is frequently used to describe the attributes of country life is 'homely': 'my coat is made of homely grey', 'we country lasses homely be', 'a homely hat is all I ask';[123] 'in homely frieze';[124] 'homely cottages'.[125] We can interpret the word in two ways: first, to denote a wholesome, uncomplicated and *honest* way of life, characterised by comfortable domesticity, and second, to mean 'of or belonging to a person's own country or native land'.[126] The second meaning is consistent with the general tenor of these ballads which use clothing to create a vision of the countryside as inherently *English* in contrast to the city which is depicted as *foreign*.

Conclusion

The country men and women that we encounter in these ballads expound a sartorial virtuousness that in the contemporary view was largely absent from the rest of the population. They appear to be immune to the 'giddy humour' that had infected the population at large, driving it into ever greater acts of acquisitiveness and sartorial display. The difference between these country men and women, as depicted by ballad writers, and their urban counterparts is that they are entirely contented with their lot; living in their 'homely cottages' they experience none of the social competitiveness that characterised the inhabitants of the city and supposedly encouraged competitive consumption. Instead, they live within their means; even the poorest rural inhabitants were able to live 'wondrous well'. Moreover, because their clothing is made out of English woollen cloth their consumer behaviour supports England's economic wellbeing rather than undermining it.

Perhaps most importantly, their clothing is entirely consistent with their social position; there is no 'mimicry' here. One of the most unsettling aspects of contemporary sartorial habits was that men and women used clothing as a disguise; tradesmen dressed like merchants, the old dressed like the young and prostitutes dressed like ladies. This kind of trickery undermined the contemporary understanding that clothing should act as an external marker of society's divisions. It also, of course, caught out the naïve – men like the 'north country gentleman' or Sir Mannerly Shallow who were incapable of deciphering complex *urban* sartorial codes. As we have seen, the sartorial confusion of the city presented the country dweller with a particularly acute set of difficulties as he sought to make sense of its unique language of dress.

One of the things that emerges from the eclectic selection of literature examined in this chapter is the consistency with which certain themes were being expressed. Indeed, many of the criticisms levelled at the contemporary consumer were the same at the beginning of the seventeenth century as they were at its end. The only area where a new set of ideas emerges is that of excessive consumption where, as we saw, writers like Houghton and Barbon dissented from their peers in arguing that it was a spur to, rather than a brake on, trade. However, these new ideas did not immediately supplant the more traditional view that excessive consumption was both a personal and a public vice. The consistency of ideas about clothing in various literary forms suggests that they were relatively well entrenched in seventeenth-century society and that even provincial consumers would have encountered at least some of them in one form or another, perhaps listening to a sermon in church on Sunday or through the rendition of a new ballad. We know that Giles Moore owned copies of three of the works that feature in this chapter, Henry Peacham's *The Complete Gentleman*, Richard Allestree's *The Ladies Calling* and Thomas Shadwell's *Epsom Wells*, the first two offering him a conservative and highly traditional view of gentlemanly status and male and female conduct, the third a more anarchic view of social groupings and their somewhat chaotic interactions.[127]

3

Clothing and Textile Production, Distribution and Acquisition

This chapter examines the way in which cloth and clothing were being produced, distributed and acquired in seventeenth-century Sussex.[1] As we will see, the clothing market was remarkably complex, involving overlapping spheres of production, distribution and consumption.[2] Many individuals were producers and distributors in the sense that they had some involvement with the textile industry; at the same time they were consumers of manufactured products. There was considerable overlap between trades: for example, tailors and mercers both sold (or supplied) cloth and both made up clothing for their clients; mercers and chapmen stocked many of the same goods and shopkeepers and itinerant traders took their stock to markets and fairs to sell. Similarly, there was a wide range of methods by which men and women could acquire their clothing: women could process and spin flax and wool themselves, take their yarn to a weaver to be woven into cloth and then take the cloth to a tailor to be made up into a garment; they could purchase linen cloth direct from a mercer or chapman and make it up themselves or they could employ a seamstress to do it for them; alternatively they might buy linen clothing ready-made from a mercer, a seamstress or a pedlar. Men and women might buy a ready-made woollen garment from a mercer; they could also purchase a second-hand garment from a port sale or public auction, or from a passer-by; they might be given cast-off clothing by their employer or they might inherit it from a family member or friend. Most men and women were linked into, and participated in, all of these modes of production, distribution and consumption to some extent.[3]

The supply of woollen cloth and clothing

Sussex was not known as a cloth-producing region and for the most part the organisation of its woollen textile industry was fragmented, with the various components of the process interlinked but conducted as separate businesses. Much of the evidence for how it operated is anecdotal, which inevitably makes gauging its extent or commercial significance difficult. There were, nevertheless, some substantial clothiers in Sussex, men like John Bishop of Midhurst, whose will of 1640 records that he had his own dye house and fulling mill and was employing three weavers.[4] There were also some important centres of production, like Chichester, which had a sizeable woollen textile industry in the first half of the seventeenth century.[5] The best Sussex wool is likely to have supplied the broadcloth and kersey industries of the Kentish weald or to have been shipped around the coast to London.[6]

Most rural parishes in Sussex had a resident weaver, serving the needs of the local community. There is little direct evidence of the type of woollen cloth that they were producing but it is likely to have been coarser varieties such as 'russet' or 'homemade' or mixed-fibre cloths like linsey-woolsey and fustian. Russet, a coarse but relatively light cloth, is the type of woollen cloth that appears most frequently in testamentary clothing bequests of those of husbandman or equivalent status. It could be used for almost any outerwear, including petticoats, waistcoats, gowns, aprons and safeguards for women; and breeches, jerkins and cloaks for men; as well as for blankets.[7] Where it appears in wills it is typically as a made-up garment. For example in 1609 Joanne Gratwick of West Angmering bequeathed her best gown, her best red petticoat, her russet petticoat, her best hat and her wearing linen to her daughter Sibyl and her russet gown and her black worsted apron to Thomas Wakeham's wife, and in the same year William Napper of Wisborough Green bequeathed a russet jerkin, a russet pair of breeches, a hat and a pair of stockings to his brother, Thomas Napper.[8] However, in some cases, the testator was bequeathing a length of cloth that they had in their possession. In 1602 Alice Pettit of Oving left a piece of new russet cloth, a pair of sheets and 18s to her kinsman, Thomas Banks.[9]

The term 'homemade' to describe woollen cloth refers to a professionally woven, locally produced cloth rather than something that was 'homemade' in the sense that we would understand it. This is clear in a case heard in the court of quarter sessions in 1609 over the alleged theft of six yards of 'homemade' woollen cloth. The alleged victims, Robert and Joan Marden, told the court that their house in Robertsbridge had been broken into and a piece of 'homemade cloth of colour white of the length of six yards, lacking a quarter and of the breadth of a yard and three fingers' had been stolen along with two flitches of bacon. Joan said she had later seen her cloth 'dyed into red' but 'of the same breadth and length and weaved after the same fashion kersey-like'. She was persuaded that it was the same piece of cloth 'for that at one end ... it appears that there was a piece of russet yarn weaved into the end of the said cloth which is out of all saving the end of the thread at one corner.'[10] What Joan was describing is the identifying mark used by the weaver: in another case of stolen homemade cloth heard at the court of quarter sessions in 1649, one of the deponents told the court that 'the mark set in by the weaver in this piece of cloth [had] been picked out and another mark (*vide* a letter B) sewed in'.[11]

Most, if not all, rural households were involved with woollen textile production to some degree, but typically only with parts of the process. Giles Moore records intermittent purchases of wool, usually between two and four pounds, which was then carded, spun and knitted into stockings for him by local women. In 1659 he bought two wool fleeces weighing three and a half pounds from his stepson, John Brett, for 2s. He paid Joan Henfield 2s for 'picking' the wool and spinning two and a half pounds of it and Widow Vinall 5s for knitting him two pairs of stockings.[12] Moore's woollen stockings are likely to have been the only locally produced woollen garments that he wore: most of the woollen cloth that he bought was English but not local, for example broadcloth and serge.[13] Many of his female parishioners would have had a greater involvement with the production process than this – cleaning and oiling the wool, carding and spinning it, then taking the yarn to a weaver, collecting the cloth, taking it to a fuller, dyeing it (or having it dyed) and, finally, taking the finished cloth to a tailor or, in some cases, making up the clothing at home.[14] Wills and probate inventories sometimes record quantities of wool, yarn and cloth in the testator's house at the time of his or her decease, as well as woollen spinning wheels and stock cards.[15] We have seen that Alice Pettit of Oving left 'a piece of new russet cloth' in her will of 1602; in her will of 1605 Alice Bartholomew of Treyford left her two daughters 'one tod of wool and eight pounds of woollen yarn to be equally divided between them and all the coarse wool that is broken' and in 1608 Alice Burt of Binsted bequeathed to Anne Fry 'a new coat to be made of my cloth which is now at the weaver's'.[16]

We can get a clearer idea of how an individual might engage with the production process by looking at the case of Elizabeth Coulstocke of Ditchling, who was indicted at the court of quarter sessions in 1651 for the alleged theft of one and a quarter pounds of woollen yarn of 'a mingled colour of green and tawny' from a weaver called John Copper. Copper told the court that the yarn was 'part of a parcel ... brought to him by the wife of John Awcocke of Keymer to make a piece of cloth' and claimed that the yard and a half of linsey-woolsey found in Coulstocke's possession had been made from it. In her defence,

Coulstocke claimed that about two years previously she had bought five pounds of wool from Goodwife Earle, two and a half pounds of wool from Thomas Styan and that she already had three pounds of wool of her own. She dyed about one and a half pounds of the wool a green and tawny colour using dye stuffs she bought from the wife of John Buckall of Ditchling. She then spun all the wool and subsequently gave the dyed wool and ten pounds of white yarn to John English to weave into linsey-woolsey, instructing him to use the dyed yarn for one end of the piece so that she could have a waistcoat made from it. The fact that someone, probably Coulstocke herself, was lying does not undermine the usefulness of this case as an illustration of the complexities of cloth and clothing production for rural households.[17]

Not all rural households owned sheep, which meant that the wool that was being spun for domestic use was usually bought by the pound. For the truly indigent, wool could also be gathered from tufts caught on branches and undergrowth where sheep were pastured, or 'pulled' or 'picked' illicitly from someone else's sheep. Whilst this might not provide enough for a length of cloth it could be sufficient to knit a pair of stockings. In 1696 Elizabeth Hills was indicted for the suspected theft of two shirts and two smocks from John Peter's hedge, where they had been hung out to dry. Peter suspected her because she was seen walking away from his house with something bundled up in her 'lap' (i.e. her apron) and subsequently near her house with 'her apron very wet'. Hills deposed that she had acquired the clothing legitimately from a travelling woman and that she had been carrying wool in her apron, which she had 'picked off' from a dead sheep to make stockings for her children.[18] Rural women might also knit stockings for others in return for cash or payment in kind. We have already seen that Giles Moore paid Widow Vinall to knit stockings for him and in a case of suspected goose theft heard in quarter sessions in 1657, Mary Numan deposed that she had promised to knit Robert Hammond (the alleged thief) a pair of stockings in exchange for two geese.[19]

Sussex mercers stocked a wide variety of woollen or woollen-mix cloth, including locally produced types such as russet, homemade and fustian and those produced elsewhere in England or Wales. The latter can be broadly divided into traditional English woollen cloths (the 'old draperies') such as kersies, worsteds and broadcloth and the newer varieties of lighter-weight woollen cloths (the 'new draperies') such as serges, perpetuanas and shalloons.[20] Of these, it was only kersey that appears to have been worn by the poor. The overseers of the poor in Rotherfield, for example, made intermittent purchases of kersey (probably 'Kentish kersey') to clothe their paupers in the 1660s. It cost between

2s 8d and 3s 8d a yard in comparison to the better-quality Devonshire kersey that Moore bought for his niece, Martha, in 1668 which cost 6s 6d a yard.[21] Much of mercers' stock of woollen cloth would have been purchased by more 'middling' customers like Giles Moore. He made regular purchases of serge from mercer, William Marshall, in Lewes which was used to make his breeches, waistcoats and doublets and less frequently he bought black broadcloth from him to make new cloaks.[22] Moore also made regular local purchases of 'paragon', a type of worsted, which was used to make his cassocks. In June 1669 he bought six yards of paragon from tailor, Edward Waters, which was made into a cassock for him by another tailor, Richard Harland.[23] Martha's clothes were also made of English, but not local, woollen cloth including Devonshire kersey, broadcloth, paragon, penistone and serge.[24]

Tailors

Woollen cloth was usually made up into garments by a professional male tailor. Moore relied heavily on the services of his tailors when it came to acquiring new clothes, and generally did not make significant purchases of cloth without their advice. Unlike members of the middle and upper gentry who were more likely to use London tailors, all of Moore's tailors were local. He used a number of tailors during the period covered by his book, including Richard Harland, Edward Waters, William Best, Thomas Pelling, 'Mr Hull' and 'Watkins'. Some of his clothing was also made up for him by Horsted mercer, James Holford (discussed below). These men made and mended his and Martha's clothes, supplied him with cloth, accompanied him on shopping trips to Lewes or London and also shopped on his behalf. He must, inevitably, have known them very well: not only did he spend considerable time in their company, but his relationship with them was a relatively intimate one, given that they saw him in a state of undress whilst measuring and fitting him for his new clothes. He also needed to know that he could trust them. At the most elementary level Moore, like other customers, had to be confident that a tailor was using the minimum amount of cloth needed to make a garment and not charging him for a larger amount and retaining the surplus. Moore also relied on his tailors to choose and buy cloth and haberdashery on his behalf. We get a sense of the complexity of the relationship in Moore's payments to, and comments about, Richard Harland.

Harland and his wife must have been regular visitors to the Moore household. He made and mended Moore's woollen clothes and presumably those of

Figure 3.1 Trade token of Edward Waters of Horsted Keynes, tailor (1668), British Museum, T.5371. Between 1649 and 1672 there was no government provision of small change in England. Instead, thousands of shop- and inn-keepers issued private tokens, usually of a halfpenny or a farthing. © The Trustees of the British Museum. All rights reserved.

his wife, and his wife made linen clothing for the household, including shirts, handkerchiefs, bands (i.e. collars) and cuffs.[25] On 10 May 1666 Harland accompanied Moore on a shopping trip to Lewes where they visited the shop of mercer William Marshall. Moore bought two yards of scarlet serge, five and a half yards of galloon (thread or tape used to edge garments), quarter of an ounce of silk thread and four dozen red silk buttons, together with lining, padding, trimmings and fastenings for a waistcoat, three and a half yards of Spanish cloth, six dozen buttons, black silk thread and canvas for a doublet and two pairs of breeches and ten yards of hair prunella (a coarse woollen cloth used for clerical gowns), three yards of ribbon and quarter of an ounce of silk thread for a cassock. Harland's role would have been to help Moore select the type of cloth and to advise him on the quantities he needed to purchase and the type and quantities of trimmings, linings and fastenings. The total bill for Moore's purchases was £6 12s. He was evidently a little short because he records that on 22 May he repaid Harland the 25s (£1 5s) that he had borrowed from him in Lewes 'to pay for my clothes'. On the same trip Moore bought five yards of black cloth, half a yard of buckram (a coarse linen), half an ounce of silk thread and one button for a cloak, which cost him £4 8s 10d. Since he did not have the cash on him, Harland stood witness that he would pay Marshall 'sometime between this (i.e. 10 May) and Michaelmas next (i.e. 29 September)'. In addition to the money spent at Marshall's, Moore spent 2s 9d on beer and food for him and Harland at the Star Inn, 9d on the ostler who took care of their horses, and he paid Harland 1s for the cost of hiring his horse and 'going along with me'. Harland was then paid £1 for making Moore's new clothes and for mending his old cloak, cassock, cap and stockings.[26]

In August 1667, a month after Martha's arrival in the household, Moore paid Harland £1 7s 1d for a straw hat and for cloth, bindings and trimmings for a new 'suit' and coat for Martha which Harland had purchased from Frank West. Harland also received 4s 1d for making up the garments and for lining the hat.[27] However, Moore's relationship with Harland soured later that year when he suspected that he had overcharged him. In October 1667 Moore paid him for the purchase of ten yards of hair prunella that Harland had bought 'of Snatt in Lewes' (Stephen Snatt, woollen draper) which cost £2 10s 'as he (i.e. Harland) says', noting that '2s more being paid for this prunella than was for the former' (i.e. that he bought from William Marshall the previous year).[28] At the same time Moore paid Harland for 'footing and mending four pairs of stockings', noting that 'the four pairs of stockings cost the footing 3s 6d which was unreasonable'. Immediately after this Moore withdrew his custom from Harland, using different tailors, Edward Waters, Thomas Pelling and William Best.[29] For Harland, this must have been a blow, representing not only a loss of income but also the prestige that came with having a customer like Moore.

Moore was not the only customer to worry that tailors were overcharging by using too much cloth.[30] There is a scrappy note from 1715 amongst the personal papers of Sir Edward Turnour (c. 1646–1721) of Great Hallingbury in Essex in which he recorded 'the difference of Hood the tailor and other tailors in the quantities of cloth and other things he took to make a suit of clothes'. According to Turnour's calculations, Hood had used five yards of blue cloth to make one of his household servants a suit of a coat, breeches and a waistcoat, and a further eight and a half yards to line the coat and waistcoat. In contrast, a tailor called 'Woodnot' has used only four and a half yards of cloth to make the same servant a suit and only seven and a half yards to line it.[31]

The relationship someone like Elizabeth Coulstocke had with her tailor is likely to have been rather different to that of Moore. As we have seen, Moore's tailors came to his home to measure and fit his clothes, they accompanied him on shopping trips to Lewes and London to help him choose his cloth and accessories and they also shopped on his behalf. In contrast, a poor woman like Coulstocke would have taken the cloth to the tailor's premises, presumably been measured and fitted there, and returned to collect the completed garment. In 1655 a young female servant, Mary Charman, told the court of quarter sessions that she had gone to her tailor's to 'fetch home' a waistcoat and petticoat that he had made for her. Like Moore and Turnour, she was concerned that the tailor might cheat her out of some of her cloth and asked him 'if there were any pieces left of it'. He gave her back a small remnant, promising 'as God shall judge my soul there is all'.[32] For the parish poor clothed at the parish's expense, the relationship would have been even more distant. Parish overseers bought woollen cloth directly from mercers and then had it made up by local tailors, as well as buying what appear to have been ready-made clothes (discussed below).[33]

The supply of linen cloth and clothing

If we turn to linen cloth and clothing production we can again look at what was going on in Giles Moore's household. Moore grew hemp and flax and his book records the various stages of its production from ploughing the land to whiting the cloth, as well as payments to the men and women involved at each stage. The cloth produced was used for household linen, including sheets, pillow cases, napkins, table cloths and cupboard cloths, or occasionally sold. For example, in March 1660 Moore sold 24 ells of woven flax tow to tailor, Edward Waters, for 26s.[34] Moore's hemp was grown in his 'hemp land', with seed bought from London or from one of his neighbours, Widow Ward.[35] The crop was sown in April; 'summer hemp' was harvested in July and 'winter hemp' in September or October.[36] Digging or ploughing the hemp land and sowing the hemp seed was a job usually undertaken by men, such as Andrew and John Devoll, who in April 1668 were paid 2s for digging, sowing and 'mulling' the ground.[37] Women usually harvested the crop, a relatively easy process since it was pulled up by the roots by hand, and undertook the initial phases of conversion, including retting (soaking the harvested hemp in ditches or in specially dug pits), drying and breaking (crushing the stems using a 'brake' to separate the fibre from the core).[38] In 1657 Moore paid Bes Mills 9d for three days' work 'in drawing the summer hemp' and eight breakers (seven women and one man) 1s each, plus their food and drink, for breaking it. After this the hemp had to be 'swingled', beaten and 'heckled' to break down the woody stems and to extract and comb the fibre. It could then be 'dressed' – essentially a repetition of the previous three stages to refine the fibre so that a finer linen cloth could be achieved.[39] For this Moore employed male hemp dressers, such as John Ashby and Enoch and Philip Brown.[40] The processed fibre was then ready for spinning, a task undertaken by a number of different women who were paid by the spun pound, the rate varying depending on the quality of fibre.[41] For example, in 1658 Moore paid Widow Ward 5d a pound for spinning 7lb of 'fine hempen tow' and 4½d a pound for spinning 12lb of 'course hemp tow' and in 1659 Thomas Norris's wife was paid 11d a pound for spinning 13lb of hemp tire.[42] Yarn was sent to the weaver, William Rigglesford, to be woven into cloth before being returned to Moore to be 'whited' or bleached, which involved soaking it in lye and ashes before spreading it out on the grass to dry.[43]

Moore's account of flax and hemp production suggests that he was managing the various stages himself but some of the spinning was evidently managed by his wife. There are odd references in Moore's journal to his wife's involvement in linen textile production. For example, in January 1657 Moore recorded that he 'sent by my man (i.e. his servant) to my wife to get spun eight heads of summer tire being 8½lb, together with 12½lb or thereabouts of the best tow and 8lb of coarse tow', which his wife then re-weighed, finding the amounts to be 7lb, 10lb and 6lb respectively. In April 1657 Moore recorded that he 'sent to my wife by my man for 8lb of summer tire spun at 10d the pound and for 10lb of coarse tow at 3d the pound' for which he records a payment, presumably to her, of 10s 8d; the following April Moore again paid his wife for 10lb of spun flax tire.[44] All the women living in the Moore household are likely to have spun: in December 1669 Moore gave Martha 1s 6d 'at Christmas to play withal' in payment for her spinning and in April 1670 he gave one of the household servants, Bes Falconer, 1s 'for ending her spinning before Easter'.[45]

In addition to his 'home-produced' cloth, Moore also bought flax and hemp cloth from local women, such as Goodwife Cornford, Goodwife Seaman, Goodwife Buckwell and Goodwife Vinall, as well as from his tailor, Richard Harland and mercer, James Holford. Most of this was used to make household linen, shirts and smocks.[46] Finer holland linen was also bought locally, either from local women such as Goodwife Cranfield and Goodwife Pignall, itinerant traders like 'Seldon's wife, itinerant pedlar of Brighton' or 'Scotch men', James Barton, Patrick Heron and John Macrery, from mercer, James Holford, or from one of the local fairs.[47] Some household linen and clothing was made up at home, such as the two smocks Susan made for Martha in 1667.[48] Other linen and clothing was put out to local women: Moore paid his tailor Richard Harland's wife 1s 6d in March 1663 for making him three new shirts of homemade cloth and 1s 8d in November 1665 for making three new shirts and 'marking' caps.[49] Household linen and linen clothing were 'marked' with his and his wife's initials (G^MS).[50]

Moore's meticulous record keeping provides a detailed account of linen cloth and clothing production and acquisition in his household which is a useful addition to the more anecdotal information available from other sources. In many respects his household was relatively typical in the sense that its members were involved with some but not all stages of linen cloth and clothing production but were dependent on the professional services of others for the remainder. Most rural households also used a mixture of locally produced and imported linen. The best quality linen was 'holland', which was particularly favoured by poorer women for head and neckware and 'best' aprons. It is reasonable to assume that much household linen and linen clothing was made up at home but even relatively poor households might use the services of a seamstress. Although it might be argued that paying someone else to make up linen clothing was an unnecessary expense for the poor it should be borne in mind that the major cost of any garment was the fabric; the cost of making it up was comparatively low. For example, in 1663 the overseers of the poor for the parish of Rotherfield spent 4s 10d on 4¾ ells of lockram and thread to make Margaret Martin two smocks; the cost of making them up was a mere 8d.[51] Moreover, it is unlikely that all women had the necessary cutting and sewing skills to make more complex garments like smocks and shirts. Poor eyesight and arthritic fingers must also have hindered many women's ability to sew as they got older.

Linen clothes (smocks, shirts, head and neckwear) were washed regularly, which means that all but the truly indigent would have had a minimum of two sets.[52] The expectation that smocks and shirts would be changed regularly is reflected in the fact that they were frequently referred to as 'changes'. This is made explicit in an entry in Moore's journal where he records paying tailor, Edward Waters, 7s 'for 5 ells of lockram to make Mat [Martha] 2 changes with all … which smocks my wife made for her'.[53] Women who did not have a water supply in or adjacent to their property washed their linen in a local pond or stream or, if in a town, at a public conduit.[54] Washed linen was hung out to dry on hedges around the house, which made it particularly vulnerable to theft. We have already encountered Elizabeth Hills, suspected of stealing shirts and smocks from John Peter's hedge.[55] In January 1639 Francis Pankhurst confessed to having stolen a shirt and two smocks from Edward Parson's hedge.[56] Once linen was dry it was smoothed or ironed before being folded and put away in household chests and boxes.

All Sussex mercers for whom probate inventories survive stocked some linen cloth, although in some cases it was limited to coarser types such as canvas and buckram.[57] Michael Woodgate of Horsham had a wider range in stock at the time of his death in 1679 including 'hamborough' or hambrow, buckram, canvas, blue linen, holland and 'genting' or gentish.[58] It was also an important part of the stock of itinerant traders like those Moore was buying from.[59] Petworth chapman, Thomas Allen, was stocking a variety of linens at the time of his death in 1692 including osnaburg, silesia, hambrow, dowlas, scotch cloth, garlicks, burlap and holland. Whilst he appears to have had a shop, some of his stock would have been taken out onto the road by his 'man', Hugh Mitchelson.[60] As their names suggest, much of this linen originated in Europe: in 1700 linen was the second largest manufactured import into England.[61] The port book for Rye for 1675 records large quantities of 'Normandy canvas' and lesser quantities of silesia coming into the port and Samuel Jeake's first venture into business in 1674 was to import a small parcel of linen from St Malo.[62] He subsequently developed a lucrative import trade in lockrams but was dealt a severe blow by the ban on French imports that came into effect in March 1678.[63] After the trading ban was lifted in 1685 Jeake again began importing lockrams. His business accounts for 1687 show that he was selling parcels of linen to fifteen different customers in Rye and its environs, including Rye draper, David Barham.[64]

Indian cotton cloth was beginning to make an appearance in Sussex by the second half of the seventeenth century. The 1678 probate inventory of Harting mercer, Thomas Vallor, listed eighty-four yards of coloured calico and an unspecified quantity of white calico and muslin and in 1692 Petworth chapman, Thomas Allen, was stocking muslin and a variety of calicoes including 'painted', 'marbled' and 'red'.[65] There must have been a market for Indian cottons in Sussex otherwise these traders would not have stocked them but there is limited evidence for their use. It is possible that their main use in Sussex in the late seventeenth century was in household textiles such as sheets, bed and window curtains although there is little evidence of this either.[66] The limited impact of Indian cottons in the provinces in the late seventeenth century is something that has been noted by Audrey Douglas. She suggested that this may have been partly down to uncompetitive pricing, which meant it was unaffordable to the majority of men and women. However, the cost of calicoes varied widely depending on their type or whether they were plain, dyed or painted. The plain calico stocked by Thomas Allen, for example, was 13d a yard, which compared favourably to the price of some of his linen cloth. His scotch cloth cost between 10d and 18d a yard whilst some of his silesia was 12d a yard.[67] The limited take-up of Indian cottons may, as Douglas also suggests, simply be due to the innate conservatism of the rural population.[68]

Shopping

As we have seen, seventeenth-century Sussex offered the consumer considerable choice in the type of fabrics that could be purchased. There was also a wide choice in the range of locations where purchases could be made. The widest range of shops and tradesmen were obviously to be found in the larger market towns but to some extent even the smallest towns can be seen as centres of consumption as well as distribution, serving a broad rural hinterland. Mercers were the type of shopkeepers most closely connected to the clothing trade, selling a variety of cloth, haberdashery, clothing accessories as well as some ready-made clothing (discussed below).[69] They also made up clothing and on occasion acted as pawn brokers. The 1611 probate account of Richard Barker of Arundel records that at the time of his death he had a number of items of clothing 'in gage' to a mercer called Nathaniel Fenn for which Fenn had lent the sum of £5.[70]

In villages and small towns, mercers' stock was typically mixed, including 'mercery', 'haberdashery' and 'grocery' but it could still be quite extensive.[71] In 1661 the shop stock of Walter Deane of the village of Rudgwick included a range of woollen, linen and cotton cloth, haberdashery, stockings and gloves, animal skins, dye stuffs, spices, loaf sugar, sugar candy and tobacco along with an eclectic range of other items such as scissors and knitting needles, candles, spectacles and combs.[72] Michael Woodgate, who had a shop in the market town of Horsham, six miles west of Rudgwick, had a similar range of stock in 1679 – a variety of woollen and linen cloth, haberdashery, some ready-made clothing, 'grocer's ware' such as spices, dried fruit, tobacco, sugar, soap and dye stuffs and miscellaneous items including hornbooks, primers, 'two bibles, five testaments, three grammars and two other small books and a construing book', snuff boxes, inkhorns, children's leading strings, nutmeg graters and shoe horns.[73] Men like Deane and Woodgate could not afford to be exclusive; their shop stock was intended to appeal to a range of customers from the relatively wealthy to the relatively poor. Mercers' clothing stock was marked to record its provenance and presumably to help identify their goods if they had been stolen. A theft case heard in the court of quarter sessions in 1648 centred on the identification of a pair of 'grass green' woollen stockings supposedly stolen by Mary Phillips. When the theft was first investigated the stockings had 'a mark on them such as mercers usually put on their commodities' but it was subsequently discovered that the mark had been pulled off.[74]

To get a better idea of how an individual shopped in Sussex we can look at the shopping activities of Giles Moore. In Horsted Keynes, Moore patronised mercer James Holford, making regular purchases of clothing-related items, including hemp and fine linen cloth, stockings, buttons, ribbon, galloon and sewing silk, as well as a range of other items such as cheese, soap, sugar, spices, vinegar,

Production, Distribution and Acquisition 59

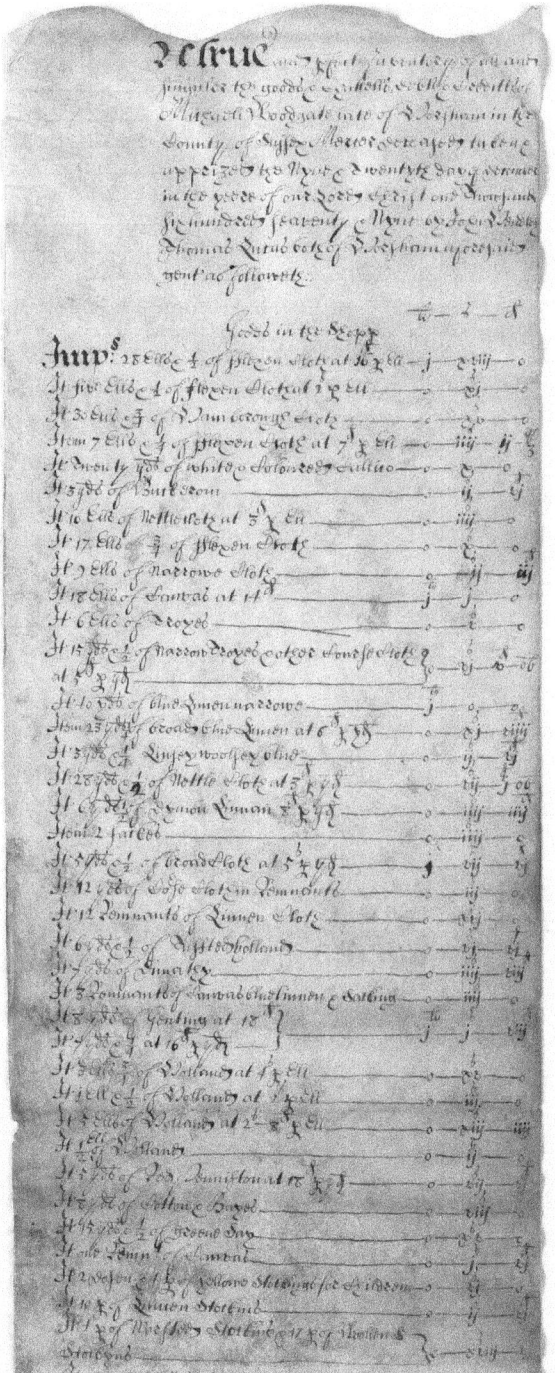

Figure 3.2 Extract from probate inventory of Michael Woodgate of Horsham, mercer (1679). West Sussex Record Office, EP I/29/106/165. Reproduced with the permission of West Sussex Record Office.

earthenware, glassware and curtain rings.[75] Holford also made up some of Moore's clothes, including 'a suit of apparel and a coat' and a serge waistcoat in 1656, undertook some 'mending work' for him and made up some of his household textiles, such as the feather mattress and tick he made in 1656 and the pair of window curtains he made in 1659.[76] Whether Holford was actually doing the tailoring and mending for Moore himself or employing someone else to do it is unclear. Either is a possibility. The 1632 inventory of mercer, Anthony Mutton, of Rusper included two pressing irons and two pairs of shears, the type of equipment usually found in tailors' probate inventories.[77] However, in the late eighteenth century Sussex mercer and diarist, Thomas Turner, was putting clothing commissions out to Framfield tailor, Charles Diggens. In 1765, for example, he recorded in his diary that Diggens had come over to 'take up a suit of clothes for Mr Porter'.[78]

Moore purchased a variety of goods from Lindfield, which was about four miles from Horsted Keynes, including furniture and bedding, candles and horse tack, but clothing-related items were limited to the purchase of a new pair of boots from shoemaker, Richard Parson, in 1660 and leather skins for 'linings' (that is, linings for his breeches) in 1673.[79] In Cuckfield, seven miles away, Moore made limited purchases from mercer, Francis (or Frank) West. In 1667 West supplied the cloth (broadcloth, penistone, paragon and bays) and haberdashery to make Martha a 'suit' (waistcoat and petticoat) and a 'coat' and in 1674 he supplied kersey, serge and buttons to make a 'soldier's new coat' for Moore's servant, Henry Plaw, when he attended the militia muster at Lindfield on Moore's behalf.[80] Moore himself made no clothing-related purchases from West, but in 1664 he paid him 4s for 'a pair of trousers which he bought for me at London'.[81] Moore bought a variety of other items in Cuckfield, including sugar cakes, brass, pewter, bedding and furniture.[82] He used a number of local shoemakers to make and mend his shoes and boots, including Thomas Stone of West Hoathly and George Norton of Chailey.[83] These shoemakers may have visited him in his own house to take his measurements and to fetch and return shoes.

Moore did not need to rely on local mercers and other traders because he could shop in Lewes, which was fourteen miles south of Horsted Keynes, or in London. As we saw in Chapter One, Lewes was a prosperous and attractive town with an extensive range of shops, selling luxury and exotic goods, some of which were imported through Newhaven and shipped the seven miles up the Ouse to the town's docks. Wealthy mercers, haberdashers, drapers, hatters, shoemakers and grocers clustered along the High Street, offering the consumer considerable choice.[84] Moore made regular visits to Lewes, combining clerical business with shopping. On the whole, his purchases were limited to mercery and haberdashery and for these he favoured mercer, William Marshall, who had a shop beside the Star Inn on the High Street. His book records that he made six trips to Marshall's shop between 1666 and 1670. For example, in June 1670, with the help of his tailor, William Best, he bought just over thirty yards of serge 'seraphico' to make a canonical coat, vest and a pair of trousers and just over two yards of scarlet serge to make a waistcoat, together with linings, tape, buttons (scarlet silk buttons for the waistcoat), silk thread and trimmings. He evidently thought that he had been overcharged for the scarlet silk thread for his waistcoat because he noted in his book that 'the colour makes [it] as dear again as any other silk that is not of a scarlet dye, he [i.e. Marshall] solemnly protesting that himself paid as much at London within 4d of what I paid him'. The following month he returned to Marshall's to buy four yards of black broadcloth and a set of black mohair buttons to make a cloak.[85]

Richard Harland made one unaccompanied trip to woollen draper Stephen Snatt's shop in October 1667 to buy cloth on Moore's behalf, but there is no record of Moore patronising Snatt himself and, as we have seen, Harland's purchase did not meet with Moore's approval.[86] In 1675, 1676 and 1677 Moore patronised mercer, Hercules Courtney, buying from him, amongst other things, ten yards of 'italiano' (a type of worsted) to make a canonical coat, and five and a quarter yards of purple bays to make a nightgown, which Courtney then made up for him.[87] Moore made one visit to mercer or haberdasher, Edmund Middleton, in July 1678, this time taking tailor, John Waters, with him, where he bought seven yards of Devonshire cloth (probably kersey), two and three quarter yards of dimity and a gross of doublet buttons to make a doublet and two pairs of breeches.[88] There were other mercers and drapers trading in Lewes during this period, including John Lopdell, Richard Barnard, Thomas Mathew, Thomas Norton, William Claggett and Francis Challoner. In choosing Marshall, Courtney and Middleton, Moore was evidently making a judgement about which trader was going to offer him the best service and range of goods at the most competitive prices.[89]

Shopping opportunities in Sussex were not limited to shops, however. Fairs were important shopping locations for a range of small consumables, including household utensils, clothing accessories and haberdashery.[90] All the members of Moore's household shopped at the local fairs, the bi-annual Lindfield Fair, held on 1 May and 25 July, and the Horsted Fair held on 1 September.[91] Both Giles and Susan bought domestic items: in 1656 Moore recorded that he had given his wife 15s to 'lay out' at Lindfield Fair with which she had bought three pails, a 'bucking basket', a soap basket, wooden dish, ladle and skimming dish, a 'tunning' dish, a

Figure 3.3 Trade token of Edmund Middleton of Lewes, haberdasher (1666), British Museum, 1913,1204.47. © The Trustees of the British Museum. All rights reserved.

milk dish, 'another dish and 7 ordinary dishes', noting that she had 2s 6d left over 'which she never returned me' and in 1673 he bought three pewter dishes at Horsted Fair.[92] Susan bought linen cloth at both fairs, for which Moore reimbursed her.[93] She is likely to have also bought herself small linen, accessories and haberdashery like gloves, hoods, stockings, pins and lace, which she paid for herself. Moore records a range of items bought either 'by' or 'for' Martha at the Lindfield and Horsted fairs, including hoods, whisks (a broad linen band or collar that covered the shoulders), stockings, gloves, ribbons, pins and fine linen.[94] Moore also gave Susan, Martha and his household servants 'fairings', small amounts of money to spend at the fair: in 1668 Anne Sayers received 6d and John Devoll 1s; in 1673 Mary Holden received 6d and in 1678 Sarah Bexly received 5s.[95]

Whilst Moore does not record who the stall holders were, theft prosecutions heard at the courts of quarter sessions provide detail about their likely identities. Many of the stall holders that the Moore family bought their linen cloth, accessories and haberdashery from were probably women, reflecting their close involvement with the linen trade. In a case that came before the courts of quarter sessions at Chichester in 1668 Katherine Young, who described herself as the wife of Thomas Young 'gentleman' of Arundel, alleged that Jane Taverner had stolen a 'laced holland peak' (that is, a fine linen neck cloth edged with lace) and a yard of lace from her stall at Steyning market where, about two weeks before Christmas 1666, she had been selling linen cloth and 'seamstress's ware'. In her defence, Taverner claimed that she had bought the items from a seamstress at Tarring Fair shortly before Michaelmas 1666.[96] Young appears again as a witness in a case heard in the court of quarter sessions at Petworth in 1679, now describing herself as a widow. On this occasion, Young claimed that she had been at her 'standing' in Arundel market when Sarah Tupper had come up to her asking for the two whisks that Young had starched for her. Young handed them over in a whisk box, into which Tupper then tried to hide a yard of bone lace stolen from Young's stall.[97] Other stall holders were chapmen like Humphrey Bell who in 1615 had 'one dozen yards of bone lace' stolen from his stall at Wisborough Green Fair and haberdashers like Henry Martin who had a hat stolen from his stall at Mayfield Fair in 1617.[98]

Fairs were also places where you could negotiate business deals, socialise, eat, drink and be entertained. In 1649 the Quaker preacher, George Fox, was preaching at markets and fairs in the Midlands where he took the opportunity to 'cry against all sorts of music, and against the mountebanks playing tricks on their stages', which he saw there.[99] Giles Moore recorded that in September 1663 he spent 2s 6d at Horsted Fair 'seeing the camel and lion', and no doubt there were other sights and entertainments that he and his household encountered that are not recorded.[100] In May 1694 Samuel Jeake attended Winchelsea Fair to 'speak to several debtors ... to pay their debts and to enquire if I could borrow any sums'.[101] The crush and social mix of people meant that they were also, as we have seen, sites of crime: stall holders had their stock stolen and fair goers had their purses cut.[102]

The type of goods that could be bought at fairs could also be bought from itinerant traders selling door-to-door. As Spufford has shown, by the late seventeenth century England had a well-established network of itinerant traders (variously described as pedlars, chapmen and Scotch men), which covered the whole country. Their stock-in-trade was linen cloth, haberdashery (needles, pins, buttons, hooks and eyes, thread, lace, ribbons, tape), small items of ready-made clothing (gloves, stockings, coifs, hoods, caps, handkerchiefs and neck cloths) and miscellaneous items such as combs, hand mirrors, scissors and whistles. Whilst they may have specialised in what Spufford describes as 'cheap and pretty goods for the poor' their stock was sufficiently diverse to ensure them a custom base at all social levels.[103] Moore records intermittent purchases from a range of itinerant traders, both men and women, mostly of linen cloth but occasionally of other items such as band strings (for example, '6 pairs of band strings bought of a travelling woman at Horsted Keynes' in March 1657), ribbon (for example, 'ribbon bought of an itinerant woman for cuffs and shoestrings' in July 1676) and stockings (for example, '2 pairs of black worsted stockings bought of a Scotch youth coming to the door' in March 1678).[104]

Figure 3.4 Pedlar with his pack from 'Sorrowful Lamentation of the Pedlars and Petty Chapmen for the Hardness of the Times and the Decay of Trade' (1685–8), British Library, c.20.f.8 (404). © British Library Board.

The socio-economic status of chapmen and pedlars was highly diverse. At the upper end of the scale was someone like Thomas Allen, 'chapman' of Petworth whose stock was valued in 1692 at £214 12s 7d. Whilst Allen himself is likely to have had a shop, his probate inventory lists separately 'goods belonging to Thomas Allen carried by his man, Hugh Mitchelson'.[105] At the bottom end was someone like Mary Pierce who for a period of twenty years had 'never had any constant habitation but went from place to place with pins and needles and such like small wares to sell'. An itinerant trader like Pierce ran the risk of falling foul of anti-vagrancy legislation (discussed in Chapter Seven); however, despite her transient lifestyle, she had 'not taken a begging or ever was punished as a vagrant'.[106] Pedlars and chapmen were also associated with criminal behaviour, either stealing goods themselves or selling on goods stolen by others. Agnes Russell told the court of quarter sessions in 1643 that a gang of thieves who had stolen goods from Widow Bexley in East Grinstead had pulled off the silver lace from a pair of her gloves, melted it down and sold it to a pedlar for 4s. Other goods were sold on to 'a chapman being a mercer … that gives in ready money for what wares they bring him 2s in every 5s worth as it is sold in London'.[107] All pedlars and chapmen posed a potential threat to the trade of established shopkeepers like mercers because they sold the same kind of ware and, according to some of the shopkeepers' complaints laid against them, operated at an unfair advantage because they did not have to pay shop or warehouse rent.[108] In 1696 the government passed an Act for Licensing Hawkers and Pedlars, which required itinerant traders selling outside markets and fairs to pay £4 a head for themselves and for their pack animal on penalty of a £12 fine. The register of licences shows that in Sussex licences were issued to thirty-four traders, of whom ten also purchased a licence for their horse.[109] Nationally, just over 2500 were licensed in the first year of the scheme although as Spufford has shown the distribution of licences was uneven, suggesting that the licensing procedure was erratically implemented.[110] Moreover, those who took out licences are likely to have been more substantial traders; many itinerant traders would not have been able to afford the fee.

The second-hand and ready-made clothing markets

As Beverly Lemire has shown, by the eighteenth century there was an extensive and well-established second-hand clothes' trade centred on London, with clothing being brought to the capital to be sorted, graded and resold to dealers operating in provincial towns and cities.[111] London had probably always been significant in the redistribution of second-hand clothing because of the size of its population: in his *Survey of London* of 1598 John Stow observed that many of the newer houses built alongside Houndsditch, which adjoined the city's eastern wall, were occupied by 'brokers, sellers of old apparel and the like' and in the 1590s, theatre entrepreneur, Philip Henslowe, was lending money on clothing and selling unredeemed stock on to Goody Watson.[112] However, as Lemire has observed, the second-hand trade was largely invisible and has left few records.[113]

In Sussex second-hand clothing was redistributed in various ways. Perhaps the most organised method was through a 'port sale', which was a public auction of household goods held after a householder's death. Notice of a port sale was given in a public place, usually the parish church, and goods were then valued by local 'appraisers' or assessors. The start of the auction might be announced by striking a drum and a 'crier' was employed to 'cry' the goods as they came up for sale.[114] Beer and bread might be served, charged to the deceased's estate.[115] There are sporadic references to port sales in quarter session records and in testamentary

Figure 3.5 Marcellus Laroon, second-hand clothes seller from his series 'The Cries of the City of London' (1688), British Museum, 1972,U.370.21. © The Trustees of the British Museum. All rights reserved.

cases heard in the church courts and more regular references to them in probate accounts. In a case heard in the Archdeaconry Court of Chichester in 1634 George Butler recounted that less than a month after Bartholomew Tiler's death the parish clerk announced a sale of his goods in the parish church of Kirdford 'on a Sunday before the whole congregation'. On the appointed day Tiler's goods were appraised by 'some of the chief inhabitants of Kirdford' and were sold off to anyone who would buy them. Amongst the goods that were sold was Tiler's best suit made of blue cloth which was bought by a sawyer called Thomas Tribe who wore it for the next seven years as his 'holy day suit' or Sunday best.[116] Overseers of the poor also used port sales to sell off the household goods and clothing of recently deceased parish paupers helping to offset the cost of their care. For example, in 1656 the overseers of the poor for the parish of Lindfield spent £1 19s 6d looking after Widow Terry in her final illness and on her subsequent burial. The sale of her goods, including her clothing, realised £1 18s 11d. The items of clothing that were sold off were a pair of stockings sold to Goodwife Gatland for 7d, a pair of shoes sold to Widow Piper for 2d, two blue aprons sold to Ann Harper and Goodwife Verall for 8d and 9d a piece, an old smock sold to Goodwife Teege for 1s, a waistcoat and coat (probably a petticoat) sold to Goodwife Coventry for 2d and an old hat sold to Goodwife Coventry for 6d.[117]

Some mercers may also have played a role in the second-hand clothing market through their pawnbroking activities, but much of the trade in second-hand clothing must have been more informal – sold to neighbours, friends and relatives, to passers-by or door-to-door. In the late seventeenth century Samuel Jeake junior's aunt, Elizabeth Bonnick (subsequently Dighton), living in Southwark, was sending down some of her old clothes to her Rye relatives to sell for her. In 1668 she sent an old coat, hoping to achieve 9s for it but Samuel Jeake senior discovered that it was moth eaten and threadbare, and told her that unless she was prepared to take the lower amount of 7s it would have to be sent back.[118] Elizabeth Hills, who we have already encountered apparently stealing shirts and smocks from John Peter's hedge, told the court of quarter sessions that she had in fact acquired the clothing from a travelling woman who claimed to have got them by begging. Since at that time Hills had no money she said that she took the clothing with a pledge to the seller that she would pay for them when she had secured some relief from her parish.[119]

Stolen clothing was usually redistributed in this seemingly casual way, with payment taken in cash or kind. For example, in 1639 Elizabeth Joab admitted to the court of quarter sessions that she had stolen three napkins and two aprons from Thomas Challoner's hedge which she had then sold to a beggar woman for a penny and a piece of bread.[120] However, there were places where stolen clothing could be brought for sale, such as the so-called 'Slowman's Fair' located in a field somewhere near Dunsfold, just over the Sussex border in Surrey. This took its name from an iron worker, Abraham Slowman, who orchestrated the event. In her deposition to the court of quarter sessions in 1618 Joanne Lunne claimed that Slowman had told her that one Lewis's wife 'did usually resort to a meadow to traffic for odd ends brought thither by rogues' and that he himself had seen her 'making herself a smock which she had new cut out of a new canvas sheet half whited'. According to Lunne, 'the byword had long been amongst the good companions of Furley Wood that the meeting of rogues and women to trade in that meadow is … called Slowman's Fair'.[121] Furnace houses attached to iron works were also popular locations for dealing in stolen clothing because they were frequented by the vagrant poor looking for somewhere warm to stay. In 1645 Joanne Booker, the wife of petty chapman John Booker of Ewhurst in

Surrey, gave evidence to the court of quarter sessions that her house had been broken into and linen bedding and clothing had been stolen along with some of her husband's stock and a sum of money. Suspecting a pair of 'wandering rogues' that her neighbours had seen near her house she procured a warrant for their arrest. They were apprehended at the furnace house in Dedisham along with a third man. Hidden in a bag under a straw 'couch' that one of them had been sleeping on were 'diverse pieces of wet linen' and a parcel of black, white, red and green thread, a paper of hooks and eyes, hair-coloured and green ribbon and white inkle.[122]

Clothing was also passed on to family members, household servants, friends and neighbours either during life or after death. In 1671 Dorothy Burgess told the court of quarter sessions that the linsey-woolsey petticoat she was alleged to have stolen had been given to her by her mother 'thirteen years since'.[123] Giles Moore gave some of his cast-off garments to his male servants, as well as to his parish clerk, George Hobbart, including a doublet, breeches and coat to Hobbart in 1663 and a riding coat and three pairs of worn stockings to his servant, John Devoll, in 1666.[124] Just over a year after the death of Anne Key in September 1665 her old taffeta gown was cut up to make hoods and scarves for her three daughters, Elizabeth, Mary and Sarah; in February 1667 three of her blue aprons were given to her stepdaughters, Jane and Anne, and in October 1667 Elizabeth was given her mother's old serge petticoat, two aprons and a pair of stockings along with her mother's 'wearing linen' including a cap, three coifs, four dressings, a forehead piece and three neck handkerchiefs.[125] Some wills reveal complex personal hierarchies of clothing, with garments being described as 'my best', 'my second best', 'my new', 'my old', 'my worst', 'my workday' or 'my holy days'.[126] Decisions about who should receive which garment were clearly highly personal, reflecting ties of love and friendship or perhaps in recompense for a service the beneficiary had provided to the testator. They were usually given without caveat although presumably with some expectation that the recipient would think of the donor when wearing the garment. However, some bequeathed garments were no doubt given away, sold on or refashioned for another use if they could not be made to fit or were simply too worn to wear.

By the late seventeenth century there was a well-established ready-made clothing market, with production centred in London and its suburbs. The growth of the ready-made market was stimulated from the 1640s by the need to clothe large numbers of army and navy personnel and by the late seventeenth century an increasing amount of London-made clothing was also being exported to the colonies to clothe settlers and slaves.[127] Those dealing in the large-scale production and distribution of ready-made clothing for the civilian market were called 'salesmen'.[128] An example of a salesman is Samuel Dalling, who had a shop in the parish of St Olave's in Southwark. His probate inventory of 1699 records a large stock of ready-made garments, including fifty-four flannel waistcoats, thirty calico frocks, nineteen women's flannel petticoats, fifty girls' cantaloon petticoats, twenty-one 'body' coats, ten pairs of boys' drawers and eight pairs of shag breeches.[129] His probate account records payments to a number of workmen and women who were involved in clothing production: Mr Johnson 'for pressing', Mr Horner 'the tailor for work in making up garments', Mrs Palmer and Mrs Thomas 'for work about the same'. As well as selling directly from his shop, Dalling sold at regional fairs, including Bristol, Stourbridge, Baldock, Maidstone and Marlow.[130] There were also salesmen operating in the provinces, men like John Wood of Sittingbourne in Kent whose probate inventory of 1704 records a stock of ready-made clothing including waistcoats, coats, breeches, frocks and drawers for boys and men and gowns, petticoats and mantuas for girls and women.[131]

It is clear that ready-made clothing was being sold in late seventeenth-century Sussex although its provenance is usually unknown. Some ready-made clothing was coming into Sussex from London through its ports, presumably on order from local mercers.[132] More might have been bought from a regional fair such as that in Maidstone. We can see stocks of ready-made clothing in some mercers' probate inventories. For example, the 1679 inventory of Michael Woodgate of Horsham records twenty-eight pairs of childrens' yellow stockings, ten pairs of linen stockings, four pairs of worsted stockings, seventeen pairs of woollen stockings, eight pairs of 'small' bodices, nine little waistcoats and six large waistcoats.[133] In 1691 the shop stock of John Penfold of Storrington included two canvas frocks, sixty-six pairs of women's hose, eighteen pairs of worsted hose, twenty-four pairs of yarn hose, thirty-six pairs of children's hose, thirteen small yellow waistcoats and twenty-eight bodices.[134] It is possible that some clothing stock listed in mercers' inventories was second hand but the quantities and apparent uniformity of sizing, colour and yarn or cloth type suggest that in the main these were ready-made items. They may have been manufactured in London but some mercers are likely to have been involved in the production of ready-made garments themselves. The overseers of the poor for the parishes of Rotherfield and Worth were both purchasing what appear to have been ready-made garments from local mercers, in addition to employing local tailors directly to make up clothing for individual paupers. In Rotherfield, the overseers dealt with at least three different mercers in the 1660s and 1670s including William Catt who in 1662 received the sizeable sum of £6 18s 6d for 'clothes and other things' for the poor.¹³⁵ In Worth in the 1690s the overseers bought ready-made clothing from mercer, James Coleman, including shifts, shirts, coats, breeches, petticoats, gowns and bodices.¹³⁶ For mercers like Catt and Coleman the parish poor were good business: not only did the overseers provide them with regular orders but payment was more-or-less guaranteed.

Hats, shoes, gloves and other accessories were bought ready-made throughout the seventeenth century. The 1687 inventory of John Waller, a feltmaker of Horsham, lists a wide range of felt, straw and 'chip' hats for children and adults, as well as hatbands (both 'course' and 'fine') and hat linings.¹³⁷ The inventories of shoemakers and cordwainers show that they made shoes in standard sizes, which customers could buy 'off the shelf'. For example, the stock recorded in the 1623 inventory of Edward Napper, a cordwainer from Chichester, included 'thirteen dozen of the bigger size of shoes', 'six dozen and eight pairs of the second size', and 'one dozen and seven pairs' of the smallest size, together with three pairs of

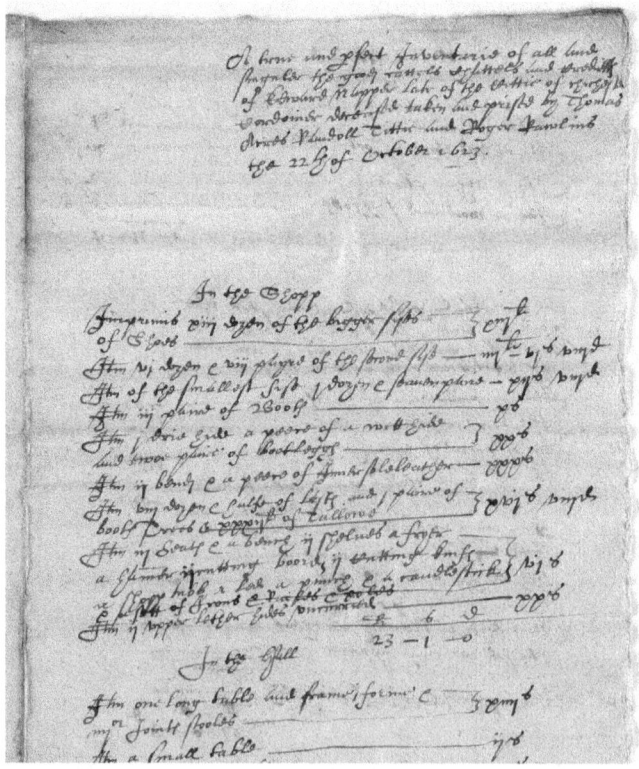

Figure 3.6 Extract from probate inventory of Edward Napper of Chichester, cordwainer (1623), West Sussex Record Office, EP I/29/541/34. Reproduced with the permission of West Sussex Record Office.

boots. Presumably Napper also made bespoke footwear for those who could afford it.[138] Shoemakers increased their customer base by taking their stock out on the road to markets and fairs: the 1621 inventory of Thomas Moore, a shoemaker from Arundel, included a 'nag', a road saddle, bridle, pack saddle and two pairs of hampers and in 1647 a shoemaker called George Palmer of West Chiltington gave evidence against Thomas Hussey who he alleged had stolen a pair of shoes from his stall at Steyning fair.[139] As well as making leather gloves and mittens, glovers made leather clothing and other accessories including doublets and breeches, purses, pockets and bags. In 1670 the shop stock of Henry Lintott of Horsham included nine pairs of breeches, two dozen pairs of men's gloves, four pairs of beaver-skin gloves as well as pouches, purses, a satchel and two leather bags.[140]

Conclusion

The reference to 'beaver-skin' gloves in Lintott's probate inventory is a reminder of how interconnected the provincial clothing market was with global trade networks.[141] Whilst only a minority of Sussex inhabitants are likely to have worn gloves made from such exotic material, even the poorest men and women were wearing garments made from European-produced linens. Indian cotton textiles were available to buy in Sussex in the late seventeenth century although they seem to have had limited appeal. The majority of woollen cloth stocked by mercers was of English manufacture but poorer inhabitants tended to be limited in their choice of woollen cloth to the coarser varieties produced in Sussex or its environs.

This chapter has highlighted the overlapping spheres of production, distribution and consumption in seventeenth-century Sussex, and the individual's interaction with these. There were marked similarities in the way that individuals of different status engaged with the clothing market. As we have seen, even a lesser gentry household like Moore's was involved with textile production; and like his poorer neighbours he had clothing made for him by tailors and seamstresses, bought haberdashery and clothing accessories from itinerant traders and from fairs and made use of his local mercer. Whilst Moore is unlikely to have purchased second-hand clothes, he did participate in the second-hand clothing market by giving his cast-off clothing to his servants.

The provincial clothing industry employed large numbers of men and women, some operating on a very small scale, others, like clothier John Bishop of

Midhurst, operating on a more substantial scale. Within the industry there were some clearly demarcated gender roles. Women carded and spun wool; men wove it and tailored the finished cloth. Home dyeing could be undertaken by women; professional dyeing was undertaken by men. Flax and hemp processing was divided between men and women, with men undertaking the more physically demanding tasks such as beating and heckling the woody stems; men also wove the yarn into cloth. Women were, however, a notable presence in the sale of linen cloth; as we have seen, Giles Moore made regular purchases of linen cloth from local women like Goodwife Cornford and Goodwife Vinall, the latter also knitting his woollen stockings for him. Women also worked as professional seamstresses, selling their wares at local fairs apparently as independent traders.

There was considerable consumer choice available in seventeenth-century Sussex, perhaps most clearly demonstrated in Giles Moore's choice of mercers. However, for many Sussex residents their consumer choice was limited by their financial means; a woman like Elizabeth Joab, indicted in 1639 for stealing three napkins and two aprons, is likely to have had little consumer choice at all. Despite the range of commodities on offer, for more affluent residents, including the conservative and money-conscious Giles Moore, the provincial clothing market was not extensive enough to meet all their consumer needs. For them, London, the greatest consumer market in England, was the place to shop.

4

London and the Provincial Consumer

For the writer Henry Peacham the city of London was a dangerous place for the country dweller; it was like a 'vast sea (full of gusts), fearful dangerous shelves and rocks ready at every storm to sink and cast away the weak and inexperienced bark', or 'quick sand', which sucked the unwary into it. What made it so dangerous were the endless opportunities it offered the consumer to spend money, whether on 'perpetual visits of vain and useless acquaintance', coach and horse hire, food and drink, new plays or 'clothes in the fashion'. Those unable to control their spending were very soon likely to find themselves napping 'on penniless bench'.[1] Despite Peacham's warnings, London remained a significant attraction to provincial consumers like Giles Moore. Not only did it offer the consumer almost unlimited choice, London-bought goods were imbued with a particular social and cultural value, which was missing from purchases made in the provinces.[2] This was especially true when it came to clothing. London was the nation's fashion capital, which guaranteed it the custom of provincial consumers wishing to remain 'à-la-mode'. London tailors and mercers supplied clothing and fashion advice to provincial clients and London's fashion news was disseminated to the provinces by London-based friends and relatives. However, as we shall see, purchasing in or from London, whether in person or by proxy, could be a complicated and frustrating affair.

Seventeenth-century London

According to the speculative builder and enthusiastic advocate of consumption, Nicholas Barbon, London was 'the heart of the nation, through which the trade and commodities of it circulate, like the blood through the heart'. It gave 'life and growth to the rest of the body'; if it declined or had its growth obstructed, 'the whole body falls into consumption'.[3] Others viewed London less positively, seeing it rather as a drain on the nation's life force through its monstrous and insatiable consumption, or as a head too big for its body.[4] Both viewpoints acknowledged the dominance of the capital in the nation's economy and its unique role in driving consumption, whether pulling it in to itself or pushing it out to the provinces. Whatever its critics might suggest, London was booming in the seventeenth century. Its population nearly trebled from approximately 200,000 in 1600 to approximately 575,000 in 1700, making it the largest city in Europe.[5] This growth led to an expansion of the built-up area. More than 20,000 houses were built in its northern and eastern suburbs between the early years of the century and the 1660s, and by the late seventeenth century much of the open land between the city and Westminster had been developed to create the fashionable and exclusive 'West End' where many of the nation's landed elite acquired second homes.[6]

The development of the West End was accelerated by the emergence of a clearly defined 'London season', coincident with the presence of the royal court and the legal terms, with the nobility and upper gentry coming to London in the autumn and returning to their country estates in summer.[7] Amongst this group was Sir Thomas Pelham (1597–1654), 2nd baronet of Halland and one of the wealthiest men in Sussex.[8] His household account book of 1626 to 1649 records his increasingly lengthy stays in London.[9] In the early years covered by the accounts Pelham stayed at a London inn called the Sugar Loaf but in 1637 he bought a house in Clerkenwell on the northern edge of the city. Perhaps deciding that this was no longer a fashionable enough London address, after his marriage to his third wife, Margaret Vane, in 1640 he took lodgings in Covent Garden. Finally, in December 1644 he took a house in the Strand, close to the house of his father-in-law Sir Henry Vane. That year the Pelhams spent Christmas in London and they subsequently adopted the regular practice of a long visit from December to about May.[10] The restoration of the monarchy in 1660 gave a new impetus to West End development as the nobility and upper gentry returned to London to enjoy a reinvigorated urban culture.[11]

As a thriving international port London was also at the heart of an expanding global trade network. Within the first twenty years of its foundation the English East India Company was responsible for five per cent of metropolitan imports and the period from 1620 to 1640 saw a five-fold increase in American tobacco imports.[12] The value of London's overseas trade continued to grow in the second half of the seventeenth century, with imports increasing by about a quarter and exports (including re-exports to regional and European ports) by a third. By the 1660s the English East India Company had carved out a dominant role for itself in the importation of cotton textiles from India and raw and finished silk from

India and China.[13] London also handled about three-quarters of the nation's trade with the Americas and, in Nuala Zahedieh's words, 'acted as the hub, or clearing house, for its Atlantic system'. By the late seventeenth century London controlled about three-quarters of English foreign trade and occupied a central position in a global trading system that extended across Europe to Asia and the Americas.[14]

London was also a centre of manufacturing. Peter Earle has suggested that about forty per cent of London's labour force was engaged in manufacture, a higher proportion than either commerce or services. The biggest industry, or group of industries, was the manufacture and finishing of textiles and their conversion into clothes or furnishing materials, which may have employed about twenty per cent of London's labour force, including a large number of women. Whilst much production was utilitarian (for example, soap production, brewing, bacon-curing and leather dressing), London also specialised in the manufacture of luxury and specialist goods, including jewellery, coaches, musical, medical and scientific instruments.[15] As John Styles has shown, the wealth of many of the capital's consumers, whether permanently or temporarily resident there, encouraged product specialisation and innovation, putting London on a par with other European centres of luxury production such as Paris and Amsterdam.[16]

Paris was the fashion capital of Europe but London was fashion capital of England. Although the Court continued to influence high fashion, fashions were also being set by London's merchants, manufacturers and elite shopkeepers. As Clare Haru Crowston has observed for late seventeenth-century France, 'the basic style of men's and women's clothing did not alter a great deal from year to year. Fashion consisted not in nuances of cut and style as it does today, but in the colours and motifs of textiles, in accessories, and in the design and placement of decorations, all of which changed from season to season'.[17] In Paris in the 1670s specialist mercers called *marchands d'étoffe de soie* set new trends each season for the colour and design of silk fabrics, working in partnership with merchants in Lyon, the centre of France's silk-making industry.[18] By the early 1680s the English East India Company was trying to anticipate new fashions by having samples of silk fabrics made in India and sent to London and Paris for market testing. Designs that found favour were then mass produced in India and returned to Europe for sale. This drive for innovative new designs was apparently consumer-led: in 1681 the Company's Court of Committee wrote to its agents in Bengal reminding them of the 'general rule that in all flowered silks you change the fashion and flower every year' because English ladies (as well as French and 'other Europeans') would pay twice as much 'for a new thing not seen in Europe before'.[19] The Company also made strenuous efforts to expand the English market for printed Indian cottons by using finer cloth that would appeal to 'gentlewomen' rather than merely to the 'meaner sort'. By 1687 they were able to report that chintzes were now 'the ware of ladies of the greatest quality' who wore them 'on the outside of gowns and mantuas [lined] with velvet and cloth of gold'.[20] These fashionable silks and chintzes would have been on sale in London's elite shops, such as those in the Royal and New Exchanges or in the mercers' shops on Paternoster Row, discussed below. Fashions could also be set by individuals. A fictional correspondent to *The Spectator* informed its readers in 1711 that it was a common expression amongst 'men of dress' that 'Mr such a one has struck a bold stroke', meaning that 'he is the first man who has had courage enough to lead up a fashion'.[21]

Dissemination of fashion information was still primarily through direct observation and word-of-mouth rather than through print or other media. From the 1670s French 'fashion' plates were circulating in London but their role in disseminating fashion information is unclear.[22] There was no equivalent to France's monthly fashion periodical, *Le Mercure Galant*, first published in 1672 (from 1677 retitled *Le Nouveau Mercure Galant*), and other types of printed material that addressed contemporary fashions were less concerned with informing its readers about what to wear as with satirising its excesses. As we shall see, London shopkeepers and tailors advised their clients on the latest fashions, not only in the cut and style of garments but also in fabric type, colour and pattern and in the choice and placement of buttons and trimmings. For those acting as proxy shoppers for friends and relatives in the provinces, communicating this fashion advice was a key part of their role. Men and women also acquired their knowledge of the latest fashions through direct observation of those they saw around them and, again, communicated this to their friends and relatives.

London's shops

In 1600 London could offer its consumers a more extensive range of shops than any other city in England. The traditional heart of London's shopping district was the area between St Paul's Cathedral and Bishopsgate, including Cheapside and St Paul's Churchyard, but as the West End developed upmarket shops could also be found on the Strand and in and around Covent Garden. Cheapside had been London's principal shopping street since the fifteenth century, noted for the splendour of its shops and houses, in particular those making up Goldsmiths' Row at its western end where wealthy goldsmiths lived and plied their trade. By the early seventeenth century many goldsmiths had moved out to new locations in the city or the West End and their shops were occupied by those of 'meaner trades'.[23] Despite the loss of such prestigious residents, Cheapside remained a centre of luxury trades and fashionable goods. The eastern end was dominated by textile dealers, most of whom were members of the Mercers' Company which had its hall there. By the 1660s shopkeepers included silk men, dealers in fashionable accessories such as bodices, lace and stockings, confectioners and tobacco and coffee sellers.[24] Cheapside was also the location of London's largest 'white' food market, which ran down the centre of the street on weekdays.[25] The Great Fire destroyed all of Cheapside but it continued to be a commercial centre after its rebuilding.[26] A 1680 print of the new Mercers' Hall, which opened in 1676, shows a row of shops with large street-facing windows, parallel counters and wall-mounted shelving and drawers.[27] In 1720 John Strype described Cheapside as a 'very stately spacious street, adorned with lofty buildings, well inhabited by goldsmiths, linen drapers, haberdashers and other dealers'.[28]

In addition to its street shops, London had a number of fashionable shopping centres or arcades.[29] The oldest of these was the Royal (or 'Old') Exchange, built

Figure 4.1 Print of Mercers' Hall, showing row of shops on the ground floor (1680), British Museum, 1880,1113.3526. © The Trustees of the British Museum. All rights reserved.

Figure 4.2 Wenceslaus Hollar, Interior View of the Royal Exchange (1647), The Metropolitan Museum of Art, 29.102.128.

in 1568 on Cornhill. From the start this had a dual function as the city's bourse or trading centre and a shopping venue. Merchants from across Europe met each day in its large central courtyard to buy and sell commodities and to receive and exchange business news whilst shoppers shopped in covered galleries or 'walks' in the ground-floor and first floor 'Pawns'. The Royal Exchange contained about 120 retail units, many of which were less than four square metres in area. From these, shopkeepers sold a range of fashionable and luxury goods, including jewellery and watches, silver ware, textiles, accessories, haberdashery and perfume.[30]

In 1609 the New Exchange opened on the Strand, built to the same plan as the Royal Exchange with a central courtyard surrounded by ground-floor and first-floor galleries. These contained about 100 small shops which were open from six o'clock in the morning to eight o'clock in the evening in summer, and seven o'clock in the morning to seven o'clock in the evening in winter. The location of the New Exchange was significant because it was outside the City, in the heart of the fashionable and exclusive West End. At first its shops were slow to let but by the 1630s it was trading successfully. Most shopkeepers dealt in luxury textiles, seamstresses's ware and haberdashery and some, like Thomas Templar, enjoyed aristocratic and royal patronage.[31] By 1693 nearly all shopkeepers were milliners or seamstresses; there were four cane sellers and two perfumers.[32]

The galleries of the Exchanges allowed shoppers to move between shops without getting wet, walking in filth or being jostled by horses, coaches or sedan chairs. An atmosphere of social exclusivity was created through the grandiose architecture and the luxury goods on display, and was maintained through the employment of beadles to keep out beggars and those of 'base quality'.[33] As Linda Levy Peck and Claire Walsh have noted, the Royal and New Exchanges were more than just shopping venues: they were social hubs where the fashionable and would-be fashionable – men as well as women – could mingle, exchange gossip and news and observe each other.[34] Daniel Defoe's fictional creation, Moll Flanders, took advantage of the excitement generated in the New Exchange by the sight of 'some great Duchess' and a rumour that the Queen was about to arrive to steal a paper of lace from a milliner's shop.[35] The destruction of the Royal Exchange during the Fire of London forced many shopkeepers to take premises in the New Exchange. Although this was intended to be temporary, trading there was so successful that many of them stayed.[36] Nevertheless, the Royal Exchange was rebuilt: its courtyard opened for trading in September 1669 and its shops in March 1671.[37]

With such an extensive range of shops in London for customers to choose from, shopkeepers tried to retain an edge over their rivals by promising novelty, exclusivity, variety, good service and competitive pricing. When James Gresham was choosing velvet for his mother's new gown in 1640 for example (discussed in more detail below), the shopkeepers assured him that the piece they showed him was 'as good a velvet as any they or any man had in London'.[38] Shopkeepers like Thomas Templar no doubt traded on their royal and aristocratic connections and London's French tailors and shopkeepers on their supposedly up-to-date knowledge of French fashions.[39] An emphasis on novelty also underpinned the more aggressive marketing strategy adopted by mercers' apprentices in Paternoster Row who, according to the author of *The Character of the Beaux* (1696), stood in their shop doorways for up to six hours at a time, 'more like actors than anything else', wearing waistcoats made of the newest 'gaudy' silk, 'invented and designed for a fashion' so that 'folks may take example by them, and they may be the first in the mode'. Customers lured into the shop to make a purchase were assured that the silk 'hadn't been made above these three days' and that it was unique 'in the whole Row'.[40] Upmarket shops, like that of mercer Joseph Floyd in Milk Street, offered their customers a relaxing environment in which to make their purchases with leather chairs to sit in and mirrors to admire themselves in.[41]

Shops were identified by a sign which helped the customer locate individual traders on busy shopping streets. Giles Moore noted many of the shop signs used by the shopkeepers he frequented in London including the 'White Lion', the 'Angel and Three Crowns', the 'Golden Anchor' and the 'Hat and Harrow'.[42] Of these, only one sign (the 'Hat and Harrow') had any relation to the type of goods being sold there; the other three were mercers or haberdashers. Trade cards, an early form of print advertising, typically displayed these signs and provided potential clients with the shopkeeper's name, the shop's location and a brief summary of the type of goods sold there. With limited space for image and text, many trade cards were nevertheless able to convey exclusivity, choice and value. For example, the trade card of glove seller, Thomas Jacomb (*c*. 1700), featured a portrait of William III with his shop address, 'the King's Head in Cheapside London' given below in English, French and Dutch, managing to suggest not only royal connections but a sophisticated European clientele. That of toymaker, John Jackson (*c*. 1700), 'at the Unicorn, the corner of Wood Street, Cheapside, London' featured a unicorn and informed potential customers that he sold 'all sorts of knives, combs, scissors, razors, canes, whips and spurs, umbrellas, buttons for sleeves, fine buckles for shoes … with other curiosities for gentlemen and ladies, at reasonable rates'.[43] By the late seventeenth century, other forms of print

Figure 4.3 Trade card of Thomas Jacomb, glove seller (*c*. 1700), British Museum, Gg,4F,52. © The Trustees of the British Museum. All rights reserved.

advertising were developing, which promoted a range of goods and services, although not yet individual shops. *The London Gazette*, first published in February 1666, included adverts for new publications, auctions of surplus and bankrupt stock, houses for sale or to let and lost or stolen goods alongside its news items.[44] By 1711 *The Spectator* was including some shop adverts such as that for Mrs Rogers's shop in Exchange Alley where 'persons of quality and others' could purchase 'the newest fashioned Venetian and brocaded gowns at very low prices'. The Golden Sugar Loaf 'right against the Horse at Charing Cross' sold bankrupt stock of men's and women's clothing, including satin, Persian and quilted petticoats, all at knock-down prices. Or those who wanted to smell sweet could buy a bottle of 'incomparable perfuming drops', exclusive to Mr Payn's toyshop at the Angel and Crown in St Paul's Churchyard.[45] The best form of advertising, however, was word-of-mouth; having secured a new customer, what shopkeepers most wanted was that he or she would recommend their services to their friends and families.

London and the provincial consumer

Those living in the provinces who had the means and the desire to access the cornucopia of goods available in seventeenth-century London had three options open to them. They could travel to London themselves and make their own purchases; commission goods by letter directly from the supplier; or find someone to shop on their behalf. In the latter case, it could be someone who lived locally in Sussex who was given verbal instructions about what to purchase or it could be someone, typically a friend or relative, who lived in London and who was sent requests and instructions by letter. The most straightforward option in terms of making sure you got what you wanted was to shop in person. However, this meant that the individual had to get him or herself to London, which was time consuming, expensive and uncomfortable.

Despite the relatively short distance between Sussex and London the poor state of the roads, especially through the clay soils of the Weald, made overland transport extremely difficult and there were no significant improvements to the road system until 1749 when the first Turnpike Act was passed, linking Chichester to Kingston-upon-Thames in Surrey, via Midhurst and Hindhead.[46] Options for getting to London widened in the second half of the seventeenth century with the advent of the stagecoach but many towns were still without stagecoach services as the century drew to a close. Thomas de Laune's *The Present State of*

London (1681), included an alphabetical list of 'all the carriers, wagoners and stagecoaches, that come to the several inns of London, Westminster and Southwark, from all parts of England and Wales, with respective days of their coming and going out'. The only town in Sussex that was served by a stagecoach was East Grinstead, close to the Surrey border, where passengers could take advantage of a twice-weekly service to Southwark. There were, however, daily coach services from Godalming in Surrey to Fleet Street and almost-daily services from Guildford in Surrey to the Strand. Those living in or near Chichester might have preferred to use the coach services departing twice weekly from Portsmouth with a dropping-off point in Southwark.[47]

Unless, like Sir Thomas Pelham, you could afford to hire a private coach each time you travelled to London, the journey was usually made in full or in part on horse.[48] Giles Moore, for example, did the whole journey on horseback, which took two days, staying overnight in Croydon.[49] Samuel Jeake, too, typically rode to London, staying overnight with relatives in Tonbridge. However, if he was travelling with his wife and mother-in-law they went on horseback to Tonbridge and then by stagecoach the rest of the way.[50] In 1684 when returning from London with his wife, infant daughter, mother-in-law and servant he hired a private coach. The journey still took two full days: Jeake noted in his diary that they left London at quarter past nine in the morning, arriving at Tonbridge at half past six in the evening; the following day they set off from Tonbridge at eight o'clock in the morning and arrived back in Rye at half past seven in the evening.[51] Stagecoach travel was not without its discomforts. The author of *The Grand Concern of England* (1673) thought stagecoaches injurious to health: passengers were squashed together all day with strangers and forced to breath in their 'nasty scents'; they were stifled with heat and choked with dust in summer and frozen and choked with 'filthy fogs' in winter; coaches were also liable to break down, forcing passengers to wait on the roadside until they could be repaired.[52] In May 1701 Elizabeth Jeake wrote to her mother in Rye to tell her about her recent coach journey to London:

> To tell you dear mother how I got to London is a difficult task but through the goodness of our gracious protector I am safe arrived. Two persons besides myself sat on my end, the gentlemen not at all less than Captain Martin when in his full bigness, the lady not inferior in bulk to Mrs Hall. Thus sat up I rode, three filling the other side, a gentleman of which held a young lady on his knee. Warm riding for us all.[53]

Since it was not possible to do the journey from Sussex to London in a day, visitors to the city were obliged to find somewhere to lodge. Before he acquired a house in London in 1637 Sir Thomas Pelham stayed at an inn called the Sugar

Loaf and his household account book records payments for lodging, diet, washing and 'horse meat' there.[54] It was to the Sugar Loaf that Pelham's seamster came for payment of his bills.[55] Giles Moore records the costs of staying in London but on only one occasion does he specify where he actually stayed. In 1660 he spent ten days in London staying with 'John West's tailor' at the 'flower de luce' (i.e. 'fleur de lys'), paying 5s 6d for his lodgings, 6s 8d for stabling and £1 1s 7d for food and drink.[56] Jeake was more fortunate than Moore in having a number of friends and relatives that he could stay with: his aunt and uncle, Nathaniel and Elizabeth Bonnick in Rotherhithe,[57] his cousins, tallow chandler John Mackley and his wife Elizabeth, in Southwark and apothecary John Jaye and his wife Mary in Fenchurch Street.[58] After 1690 Jeake and his wife Elizabeth usually stayed with his friend and former business partner, Thomas Miller, in his house in Mincing Lane, just off Fenchurch Street, and Elizabeth continued to stay with the Millers after Samuel's death in 1699.[59]

Those relaying their purchasing instructions by letter were dependent on what was at times, at least in the first half of the seventeenth century, an erratic private postal service. A series of letters from James Gresham to his mother, Judith Morley, then living in Chichester, sent between 1639 and 1643 show repeated issues with the 'foot post', not just in terms of its reliability but also its cost. For example, in a letter dated 21 December 1639 Gresham told his mother that he had waited 'this four hours for the foot post' in the hope that he would receive a letter from her with further instructions about what she wanted him to buy 'but he has not yet come, it being now dark night and rainy'.[60] In October 1640 James complained to his mother about the cost of the postal service, telling her that 'your foot post grows so unreasonable that you must agree with him by the quarter for carriage of our letters or I shall not be able to contrive any longer this our mutual conversation, for every Saturday he gets a groat of me, 2d for your letter that he brings and 2d for my letter'.[61] Delays in receiving his mother's letters meant that James often did not know whether she had got his, leading to duplication in the content of some of his letters to her and frustration on both sides about fulfilling Judith's shopping requests. The introduction of a public postal service in the late seventeenth century improved communication between London and the provinces.[62] In 1697 it took two days for a letter from Rye to get to Samuel Jeake in London and in 1701 Elizabeth Jeake could write on a Tuesday from London to her mother in Rye requesting her to send horses for her return journey from Tonbridge that Friday.[63]

Irrespective of whether someone shopped in person or by proxy, the goods still had to be carried down to Sussex. Commercial carrying services between

Sussex and London were better developed than stage coach services: Chichester, East Grinstead, Horsham, Lewes, Petworth, Shoreham and Wadhurst all had carriers or wagoners operating at least once a week, with collection or dropping off points at various Southwark inns.[64] Between 1656 and 1669 Giles Moore was using a local carrier called John Morley to bring his purchases down from London; Morley also supplied Moore with London 'news books' and carried his post for him.[65] As well as using carriers, Jeake occasionally transported his goods back from London by sea. In 1688 he spent £24 on clothes and some fashionable Japanned furniture and it was transported back to Rye on the boat of Rye mariner, Alexander White. However, when it was unloaded Jeake discovered that some of the furniture was 'dented and battered', leaving him 'excessively vexed all the day'.[66]

Shopping in person

To examine in more detail how a seventeenth-century Sussex consumer shopped in London we can turn to the household account book of Giles Moore. Moore's record keeping was so precise that he noted each item that he purchased, usually with the name of the shopkeeper and the name and location of his or her premises. This is in contrast to many seventeenth-century household accounts which offer only the most cryptic references to purchases made in London. For example, in 1621 John Everenden of Sedlescombe recorded in his account book that he had spent £30 'at London when I went to be married' and in 1628 that he had spent £20 'at London ... for two suits of apparel and other things'.[67]

Moore made approximately forty journeys to London over the twenty-three year period covered by his account book; in some years he went up only once, in others two or three times; typically he stayed for two or three nights. His longest trips were in 1660 when he stayed for a period of ten days from 26 June to 6 July and in 1661 when he stayed for a period of eighteen days from 10 June to 27 July.[68] He had various reasons for travelling to London. Sometimes, he travelled on legal business, as in June 1670 when he had been subpoenaed to appear at London's Guildhall.[69] In June 1664 he travelled to London on his way to visit his family in Suffolk; in July 1667 Moore travelled to London to meet his sister, Susan Mayhew, and to collect his niece, Martha, who was coming to live with him; and in May 1670 he travelled to London 'about putting of my hops'.[70] He does not always say who went with him, but he was usually accompanied by his 'man' (i.e. his servant) and frequently by his tailor. For example, in April 1659

Moore records his journey to London and notes that he paid 2s to 'the tailor for going along with me and helping me to buy'.[71] His wife seems to have accompanied him on only two occasions, in June 1662 and October 1670. On the first occasion, he was visiting London on legal business ('about the cutting off the entail of land') and her presence may have been required as a party.[72] On the second occasion, she was seeking medical treatment since Moore records that 'I went up to London with my wife and man about my wife's arm'.[73] His niece, Martha, accompanied him to London on two occasions. In April 1669 Moore records that he travelled to London 'carrying with me my little maid whom I there habited for school'. And in September 1672 she again accompanied him, together with his servant and a tailor, Mr Hull, buying her a new riding suit (a coat and petticoat), gown and petticoat from Captain Feages at the White Hart in Watling Street.[74] Whilst in London he went shopping in and around Cheapside, buying books, household items, exotic foodstuffs, cloth, haberdashery and accessories such as hats, gloves, shoes and stockings.

In the previous chapter we saw that Moore was a regular customer of his local mercer, James Holford, and also showed a preference for certain Lewes shopkeepers. In contrast, his choice of shops in London was more eclectic. As we shall see, he made repeat purchases from two shops, Edward Swinpane's shop at the sign of the Golden Anchor on Cheapside and Thomas and James Allen's shop at the Hat and Harrow in Bishopsgate Street, but many of the shops that Moore names benefited from his custom only once. What drew him to individual shops is unclear and of course we do not know how many shops he went into before deciding to make a purchase. He seems to have preferred London's street shops; perhaps he found the Exchange shops and their clientele too fashionable for his rather conservative tastes. It is safe to assume that his loyalty to the Golden Anchor and the Hat and Harrow reflected his satisfaction with the service he received there but with such an extensive selection of shops Moore needed to be discerning about which ones he chose. Shoddy goods, inflated prices and poor service were all a risk: in October 1670 he bought two worsted girdles for 4s, noting that this was 'more than they were worth by 8d, I buying them from a knave at the bridge (i.e. London Bridge) foot'.[75]

The sorts of cloth and haberdashery that he bought in London could have been obtained locally in Sussex, if not from James Holford then certainly from William Marshall or one of his competitors in Lewes. For example, in 1659 he bought five and a quarter yards of 'cloth' at 17s a yard from Mr Gorman at the Anchor in St Paul's Churchyard to make a coat, doublet and two pairs of breeches, two pairs of oiled skins and one black skin for 'loynings' (i.e. linings) and pockets,

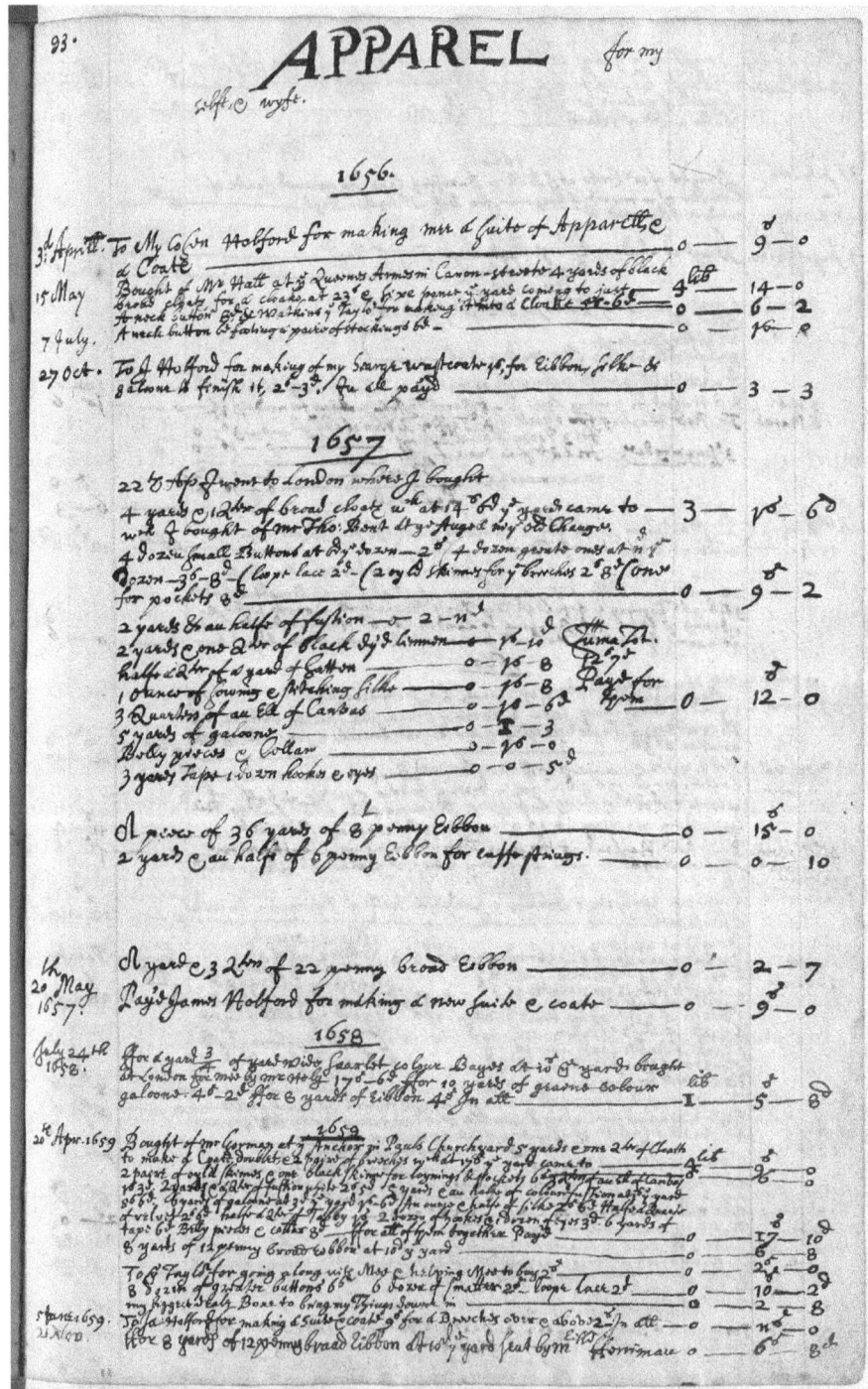

Figure 4.4 Page from Giles Moore's account book, showing entries for 1656–9, West Sussex Record Office, Par 384/6/1, p. 93. Reproduced with the permission of West Sussex Record Office.

spending in all £5 3s.[76] In 1664 he bought thirteen yards of Turkey Tammy (a type of worsted) from Mr Cawley at the Angel in Paternoster Row at a cost of £1 18s, two yards of broad cloth at 14s a yard, buttons, loop lace, silk thread, galloon, two oiled skins and a 'large piece of velvet enough to face a doublet sleeves twice' from Mr Gough at the White Lion in St Paul's Churchyard, spending a total of £2 7s 4d there.[77] As will be discussed in more detail in the next chapter, Moore was a conservative dresser and had little interest in fashion. He clearly went to London with the intention of buying cloth and haberdashery, however, otherwise he would not have taken his tailor with him. On his visit to Mr Cawley's and Mr Gough's, Moore's purchases were made with the advice of the eldest son of his tailor, Mr Hull. All his clothing was made up for him in Sussex rather than by a fashion-savvy London tailor. In shopping for cloth and haberdashery in London, therefore, what Moore appears to have been most interested in was securing the best quality at the most competitive price.

Moore particularly favoured London shops for accessories such as socks and stockings, caps, hats, gloves, girdles and slippers. He visited Edward Swinpane's shop at the Golden Anchor in Cheapside on five separate occasions between 1674 and 1679, buying black worsted stockings, satin caps and worsted girdles. In June 1679 (a few months before his death) he spent 3s 8d on two worsted girdles and 3s on a satin cap from Swinpane's and 2s 3d on three pairs of knitted socks (at 9d the pair) from Mr Collet 'a Somersetshire man of 2 camels on the other side of the same shop'.[78] For hats Moore favoured Mr Cook 'my countryman' (i.e. from Suffolk, like Moore), buying eight hats from him between 1656 and 1665, including one for his wife in 1657, a 'black shag hat' for himself in 1661 and a 'shaggy demi-castor of the new fashion' in 1665. Cook, whose premises are unidentified, also sold Moore hat bands and linings and dressed and re-cut his old hats. Between 1666 and 1675 Moore bought his hats from Thomas and James Allen at the Hat and Harrow in Bishopsgate Street, buying nine hats, including a new hat for his wife in 1674. These hats were expensive: the cheapest were 18s; Moore's 'black shag hat' cost him £1 2s and he spent £1 12s on a new hat from the Hat and Harrow in 1675.[79]

Of course Moore was buying more than cloth, haberdashery and clothing accessories in London. To give an idea of the range of items bought by Moore on his trips we can look at two examples, the first from 1663 and the second from 1673. Moore had travelled up to London on 5 October 1663 to meet his brother, Robert Moore, returning to Horsted on 12 October. On 6 October he bought a pair of enamelled spurs, half a dozen pairs of socks, three yards of black taffeta ribbon and three yards of ferret ribbon. On 7 October he bought a new hat and lining from Mr Cook and paid for the re-facing of an old one, two pairs of black worsted stockings, a horn and an ivory comb, six pounds of Brazil sugar and one pound of 'stone' sugar, a pair of girths, a deal box, four ounces of gall, one ounce of copperas, gum arabic, an extinguisher, a 'prolonger' and a pair of snuffers. On 10 October he visited two booksellers, Philemon Stevens at the Gilded Lion in Paul's Churchyard and Henry Such at the Rainbow in Paternoster Row, buying a number of books and pamphlets.[80] In 1673 Moore travelled up to London on 12 May, returning to Sussex on 14 May. On 13 May he bought four books (three works of theology and Thomas Shadwell's newly published comedy, *Epsom Wells*), half a ream of paper, gall, copperas and gum to make ink and a dozen tulip bulbs.[81] From goldsmith Thomas Sharp in Lombard Street he bought a tumbler, a caudle cup and a silver spoon, the latter items intended as gifts for two infant godsons.[82] He bought himself a periwig from Mistress Johnson 'on this side the Saracen's Head' and two pairs of stockings from Mr Trotman at the Queen's Head in Soper Lane. Possibly also from Mr Trotman, Moore bought six pairs of socks, a new pair of white kid gloves, three yards of ferret ribbon for shoe strings, four yards of satin ribbon for cuff strings.[83] Finally, he bought a new hat with hatband and case from James Allen.[84]

Moore's last trip to London was in June 1679, less than four months before his death in October. He must have seen considerable changes in the city during the twenty-odd years covered by his account book, not least its partial destruction and rebuilding, but he does not comment on them. He made only one trip to London in April 1665, shortly before the presence of plague was beginning to raise concern. His next visit was on 26 September 1666, a mere three weeks after the Fire which destroyed many of the shops he had frequented.[85] On this trip his purchases were limited: ten quires of paper, news books (possibly *The London Gazette*), two works of theology, 'Goodwin's plague bill in a frame', some candle wax and a new hat from Thomas Allen.[86] Possibly he wanted to see the city's destruction for himself. He evidently had an interest in the Fire; on a trip to London in July 1667 he bought Samuel Rolle's *The Burning of London*, Thomas Vincent's *God's Terrible Voice in the City* and the Parliamentary Committee's report into the causes of the Fire, which had been published in January.[87] In October 1666 he contributed £1 towards the city's relief fund and in 1678 he contributed £2 towards the cost of rebuilding St Paul's Cathedral.[88]

Proxy shopping

Moore seems to have preferred to shop for himself in London, perhaps enjoying the experience of browsing as much as the act of purchasing. However, other Sussex residents were less inclined or less able to make the journey to London for themselves and so relied on a proxy shopper. Proxy shopping presented a completely different set of challenges, both to the consumer and to their proxy. In addition to the vagaries of the postal and transport services outlined above, the proxy shopper had to locate the requested items and identify substitutes if they could not be found. If the proxy shopper was commissioning clothes then he or she had to liaise with the tailor over style, fabric type, trimming and size. The difficulties of proxy clothes shopping is illustrated in a series of letters sent by James Gresham between November 1640 and February 1641 to his mother, recently widowed Judith Morley, over the commissioning of a new gown (made up of two separate pieces, a waistcoat and petticoat) intended to provide her with a 'fit garment for Christmas'.[89] Her letters to him during this period do not survive. At this date Judith, aged fifty-seven, was living in Chichester at 'Mr William's house'. Gresham, then aged about twenty-three, was studying at the Inns of Court and lodging in Bell Yard, off Fleet Street but made regular visits to his family home in Fulham.[90]

Figure 4.5 Wenceslaus Hollar, The Winter Habit of an English Gentlewoman (1644), The Metropolitan Museum of Art, 23.65.35.

The story of the new gown begins in a letter dated 15 November 1640 in which Gresham informed his mother of his initial meeting with her London tailor, Pollard.

> Your tailor I spoke with yesterday who tells me that the fashion for petticoats and waistcoats is without short hanging sleeves, longer-waisted and somewhat narrower in the shoulders and that if you put six breadth in the petticoat he must have eleven yards and a quarter of velvet. He says he can cut a waistcoat out of less than three yards and a half but then it will not be all the right way of the velvet but look diverse colours which will be very ugly and that half a yard of velvet very ill favoured but which is worst of all he tells me that velvet is very scarce and dear and that I shall get none good under 24s the yards so that your £10 will not buy the outside by £3 or £4.[91]

On 6 December he wrote to his mother to let her know that he had bought the velvet for her dress from 'Alderman Gurnett' (Richard Gurney, a mercer with a shop in Cheapside) and enclosing a sample of the fabric.[92] He explained,

> When I came to Gurnett's I found that velvets were not so dear as your tailor made me believe nor had I need of more money than I carried with me for both the Alderman and his partner in the shop did dissuade me from buying three piled or two piled and a half velvet because no ladies about town wear above a pile and a half and it will do much more service than a thick one which will presently wear out in slits, and in the colour and covering there is no difference but merely in the robustness and weight. And so amongst a great many prices they advised us (for my brother was with me) to this piece, for as good a velvet as any they or any man had in London. It cost a pound a yard and came just within your money only I have 6d *ob*. left which must buy a box to send it down in but by whom I know not for I believe the foot post cannot carry it. It will be finished next week and you shall have it the next return of the carrier.

With his letter he sent his mother a pair of silk stockings, telling her that she could return them if she did not like the colour but adding that they were 'as nigh the pattern as I could get' and that if he had to change them it was unlikely he would be able to get 'so good a stocking'.[93]

By the 16 December the gown was finished and was sent down to Chichester along with a letter, a pair of worsted stockings, an account of Gresham's expenditure and a small amount of money hidden in the pocket of her new petticoat. The petticoat, as Gresham told his mother, had been bordered with black serge and the waistcoat sleeves lined with white calico. Gresham was clearly concerned about fit, writing 'for your whole form of the body and neatness of its fitting I am not able to judge unless I saw it on your body and you must abide the hazard'.[94] Unfortunately, the waistcoat proved to be too tight. In Gresham's next letter to his mother (undated, but probably around 20 January 1641) he wrote,

> Sweet mother I have been diverse times this week to speak with your tailor but failed till this afternoon or rather night when after I had received your letter and was going (according to my former intent) to Gurnett's for half a yard of velvet [needed to enlarge the waistcoat], his door lying in my way, I called and at last found him. He swears that he cut it by your first pattern which he offered to show me and he can scarce believe it should be so much too little except you be grown bigger or wear more clothes but if you will send it up with a just measure how big it must be he will mend it and it shall not cost you a farthing.

He advised his mother to send the waistcoat back in the same box with one of the local wagoners or rippiers, with instructions that it should be carried immediately to his lodgings in Bell Yard. He promised that he would be able to return it to her by Saturday, which would be fine since 'you would not have worn it before Sunday'. He gave his letter to an attorney called Mitchell who he had heard 'by chance' was travelling to Chichester the next day.[95] However, clearly in doubt about whether she had received his letter, he repeated much of what he had said about the gown in his next letter of 24 January.[96]

On 27 January Gresham wrote to tell his mother about his progress in having her waistcoat altered,

> Sweet mother your waistcoat I carried to the tailor's as soon as I received it where I saw him lay your old pattern on it and it proved the very same size, notwithstanding he will make it according to that pattern you sent. I have told him all the faults and he has faithfully promised to be very careful in the amendment which I wish may be to your liking.

Adding,

> Your sarcenet [a fine silk] and sleeves I left behind me when I removed from Fulham and went since thither for them and my brother unluckily was gone before I came and had locked and nailed up all the doors. I have been forced therefore to let him [the tailor] use that sarcenet you wrapped the waistcoat in; your scarf he used in the [waistcoat] skirts, the short sleeves and facing the hands. He says likewise that he cannot take off the skirt to make it wear like a gown unless he had the petticoat to sew to the body, all which you may make one of your tailors there do for you. If he should send you a roll [a padded roll for extending the skirt at the hips] he says your petticoat would be too short to wear with it.[97]

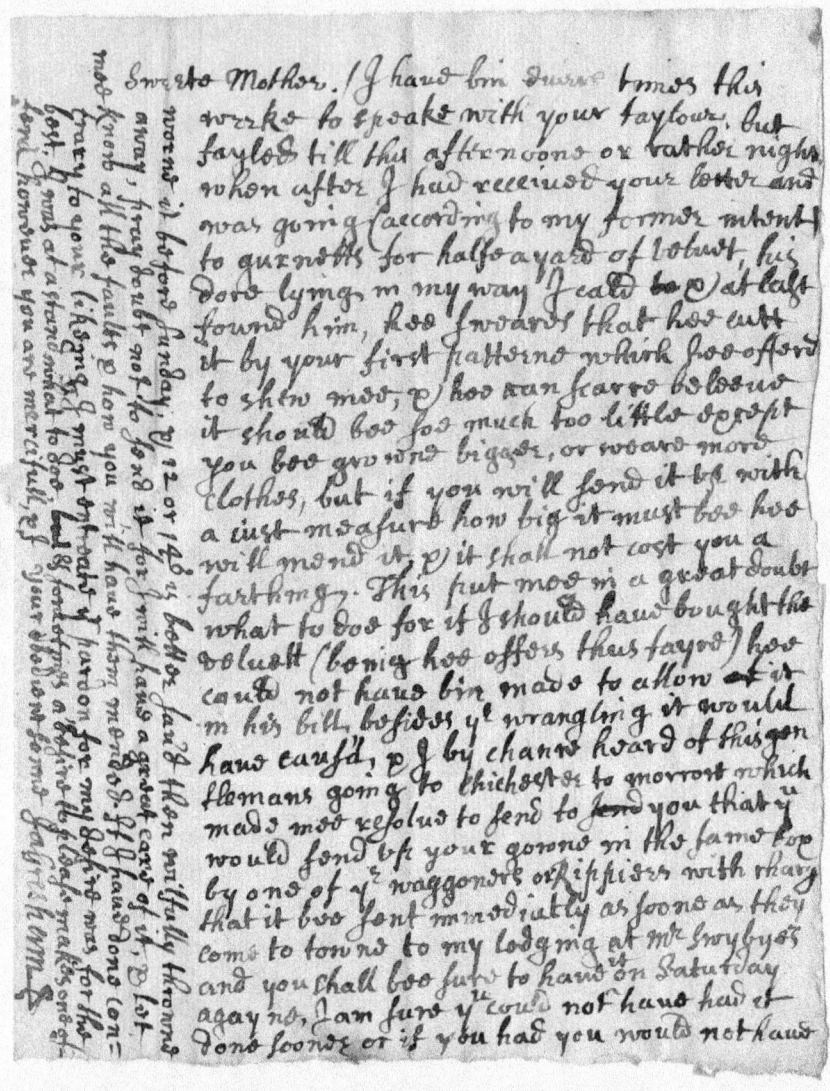

Figure 4.6 Letter sent by James Gresham to Judith Morley, January 1641, Surrey History Centre, LM/COR/7/51. Reproduced by permission of the More-Molyneux family and Surrey History Centre.

The waistcoat was altered but Gresham then faced problems with returning it to his mother in Chichester. On 7 February he wrote to her telling her that he had been

> very much disappointed and abused by the carrier's porter or else you had received your waistcoat that very week you sent it for the tailor dispatched it and sent it to my chamber by ten of the clock on Thursday that week and the porter promised to call on me for it but never came ...

Gresham decided that it would be better to keep the waistcoat in London for another few days because his brother had told him that he 'would come down to you on Wednesday or Thursday next with a coach to bring you to town', adding that he thought 'it to no purpose to send it down at charges for you to bring it up again in the coach the next day and no necessary day of wearing it happening in the meantime'.[98]

The waistcoat disappears from view after this and so we do not know whether Judith was ever satisfied with it. The process of commissioning it and having it altered had taken three months, with significant delays caused by unreliable postal and carrier services. Gresham had had to overcome a range of practical issues caused by acting as his mother's proxy shopper: the style of the gown, the cost, quantity and choice of velvet, the gown's sizing and its dispatch, return and re-dispatch. His letters show that he was highly dependent on the advice given to him by the tailor and the mercer. Gresham's frustration with the process is apparent in his letters; Judith's frustration is implicit in his repeated assurances to her that he is doing his best. One of the things that emerges from Gresham's letters is the extent to which the London tailor was willing to accommodate Judith's requests that the waistcoat be altered, not only in its size but also apparently in its style. He had, as he showed Gresham, cut it out according to the pattern that she had supplied but nevertheless he was willing to alter it at no extra cost to her. He also made his alterations swiftly, perhaps responding to Gresham's insistence that her need for it was pressing.

Commissioning directly from a London tailor or mercer

It was, of course, possible for provincial consumers to limit their use of proxy shoppers by commissioning new clothing by letter from a London tailor or mercer. This seems to have been the method preferred by Walter Roberts senior who lived in Ticehurst in the north-east of Sussex. For at least a ten-year period between 1677 and 1687, Roberts was commissioning new clothing for himself, his two sons, Walter junior and John, and his ward, Edward May, from a London mercer or tailor, John Heath. Evidence for what he was purchasing is contained in a series of 'vouchers to account' or suppliers' bills that Heath sent to Roberts for payment. Ten bills survive but whether these are all or the majority that were sent or only a small proportion is unknown. Moreover, in some instances it is difficult to tell for whom the clothes were being made, either because the bill gives no indication or because the top part of the bill where Heath normally recorded the customer's name is missing.[99] In none of the bills is Heath's occupation recorded and it has not been possible to locate him in other records. There was, as we saw in the previous chapter, considerable overlap between the occupations of mercers and tailors with both supplying made-up garments.

Although none of Roberts' letters to Heath survive, Heath sometimes scrawled notes to Roberts at the foot of his bills, explaining the decisions that he had made in making or purchasing new items or asking for further advice on what he should do if he thought that his original instructions were unclear or impractical. An example of this is on a bill dated 23 June 1687 recording the cost of making a new suit for Roberts junior, aged thirty-two. Heath wrote,

> I have here sent your bill and your son's and I desire to know what Mr Roberts would have me do with his hair camlet [a mixed-fibre woollen cloth] coat for I sent him a letter that if I dyed it, it would be spoiled and not worth anything afterwards. Therefore if he pleases I will send it to him as it is next week but I desire a line from him and if he will have it dyed it shall. Pray let him send me word how I may direct a letter or parcel to him; he ordered me to send the bill, this being all at present ...[100]

In 1680 he made a new suit for Edward May, aged sixteen, made of scarlet cloth and trimmed with scarlet ribbon. With this he supplied a 'fine hat', two cravats, a pair of worsted stockings, a rapier and a rapier knot made of scarlet, gold and silver ribbons. At the foot of the bill Heath added a short note for Walter senior,

> Sir, I have here sent you Mr May's coat with a rapier and knot for the rapier. As for the rapier I could not buy one under the price above written [£1 15s]. I have not set a cape to the coat for some wear them and some will not but if he will have it I can get one made if I hear from you and send it down or if you send the coat I'll set one on and return it the same week. I have sent the bills according to your order. With my services to you all I wish you a Merry Christmas and am your obliged servant ...[101]

As is clear from this quote, Heath was also acting as a proxy shopper for Roberts, here describing his difficulties in locating a rapier at an affordable price. The additional items he supplied on this occasion, the hat, stockings, cravats and possibly the rapier knot would all have had to be sourced separately. Some of these purchases may have been made by Heath's wife: at the bottom of a bill dated 23 October 1684 recording the cost of making a new coat for Roberts senior Heath added a note for John Roberts informing him that his wife had bought him three cravats at a cost of 10s.[102]

As will be discussed in more detail in the next chapter, the clothes that Heath made for the Roberts men were plainer and cheaper than those he made for May and it is also apparent that Walter senior used Heath's services more sparingly for his and his son's clothes than for those of his ward, Edward May. It is likely that most of the Roberts men's clothes were sourced elsewhere, probably locally. We know that in 1672 Walter senior bought cloth, fastenings and trimmings to make a new coat from Ticehurst mercer Thomas Nash, and between 1662 and 1670 he was also using the services of a tailor or mercer, Edward Butler, who, although unidentified, is likely to have been local.[103] Heath's bills may of course only provide partial evidence of how Roberts was engaging with the London clothing market. Although there is no evidence that Walter senior was travelling to London to shop, or indeed, shopping there by proxy, it is unlikely that he managed to avoid London altogether since legal business took most gentlemen there from time to time. Moreover, Roberts did have a London connection through his brother-in-law, London silk merchant Thomas Busbridge, and from 1677 through his son John, Busbridge's apprentice, but whilst Busbridge supplied miscellaneous goods, including cloth and clothing accessories, to some of his Sussex relatives, Roberts does not appear to have been amongst them.[104] The weight of evidence suggests, however, that Roberts' London connections were limited and possibly under-exploited. Despite this, he was willing to invest in London-made clothes; his loyalty to John Heath shows that he placed considerable trust in his honesty, workmanship and professional judgement about what would be suitable for him and his family to wear.

The Jeakes and metropolitan consumption

The Sussex men and women we have encountered so far shopping in London in person or by proxy were all members of the lesser or middle gentry. However, the Rye merchant Samuel Jeake and his wife Elizabeth were also enthusiastic participants in London's fashionable consumer culture. As will be discussed in more detail in Chapters Five and Six, both were determined to put in a fashionable appearance in provincial Rye and understood very well that this meant staying abreast of London fashions and, wherever possible, wearing London-made clothes and accessories.

Jeake first visited London in November 1667 aged fifteen, on a sightseeing trip with his father. Together they visited the tombs and Henry VII's chapel in Westminster Abbey, the Tower of London, Deptford and Greenwich and 'saw the ruins made by the great fire at London' the previous year.[105] The following year he spent six months in London 'for diversion', staying with his aunt and uncle in Southwark.[106] Thereafter he visited London irregularly, some years not going at all, others going two or three times. His reasons for visiting London varied: in May 1672 he travelled to London to 'find medicine for my eyes'; in May 1682 he spent a month in London with his wife and mother-in-law 'for diversion'; other times he went on business.[107] In October 1683, accompanied by Elizabeth, then pregnant with their second child, he attempted to move to London permanently to avoid prosecution for nonconformity. Once there, he looked for a post with the East India Company or as a merchant's accountant but without success and the family were forced to return to Rye the following May.[108] Elizabeth visited London again in 1691 and 1693, on both occasions accompanying her husband.[109] As a widow, she spent two months there between May and July 1701 trying to resolve a property dispute that had ended up in the court of Chancery.[110]

During their trips to London, Samuel and Elizabeth were able to make purchases for themselves, their household and their Rye friends and family. For example, after their month-long stay in London in 1693, Jeake noted in his diary that 'things fitted very well for pleasure this journey, but expensive, I furnishing myself with a great deal of clothes, wherein and with other expenses laid out near £40'.[111] In addition to clothes, the Jeakes bought a wide variety of goods in London, some utilitarian such as hair powder and wash balls, some relatively exotic such as chocolate and oranges, and some highly fashionable such as the green and white hangings with a 'very large leaf and pretty figure' and the 'Japanned' furniture bought by Jeake in 1686 and 1688.[112] When not in London, they were dependent on their friends and relatives to make purchases for them and to provide them with up-to-date fashion advice.

As the less frequent visitor to London Elizabeth was especially dependent on her husband to shop on her behalf. To do this he took advice from Elizabeth Miller, the wife of his friend and former business partner, Thomas Miller. Living in Mincing Lane, very close to the Royal Exchange, Elizabeth would have been well placed to observe what fashionable female shoppers were wearing and may have enjoyed browsing and making the occasional small purchase there herself. As well as advising Samuel and Elizabeth on the latest women's fashions she also bought some of Elizabeth's clothing for her: in a letter to his wife dated 28 October 1697 Jeake told her 'I intend to send your coat and things Madam Miller has bought tomorrow per carrier', adding 'she will send you a letter to tell you your coat must be lined ...'.[113] As we saw with James Gresham, proxy shopping could be onerous especially when it had to be fitted in around other business activities: 'pray don't trouble me with any errands', Samuel wrote to Elizabeth on 14 September 1697 and on 15 April 1699 he wrote 'I have not had time yet to consider your letters about what you desire to be bought but I shall mind it next week'.[114] Whilst in London in 1701 Elizabeth also found herself inconvenienced by the endless shopping requests of her Rye friends and family, complaining in one of her letters to her mother that she had been unable to accept a social invitation because of her 'perpetual hurry of buying things'.[115] Moreover, she felt that those for whom she was buying were not always fully appreciative of her efforts on their behalf,

> I am sorry, dear mother, I incur so much displeasure for my good will; I know of no advantage I shall reap by what I buy for people. My readiness to serve them should not encourage them to be so severe on me for it is most certain if greater motives than those commissions received had not induced me to go [to] London I should not have been there on purpose for their occasions. My aunt's lace I bought long ago as likewise cousin's stuff, but for making it up I never understood it was to be done here nor can it be unless her stays were with me; I shall send it this week with Mary Wall's. I wish I could as easily dispatch my affairs which are of more importance, but I know not what to do.[116]

As we saw with James Gresham and his mother, Judith Morley, the difficulties of communicating shopping requests adequately by letter could lead to confusion and shopping mistakes, generating frustration and resentment on both sides.

Conclusion

This chapter has explored the relationship between the provincial consumer and seventeenth-century London, emphasising the city's dominant role in consumer culture made possible by an extensive and highly sophisticated retail network. London's consumer appeal was not solely based on its unparalleled range of goods, however, but also on its role as the originator and arbitrator of fashion.

London tailors and mercers were particularly valued by provincial consumers for their understanding of what was in fashion and what was not. As we have seen, provincial consumers could shop in London in person (as Giles Moore seems to have preferred to do), by proxy or by commissioning goods by letter directly from the supplier. Each of these methods came with its own challenges. Those shopping in person had to get to London, no easy feat given the state of the roads and the limited means of transportation. Once in London they had to cope with its congestion, filth and noise and find their way around its complex shopping landscapes. Those shopping by proxy had to put up with miscommunication, whether caused by an erratic postal service or the difficulties of communicating shopping requests by letter, and the chance that their London-made clothes would not fit them properly. All provincial shoppers, whether shopping in person or by proxy, then had to deal with the difficulties and expense of getting their London-bought goods back to Sussex. Nevertheless, the lure of London's shops and the cachet attached to London-sourced goods meant that they were challenges that the provincial consumer was willing to overcome. There was, however, a gendered dimension to London shopping.[117] As we have seen, Susan Moore and Elizabeth Jeake had considerably less access to London than their husbands. Susan went to London only twice between 1656 and 1679, on both occasions accompanying her husband; in contrast Giles went to London approximately forty times during the same period. Elizabeth fared slightly better, travelling to London with her husband on at least four occasions between 1682 and 1693. Whilst she inevitably had less consumer choice than Samuel she was still able to participate in London's consumer culture by using her husband and her good friend, Elizabeth Miller, as her proxies.

5

The Clothing of Provincial Gentlemen

In *The Complete Gentleman* Henry Peacham advised his readers to adopt a 'moderate and middle garb which shall rather lessen than make you bigger than you are'. It was 'a poor pride to seek your esteem and regard from worms, shells and tailors and [to] buy the gaze of the staring multitude at a thousand or fifteen hundred pounds'.[1] In Peacham's view, the true gentleman displayed his status through his behaviour rather than through his clothing. But who was a true gentleman? Peacham's definition was quite expansive, including members of the professions such as lawyers and doctors and allowing that even the 'ignoble and inglorious may acquire nobility by virtue'.[2] Merchants could not be gentlemen, but Peacham acknowledged their importance to the country 'since commonwealths cannot stand without trade and commerce'.[3] *The Complete Gentleman* was a conduct book that instructed its readers in the essential modes of gentlemanly behaviour. It had a wide and mixed readership – Giles Moore and Samuel Jeake both owned copies – suggesting that its content had a broad appeal.[4] Arguably, any of its readers who were able to display an acceptable range of gentlemanly behaviour might be viewed as 'gentlemen' or at least 'genteel', whatever their birth or profession. By the time Moore and Jeake were reading *The Complete Gentleman* 'gentility' was increasingly being defined by an individual's appearance, manners and education.[5] In other words, the way that a man dressed was as vital to his presentation of himself as a gentleman as his ability to engage in polite and learned discourse.

This chapter looks at the clothing of provincial gentlemen through a series of case studies of men living in Sussex from the 1650s through to the early 1700s. The men's background was introduced in Chapter One and, with the exception of Richard Stapley, they have all been encountered previously, shopping in Sussex and in London. In comparison with the majority of the Sussex population, each of them was relatively wealthy and enjoyed a high standard of living. With the exception of Samuel Jeake, all of them were members of the lesser or middle gentry. It was suggested in Chapter One that Jeake's liberal education and fashionable consumption placed him amongst the 'urban gentry' although it should be pointed out that he was only ever referred to in contemporary records as a merchant.[6] From a national perspective, to qualify the contemporary language of 'sorts', Giles Moore and Samuel Jeake can perhaps be described as belonging to the upper end of the 'middling sort', the Roberts men and Richard Stapley to the lower end of the 'better' or 'best sort' and Edward May towards the middle of the 'better sort'. Within their own communities, however, all would have been amongst the 'best' or 'better' sort. The differences in their social and occupational statuses meant that they moved within distinct social milieus. Moore's social and familial connections lay mainly within the clerical profession, the minor gentry and the trades. The Roberts men were connected through marriage to several other middle gentry families in eastern Sussex including the Everendens, the Busbridges and the Farndens as well as the more substantial middle-gentry families living in Ticehurst, the Mays, the Courthopes and the Apsleys. Jeake's main social and familial connections were with affluent merchants and tradesmen, in Rye and elsewhere. Of the men considered in this chapter, he had the strongest personal connections with London, with a number of friends and relatives living there.[7] As we saw in Chapter One, although a middle-gentry family, Richard Stapley's familial connections were quite mixed, including a number of other local gentry families but also a family of wealthy tanners and butchers in nearby Cuckfield. His social milieu was geographically limited to Twineham and its surrounding parishes and his closest friendship appears to have been with the local curate and subsequently vicar, William Sheward.[8]

The case studies are drawn from a disparate body of sources. The most extensive in its coverage of clothing purchases is Giles Moore's household and personal account book which, as we have already seen, provides detailed information about what he purchased and where he purchased it from. For Jeake we have his correspondence, diary and some personal accounts. Some of the letters provide detailed information about a new watch and suit that Jeake commissioned in 1681, but on the whole, the information provided by this disparate source material is uneven in its coverage and often lacking detail. For the Roberts men and Walter Roberts's ward, Edward May, there is a series of 'vouchers to account' or tradesmen's bills, some of which we have already encountered, covering the period from 1677 to 1694. These offer a useful insight into what these men were wearing but they are unlikely to represent a full account of clothing purchases made by the Roberts's household. For Stapley there is his memorandum book, a printed almanac in which he recorded purchases of clothing and accessories between 1684 and 1724.⁹ Again, this is unlikely to provide a complete record of his clothing purchases during this period. So, with the exception of Moore's account book, all of the information about what these men were wearing is intermittent and incomplete. The other limitation of the source material, which applies too to Moore's book, is that it reveals little about the individual's motivation in making his sartorial choices. However, a careful reading of the sources alongside other documentary evidence for these men's lives and lifestyles can provide an insight into their consumer behaviour and the role their clothing played in the construction and maintenance of their social identities.

The style of men's clothes

In the 1650s when Moore's household account book begins, the basic items of male outerwear were the doublet and breeches, which together made up the 'suit'. A waistcoat, of similar cut to the doublet, might be worn underneath it to provide an extra layer during periods of cold weather, or, with the doublet worn open, might be worn for show. Fashionable doublets were cut boxy and short to sit on or slightly above the waistband of the breeches – 'little lower than our breasts' in John Bulwer's words – with the gap between the two filled in by the shirt; those wishing to dress more modestly could wear a longer and closer fitting doublet, which covered the hips.¹⁰ 'Falling bands' were worn around the neck; these could be a small turned-down collar with a reversed 'V' opening or a broad band stretching across the shoulders meeting edge-to-edge in front. Both were tied with tasselled ties or 'band strings'. Breeches could be close-fitting (sometimes so tight that, according to John Evelyn, the wearer needed a 'shoeing horn' to get them on) or full and open legged.¹¹ The widest breeches, still worn by fashionable men in the 1670s, were known as petticoat breeches, which sat on or below the knee. As Pepys recounts, the legs of these breeches were so wide that it was possible for a man to fit both of his legs in one side and still walk with ease.¹² Petticoat breeches featured elaborate ribbon loops at the waistband and knees, often with an extra bunch on the outer side of each leg. Over garments included the cassock, which was a loose fitting, thigh length coat, fastening down the front, the riding coat, and the cloak.¹³

Shirts were regarded as undergarments and, unlike outerwear, were washed regularly; like women's smocks they are sometimes referred to in contemporary accounts as 'changes'.¹⁴ Men and boys might also wear drawers, usually made of

Figure 5.1 Short doublet and petticoat breeches made in England or France (1660), Victoria and Albert Museum, T.324-1980. Watered silk lined with cream silk taffeta, trimmed with parchment lace. The breeches shown here are reproduction, but follow the exact style of the originals. © Victoria and Albert Museum, London.

linen, but their use does not appear to have been ubiquitous. There are no references to drawers in Moore's account book; even if these had been made for him at home it is likely that he would have recorded them since he was meticulous in noting the uses to which his linen cloth purchases had been put.[15] It is possible that the detachable 'loynings' or linings he wore inside his breeches effectively acted as underwear. These were mostly made of leather, sometimes described as 'oiled', but on two occasions were made of 'million' or 'Milan' fustian.[16]

The style of male outerwear changed after 15 October 1666 when Charles II appeared in public in a long-line close-fitting 'vest' or waistcoat with a long-line coat over the top of it. According to Pepys, in adopting the new vest it was the King's intention to set 'a fashion for clothes, which he will never alter ... to teach the nobility thrift'.[17] The King's sartorial statement needs to be seen in the context of the panic engendered by the Great Fire of the previous month, which was viewed by some as a punishment for the nation's obsession with the luxury consumption of foreign, particularly French, goods and French fashions.[18] The new, longer-line, suit appears to have been rapidly adopted by the fashion-conscious man: Pepys commissioned a new suit from his tailor's on 29 October and wore it for the first time on the 4 November.[19] Looking back from the early 1680s on the first years of the longer-line suit the author of *England's Vanity* described it as 'perhaps the most grave and manlike dress that ever England saw' but lamented that 'it had the unhappiness to be brought in too late, and the hard fate to be sent out again too soon ...', blaming the English obsession with French fashion for its demise.[20] This view of the early 'three-piece suit' as especially 'manlike' is shared by David Kuchta who sees it as representing a 'new modest masculinity' but early illustrations of it suggest that there was never anything particularly modest about it. Full-skirted, long-line coats were worn over wide breeches giving their wearers a bottom-heavy appearance; flared coat sleeves might end at the elbows to reveal billowing linen shirt sleeves with wide lace cuffs and both the coat and the breeches could be heavily decorated with ribbons, brocade or braid trim.[21] The new-style suit was worn with a linen and lace cravat rather than a falling band or collar, sometimes tied in a bow under the chin. A fashionable man would also wear a 'shoulder knot' – a bunch of ribbon loops or looped cord worn on the right shoulder – possibly with a matching 'sword knot'.[22]

A significant change to fashionable men's appearance in the 1660s was the adoption of the wig. Wig-wearing was not unknown before the 1660s: in *The Loathsomeness of Long Hair* (1654) Thomas Hall had noted with disgust that 'periwigs of false-coloured hair' had become 'rife, even amongst the scholars in the universities'.[23] However, they became *de rigueur* for the fashionable gentleman in the early 1660s. Pepys first wore a wig on 3 November 1663, motivated by overhearing the Duke of York the day before saying that both he and the King intended to wear one.[24] The best wigs were made of human hair; cheaper wigs might be made of horse or goat hair.[25] As Ribeiro notes, 'wigs were status symbols precisely because they were expensive, difficult to wear with ease, and required correct manners and deportment'.[26]

Over the next twenty-odd years the cut and style of the three-piece suit altered and the accessories worn with it changed, but as an ensemble, fashionable male clothing remained elaborate and showy. In the 1680s and 1690s the knee-length coat was worn closer to the body with a slight waist emphasis and a flared skirt, waistcoats followed the line and length of the coat, and breeches were knee-length and close fitting, fastening at the knee with a buckle, buttons or ties.[27] In the 1690s fashionable coats became more muted in pattern and colour but they could still be highly decorated with metallic braid and large buttons. If coats were muted, waistcoats in contrast could be flamboyant, made of brightly coloured and patterned fabrics and decorated with braid or fringe. The showiest accessories like shoulder and sleeve knots had gone but other accessories remained important, in particular the cravat and the wig, the latter becoming increasingly full and high crowned by the end of the century.[28] Fashionable men began to wear their cravats very long and loosely tied with the ends twisted and tucked through their coat button hole. This type of cravat, which could also be worn by women, was known as a 'steinkerk' or 'steenkirk', named after the battle of Steenkerque of August 1692.[29]

Accessories were an integral part of men's appearance, both for those wishing to appear 'à la mode' and for those seeking to display their 'gentlemanly' status. The way that men wore and used their accessories formed part of a complex sartorial code, expressing the wearer's own perception of his social identity as well as acting as a visual short hand of social persona for those who observed him. The use and misuse of accessories feature as a key comic trope in Restoration comedy. For example, in George Etherege's *The Man of Mode* (1676), arch-fop, Sir Fopling Flutter, and gentlewoman, Mrs Loveit, discuss 'three ill-fashioned fellows' that they encounter in London's fashionable Mall in St James's Park. Flutter remarks, 'did you observe, madam, how their cravats hung loose an inch from their neck, and what a frightful air it gave 'em?' To which Mrs Loveit replies, 'Oh! I took particular notice of one that is always spruced up with a deal of dirty sky-coloured ribbon'.[30] For the fashion and status-conscious Sir Fopling Flutter and Mrs Loveit, therefore, the failure of these men to wear their neckwear correctly, and as importantly to keep it clean, means that they lack gentility and

Figure 5.2 Brown worsted coat and breeches (*c.* 1680) shown with brown worsted cloak (*c.* 1670), Victoria and Albert Museum, T.62-1978. The coat is trimmed with black silver and silver-gilt thread braid and faced and lined with blue wool; the cloak is embroidered with silver and silver gilt thread. © Victoria and Albert Museum, London.

Figure 5.3 Jean Dieu de Saint Jean, 'Homme de Qualité en Habit d'Hiver' (1678), Victoria and Albert Museum, E.21438-1957. © Victoria and Albert Museum, London.

can never be part of their social circle. The wearing of a sword was perhaps the clearest indication of an individual's status as a 'gentleman'. In law, only those with the right to bear arms were entitled to wear swords but in practice they were worn by any man with aspirations towards gentility including, as we shall see, Samuel Jeake.[31] By the 1660s the 'small sword' or 'town sword', which sat close to the body, had become fashionable. These were more practical for daily wear than the large cavalier rapiers popular in the 1640s and 1650s, which had a tendency to catch passers-by when worn on crowded streets.[32]

Men adapted their clothing to the seasons with lighter-weight suits worn during the warmer months. Pepys noted that on the 1 May 1669 he went to his tailor's and 'there first put on a summer suit this year'. This was a woollen 'stuff' suit that he had had made the previous year, rather than his 'fine one' of flowered silk tabby and coloured camlet because he feared that, with its gold lace at the wrists, others would deem it 'too fine' for him. He did, however, put it on later that day when he and his wife rode in their new carriage to Pall Mall. Disappointingly for him the weather was cold and windy with 'a little dribbling rain'.[33] The changing seasons also allowed for the introduction of new styles: Nicholas Barbon's observation that 'it is an invention to dress a man, as if he lived in a perpetual spring' succinctly captures the cyclical nature of contemporary male fashions.[34] From the 1670s French fashion prints were illustrating summer and winter fashions for men and women and it is likely that, as in Paris, London's upmarket mercers' shops set new trends each season to promote sales; as we saw in Chapter Four the fictional mercers' apprentices of Paternoster Row, satirised in *The Character of the Beaux* (1696), enticed customers into their shops with the promise that the newest 'gaudy' silk 'hadn't been made above these three days'.[35]

The country gentleman

When Arthur Ingram, third Viscount Irwin (1666–1702) had his portrait painted in 1700 aged thirty-four it was in the guise of the country gentleman. Wearing a long buff-coloured coat, close-fitting black or brown breeches, brown stockings and sturdy black shoes he stands with his legs astride loading a gun. He sports a modestly curled grey wig, his plain white linen 'steinkerk' cravat is sensibly pushed through his top coat buttonhole whilst his black 'Carolina'-type hat (a beaver hat with a wide and floppy brim) lies on the ground behind him. His other accessories are a powder flask worn on a string across his body and a

Figure 5.4 Leonard Kynff, Portrait of Arthur Ingram, 3rd Viscount Irwin (1700). © Leeds Museums and Art Galleries (Temple Newsam House) UK/Bridgeman Images.

leather pouch worn on a belt around his waist. In front of him a pointer carries a dead pheasant in its mouth; besides him a dead hare hangs by its feet from a tree and a pile of dead game lies on the ground; three mallards fly past overhead.

For fashion-conscious Londoners, Ingram's portrait would have reinforced their perception of the country gentleman as coarsely and unfashionably dressed, obsessed with hunting and lacking any social finesse – a 'dull country clown' leading a 'melancholy country life'.[36] This representation of the country gentleman was well established in late seventeenth century comic and satirical literature, aimed primarily at a metropolitan audience. We encountered three such literary stereotypes in Chapter Two in the characters of Hugh Clodpate, Sir Mannerly Shallow and the 'Country Beau'. The 'Country Beau', it will be recalled, arrives in

London for the first time wearing his 'best leather breeches, tied at the knees with red taffeta', a new blue jacket and a grey coat 'with buttons no bigger than nutmegs'.[37] In Shadwell's comedy, *Epsom Wells* (bought by Giles Moore in 1673), Sussex JP Clodpate presents young heiress, Carolina, with a brace of partridges that he has hunted with the help of his beloved Sussex dog, Tray. He takes Carolina by surprise by urging her to kiss Tray and when she refuses tries to interest her instead in the beauty of his dappled mare, 'the finest fore-handed mare in Christendom'. His vehemence is such that one of the other characters offers as an aside, 'he describes his mare so passionately I shall begin to suspect her virtue'.[38] Sir Mannerly Shallow, too, is depicted as obsessed with dogs and horses and with a social milieu in remote rural Cumberland that is limited to 'fairs, cock fights and horse races'. Arriving in London for the first time he dresses himself for his forthcoming marriage to Christina Rash in a 'fine country-fashioned suit'.[39]

In the metropolitan view country fashions lagged some years – even decades – behind city fashions and it was almost impossible for a country gentleman (or gentlewoman) to be 'à la mode'. The difficulties of staying in fashion were such that the fictional narrator of *The Spectator*, 'Mr Spectator', advised his country friends to avoid trying to follow fashion at all. Rather than make themselves look ridiculous in outmoded styles, they should remain 'fixed in one certain habit' which at some point would come back into fashion just as a 'clock that stands still is sure to point right once in twelve hours'.[40]

Like all good stereotypes this one had a firm basis in fact but the sartorial choices and social behaviour of country gentlemen were far more complex than this. As we have seen in Chapter Four, an increasing number of the peerage and upper gentry were spending part of their year in London, maintaining second homes in the fashionable West End and enjoying the capital's social, cultural and shopping amenities. They are likely to have practised a kind of sartorial bifurcation, with fashionable city clothes worn whilst in London and more robust, practical clothes worn whilst resident on their country estates.[41] This is suggested by an earlier, undated, portrait of Arthur Ingram in which he is depicted wearing a close-fitting red satin coat with a fashionable blue satin knot on his right shoulder, a lace cravat and a full-bodied curled brown wig.[42] The middle and lesser gentry, however, spent considerably less time in London, perhaps visiting once or twice a year and for the most part their social milieu was more local. For them, fashionable 'city' clothes may have been less of a priority than hard-wearing 'country' clothes that allowed them to display their gentlemanly status whilst getting on with their day-to-day lives.

Giles Moore

Giles Moore's engagement with the complex early modern clothing market has been explored in Chapters Three and Four. As we have seen, Moore made purchases of cloth and clothing accessories from itinerant traders, local tradesmen, shops and fairs as well as in Lewes and in London. His carefully recorded purchases show that he had considerable consumer choice but that he exercised that choice with some discretion, motivated by a concern to achieve the best quality at the most affordable price. Moore's woollen outerwear was made up for him by a number of different local tailors and mercers; his linen clothing was made up for him either at home or by local women such as his tailor Richard Harland's wife. This section addresses more directly what Moore was wearing during the period covered by his household account book and what his sartorial choices suggest about his social status as a Church of England clergyman and minor gentleman and his personal preferences.

A household and personal account book does not offer the historian the same sense of the individual as a diary or a series of personal letters. Nevertheless, a careful reading of Moore's book along with the limited additional biographical information that exists for him does allow some insight into the sort of man that he was. As we saw in Chapter One, Moore was politically and religiously conservative, a Royalist sympathiser during the Interregnum and a supporter of Charles II after the Restoration. His choice of reading matter also suggests that he was concerned with status – or perhaps more accurately the maintenance of traditional social hierarchies.[43] His occasional more personal interventions in his account book also suggest that he was cautious with money but not frugal and that he could be extremely judgemental of the moral lapses of others.[44]

Clerical vestments were prescribed by canon law promulgated by the Church of England in 1604. In church, when saying public prayers or administering the sacraments, ministers were required to wear a 'decent and comely surplice with sleeves' – what Moore describes as his 'canonical coat'.[45] In public, ministers had to wear cassocks, sleeved cloaks, plain black silk, satin or velvet caps and dark-coloured stockings.[46] Moore's cassocks were made of a variety of mid-priced woollen cloths, including calamanco, prunella and paragon, fastened down the front with black silk buttons.[47] His cloaks were made of more expensive black broad cloth, fastened at the neck and down the front with black silk or mohair buttons.[48] Moore favoured satin caps, which he bought in London.[49] His black worsted stockings were bought from itinerant traders turning up at his door, from local mercer James Holford, from Lewes or from London.[50]

Figure 5.5 Unknown artist, Edward Sparke (d. 1693), vicar of Tottenham and chaplain to Charles II, wearing skull cap, bands and gown (1666). There is no known portrait of Giles Moore but Sparke's portrait shows us what clerical vestments would have looked like in the second half of the seventeenth century. © The author.

As a rector, Moore was expected to dress soberly in private. The 1604 canons prescribed that 'in private houses, and in their studies', ministers could wear 'any comely and scholar-like apparel, provided it be not cut or pinked'.[51] Whilst 'pinking' (cutting or punching the fabric with small holes or short slits to show a contrasting lining) had gone out of fashion by the 1650s, the principle contained in the canon is clear: frivolity and showiness in dress was to be avoided.[52] As the author of *Coma Berenices* complained, clergymen who immersed themselves in 'the manners and fashions of this world' undermined their status as God's messengers and made it difficult for them to reprove the excesses of others.[53] Moore appears to have held fast to this principle which probably suited his somewhat austere temperament as well as testifying to his diligence as a clergyman. His secular wear was made of good quality English woollen cloth – broad cloth, serge, tammy, bays and kersey. Although cloth colours are not always given, the references to colour that there are, together with details of buttons and silk thread that were chosen to match the colour of the cloth, suggest that his doublets and breeches were usually black.[54] But Moore was not averse to wearing bright colours: he favoured red for his waistcoats complete with red buttons and purple for his nightgowns (loose, informal gowns worn over shirt and breeches).[55] In 1669 Moore bought five yards of purple serge from a Mr West 'on the Bridge' (that is, with a shop on London Bridge) 'for a nightgown' at a cost of 22s and in 1676 he bought five and a quarter yards of purple bays at 4s 6d a yard from Lewes mercer, Hercules Courtney, for another nightgown.[56] By the second half of the century fashionable men might wear their nightgowns as informal outerwear but Moore probably wore his for comfort and warmth whilst at home, perhaps whilst reading or writing in his study.[57]

In 1670 Moore had two 'vests' made for him and in 1673 he had a 'long coat' made but there is nothing to suggest that these were intended to be worn as an ensemble and he continued to wear what he described as waistcoats, doublets and breeches up until his death in 1679.[58] Moore records two purchases of 'trousers' which were close-fitting breeches, buttoned at the knees – presumably a more practical garment for wearing under a cassock than the garments Moore described as 'breeches', which were probably fuller in the leg.[59] In 1674 he bought five yards of cloth to make a doublet and breeches, noting that there was just under a yard remaining 'towards another breeches for the making of which full and large there would be required ... one yard and a half more'.[60] As we have seen Moore's breeches had detachable leather or fustian linings; they were closed at the knee with ribbon.[61] Moore continued to wear 'bands' tied with 'band strings' into the 1670s; there are no references at all to him purchasing cravats. For example in 1677 he purchased six 'bonds' or bands and six pairs of 'bond strings'.[62] He was not completely immune to fashion: in 1665 he bought himself a 'shaggy demi-castor [hat] of the new fashion' and had his old hat dressed and cut 'to fashion'.[63]

Moore records the purchase and mending of a variety of footwear. All of his boots and most of his shoes were made and repaired for him locally but he made the occasional purchase in London such as the 'new pair of shoes' be bought there in 1656 costing him 3s 10s and the 'new pair of slippers bought at London' for 2s 6d in 1659.[64] Usually Moore bought two new pairs of shoes a year, a 'summer' pair and a 'winter' pair.[65] He owned a variety of boots, including 'black walking boots' and 'riding boots', and typically purchased a new pair every two years paying between 12s and 19s for them.[66] His shoes and boots were regularly resoled at a cost of between 1s 2d and 1s 4d. In December 1663 Moore recorded that he spent 1s 4d having a pair of shoes resoled that had been 'cut for the corns', hard and thickened areas of skin which would have caused him considerable discomfort when walking.[67] Boots required more maintenance than shoes and in addition to resoling Moore records payments for 'mending', 'tallowing', 'underlaying' 'welting', 'new vamping' and 'new strapping'.[68] Moore's caution with money is reflected in his comments about excessive footwear prices. In April 1673 he recorded that he had paid Richard Scrase 4s for a new pair of shoes 'being too much by 2d'.[69] In July 1674 he paid 4s 2d for a pair of new shoes from Thomas Stone but bargained with him that 'thenceforward' he would pay no more than 4s a pair 'be leather cheap or dear'.[70] Unusually, Moore bought no shoes in 1675. In June 1676 and October 1677, as agreed, Stone charged Moore 4s for a new pair of shoes but in April 1678 the price had gone up again to 4s 2d, Stone promising him 'that if leather fell (which as he said was almost £10 the dicker) he would fall also in his price'.[71]

The 1604 canons made no reference to clergymen's hair but they were expected to wear it relatively short. In *The Loathsomeness of Long Hair* Hall excoriated clergymen who wore their hair long, 'appearing like ruffians in the pulpit' when they should be setting an example to their congregations.[72] Wig-wearing clergymen also aroused moralists' ire. The author of the *Coma Berenices* condemned clergymen who preached whilst wearing 'long buzzled periwigs or borders of artificial hair hanging over their bands and shoulders', thereby exposing their 'persons and office to contempt, to the great detriment and hindrance of their labours'.[73] The fear of undermining his status as a clergyman probably explains why Moore never wore a wig. He went so far as to buy one in May 1673 for £1 5s from a Mistress Johnson 'on this side of the Saracens Head' in Cheapside but, as he noted, he never wore it and gave it to his neighbour, tanner John Wood, in January 1674.[74] His moral uneasiness over wig wearing evidently overcame his desire to adopt what by then had become an essential item of gentlemanly attire.

The overall impression that we get of Moore from the purchases recorded in his account book is that he dressed modestly wearing good-quality, sober garments befitting his profession and his status. His clothing also reflected his country lifestyle, with an emphasis on hard-wearing, practical garments and footwear that could withstand the rigours of the weather and arduous journeys on foot or horseback over Wealden Sussex's frequently muddy and water-logged roads and footpaths. But Moore was also a bookish man, who no doubt spent many hours in his study wrapped up in his nightgown reading books from his extensive library, writing sermons and letters and keeping up his household account book.

The Roberts men and Edward May

Walter Roberts senior's engagement with his London tailor or mercer, John Heath, has already been discussed in Chapter Four. Instructions were sent to Heath by letter, none of which survive. Instead we have a series of ten bills from Heath dating from 1677 to 1687 itemising his expenditure and requesting payment.[75] In 1677 the Roberts family consisted of Walter Roberts senior and his two sons, Walter Roberts junior, aged twenty-two and John Roberts, aged fifteen. Walter senior was also guardian to thirteen-year-old Edward May who lived at Pashley with his widowed mother, Ann. Ann submitted quarterly bills to Roberts for his board and some household expenditure.[76] Her final bill, dated October 1684, included the cost of boarding May, his new wife, Elizabeth, and three male servants.[77] In April 1685 May turned twenty-one and came into his inheritance but he only had a few months to enjoy it, dying in November.

As we have seen, Heath's bills show that in addition to making up clothing, he acted as a proxy shopper, supplying accessories such as hats, stockings, cravats and on one occasion a rapier. He added notes to some of his bills explaining the decisions he had made in making or purchasing new items or asking for clarification of what had been requested. Although it is not always possible to tell who the clothing was intended for there is sufficient detail in the bills to allow an analysis of what these men (or adolescents in the case of John Roberts and Edward May) were wearing during this period.

During his minority May's clothing purchases were made on his behalf by Roberts senior. The earliest of Heath's bills surviving for May is from 1680 when May was sixteen. The bill records that Heath had made May a red 'cloth' (i.e. woollen) suit at a cost of £7 8s 6¼d and supplied with it a scarlet, gold and silver shoulder knot, two cravats, a 'fine' hat, two pairs of worsted stockings, four and three-quarter yards of scarlet ribbon and a rapier at a cost of £4 18s, a 'fine hair camlet coat' at a cost of £1 15s and a box to send the goods down to Sussex in at a cost of 1s 2s. In all the cost was £14 2s 8¼d. As we saw in Chapter Four, Heath added a note to his bill explaining that he had not been able to find a cheaper rapier and that he had 'not set a cape to the coat for some wear them and some will not', offering to add a cape if May 'will have it'.[78]

In early 1682 Heath made May a coat of woollen cloth called *drap de Berry* costing 13s a yard with a 'hair plush' (a type of velvet) for the cape and the cuffs.[79] The coat was accessorised with fashionable 'frost' buttons – as we shall see, the same as those recommended for Samuel Jeake's new suit in 1681 – and a shoulder knot of a scarlet and silver ribbon.[80] Heath also supplied a broad scarlet hat ribbon, intended to match the shoulder knot. Later the same year Heath made May a complete new suit, with a coat and breeches of fine woollen cloth priced at 15s a yard and a waistcoat made of striped lustring (a lustrous silk taffeta) and lemon-coloured sarcenet. The coat and waistcoat were fastened with silver buttons and Heath also supplied matching shoulder, sleeve and sword knots, a white castor hat and a pair of silk stockings. The same bill records the making of a second coat for May, this one of hair camlet priced at 6s the yard with contrasting shag cuffs and cape and fastened with gold and silver buttons. Scrawled at the foot of the bill is a note that £1 1s 8d had been paid to London goldsmith, Moses Sicklemore, for a silver tobacco box engraved with a coat of arms, presumably those of the May family.[81]

The clothes that Heath made for the Roberts men were plainer and cheaper than those made for May. For example in 1677 Heath made the forty-two-year-old Walter senior a new suit made of woollen 'stuff' priced at 2s a yard. The only showy element was the Persian flowered taffeta, which may have been used to front the waistcoat (the part that would have been on show) or to line the coat and no other accessories were supplied.[82] In 1687 Heath made Walter senior another suit made of 'fine stuff', priced at 2s 6d the yard. The 'Florence sarcenet' at a more costly 6s a yard may once again have been used to front the waistcoat or line the coat (or possibly both) but otherwise the suit was relatively unadorned. As a point of comparison, the coat buttons used on Walter's suit cost a modest 6d a dozen and those used on the waistcoat 3d a dozen; those used on May's suit of 1680 cost 3s a dozen and 14d a dozen respectively.[83]

The clothes Heath made for John Roberts – two years older than Edward May – were also relatively plain. In September 1677 he made the fifteen-year-old

Figure 5.6 Silver tobacco box engraved with coat of arms, made in London possibly by Caleb Westbrooke (1691–2), The Metropolitan Museum of Art, 68.141.165a, b.

a new suit of a good-quality woollen cloth costing 10s 6d a yard. The small amount of silk tabby recorded in the bill may have been used to face the cuffs but otherwise the suit was completely plain. It was almost certainly made in anticipation of Roberts' apprenticeship to his uncle, Thomas Busbridge, since he was indentured on 17 October 1677.[84] In 1684 Heath made John – now living at Boarzell again – a fine cloth 'close coat' with velvet-faced cuffs, costing £2 16s 1d. With the coat Heath also sent John three cravats bought for him by Heath's wife costing 10s, but no other accessories were supplied.[85]

It is evident from the bills that Walter senior used Heath's services more sparingly for his and his sons' clothes than for those of his ward, Edward May. A number of the bills relating to Walter junior and John are for mourning suits and accessories and it is here that the most money was spent, reflecting the fact that late seventeenth-century funerals were as much expressions of status as they were expressions of loss.[86] For example, in April 1684 Heath supplied the twenty-nine-year-old Walter with a new suit costing £6 6s 5d consisting of a black cloth coat and breeches and a black silk waistcoat. In addition, Heath supplied a mourning sword and belt, mourning shoes with shoe buckles, black silk stockings, a fine muslin cravat, a mourning hat band and a gold ring, costing a further £3 8s 10d.[87] As was suggested in Chapter Four, it is likely that most of the Roberts men's clothing was sourced elsewhere, probably locally, including from Ticehurst mercer, Thomas Nash.[88]

In the 1690s Walter junior was buying some of his clothes from another London tailor or mercer, Samuel Jones, for whom three bills survive.[89] Items made for Walter included a 'fashionable riding coat', a 'fashionable close coat' and a 'fashionable coat, breeches and waistcoat'. The description of the items is relatively limited but does suggest that Walter was keeping up with current trends in male clothing. The fine cloth 'fashionable close coat' that Jones made for him, probably in 1693, was trimmed with braid and was to be worn over a new striped cloth waistcoat with silver buttons and silver cuffs.[90] Another 'fashionable coat' made in 1694 is described as having 'broad buttonholes'.[91] As we have seen, male coats tended to be cut closer to the body at this date with decoration provided by metallic braid trim and over-sized metallic buttons rather than the elaborate use of ribbon which we saw with Edward May's clothes.

There is, as discussed in Chapter One, very little biographical information about any of these men that would allow us to place them more clearly within their social and cultural milieu. Nevertheless, they provide an interesting case study of the different types of clothing worn by men of a middle gentry status living in the same Sussex parish at the same date. Whatever the limitations of the

Figure 5.7 'Lord Clapham', one of a pair of fashion dolls thought to date from around 1690, Victoria and Albert Museum, T.847-1974. He is wearing a red woollen silk-lined coat over a taffeta waistcoat, chamois-lined silk breeches, a 'steenkirk' cravat and a black tricorn hat. © Victoria and Albert Museum, London.

'vouchers to account' there is little doubt that May's clothing was both more expensive and more fashionable than that worn by the Roberts, reflecting the fact that his family was wealthier and that he would, on turning twenty-one, inherit a sizeable estate. Since May lived with his mother it is probable that when he was younger she chose his clothes for him. However, by the time he was eighteen he was evidently ordering them himself. On the back of the bill from John Heath dated 23 September 1682, May has written: 'Cousin Roberts, I do allow of this within written bill and I desire you to pay and discharge the same to Mr John Heath of London'.[92] The Mays had stronger connections to London than the Roberts whose connections appear to have been limited. As we have seen, there is no evidence that Walter senior's brother-in-law, Thomas Busbridge, was supplying the household with London goods, although we know from his business ledger that he was supplying miscellaneous goods, including cloth and clothing accessories, to some of his other Sussex relatives.[93]

Samuel Jeake

Of all the men who feature in this chapter Samuel Jeake is the only one for whom we have a physical description.[94] Aged nineteen, he described himself in his diary as follows:

> My stature was short, viz the same that was noted July 4 1670 [i.e. 5ft 5/8in.]. My complexion melancholy, my face pale and lean, forehead high, eyes grey, nose large, teeth bad and distorted, number 28 [i.e. 28 teeth], hair of a sad brown and curling about this age and until after 20 had a great quantity of it but from thence it decayed and grew thin. My voice grew hoarse after I had the smallpox. My body was always lean, my hands and feet small.[95]

Jeake provides a relatively unflattering description of his appearance: he was short, slight in body, with a pale, possibly angular face, a beaky nose and bad teeth. The man who wrote this description could hardly be accused of vanity, but he does reveal a certain preoccupation with his appearance. His incipient baldness in his early twenties seems to have caused him some anxiety; a tiny scrap of paper records the astrological circumstances and consequences of a haircut in 1672, noting that 'within two or three days after the curls became more fixed, solid and perceptible than formerly but by degrees decayed'.[96] The smallpox he had experienced as a child did not disfigure his face, but it did damage his eyesight and as an adult he wore spectacles.[97]

Jeake's personal expenditure accounts, which survive from January 1674 to January 1680, show that during this period his cloth, clothing accessories and footwear were mostly being bought locally and his clothes were being made up by local tailors.[98] His suits were made of serge or stuff, his riding coat was made of camlet, his shirts were made of dowlas, he wore worsted stockings and cambric cravats. There is not enough detail in the accounts to say much about the cut or style of his clothes but they seem to have been good quality but modest, in line with contemporary male fashions but not especially fashionable. There is also an emphasis on practicality: in 1676 he spent 1s 10d on a pair of buskins, 3s 6d on two pairs of oiled-skinned 'drawers' and 5s 6¼d on a linen 'frock'.[99] The countryside surrounding Rye was low-lying salt marshland, which would have been wet and inhospitable to travellers during winter.[100] Knee-length boots and waterproofed clothing would have provided Jeake with a degree of protection whether travelling on foot or on horseback. Possibly he wore his frock when shifting stock around in the warehouse. There were some signs of sartorial display, however. In 1676 he spent £2 2s 6d on a silver-hilted sword and in 1679 whilst in London he spent 2s on two pairs of silver-mounted glass buttons, 7s on a velvet cap and 8s 2d on seven yards of 'Colbertine' lace.[101]

By 1676 Jeake was twenty-three and looking for a wife, which may have heightened his concern about his appearance. His first two courtships were unsuccessful but in June 1680 he resolved to seek the hand of Elizabeth Hartshorne (then aged twelve years eight months) in marriage. This time his suit was accepted; they were betrothed the next month and married in March 1681.[102] The marriage settlement, agreed prior to the betrothal, was £1000 in cash together with Barbara Hartshorne's house in Middle Street, worth (together with its contents) about £200.[103] Jeake marked his transition to a man of substance by ordering himself a fashionable new watch from his cousin, London watchmaker James Wightman.[104] On 12 February 1681 James wrote to Jeake saying,

> ... [I] understand you would have a fashionable watch. That which I would advise you to is a pendulum watch as we call them which is with a spring under the balance which regulates the work so that it goes better than one with a balance only. As for the studded carcase, they are still in fashion only some alteration in the order of them. The price of such a watch will be £7 but if you fix upon such a one as Mr Smith's it was a shilling or two under £5 10s. Pray be pleased to send which you please to have and I shall take an extraordinary care in making it ...[105]

The balance spring (or hair spring), which Dutch scientist, Christiaan Hugyens, claimed to have invented in 1675, was a spring attached to the balance wheel in mechanical timepieces to control the speed at which the wheels turned thereby controlling the rate of movement of the hands and improving the accuracy of the device. The 'studded carcase' might have been made of leather, sharkskin or tortoise-shell, decorated in silver 'piqué-work' or studs.[106] The watch cost Jeake £6 15s, which, according to Wightman, was '5s cheaper than I have sold the worst that I have made of these sort'.[107] As an enthusiastic amateur scientist Jeake was no doubt impressed with the watch's novelty and the accuracy of its timekeeping. Despite being worn out of view in the fob pocket of Jeake's breeches this was nevertheless a fashionable piece of male jewellery and he no doubt took pleasure in displaying it whilst in company. What Jeake needed now was a fashionable new suit to wear it with. This was made for him by a London tailor, with James Wightman acting as his proxy. The details of the suit are set out in a letter from Wightman to Jeake which is undated but probably written in April 1681.[108]

> ... [I] have been with my tailor about your suit but find him unwilling to make it except he have measure sent up or else one of your coats for he says it will not be well made without one of them. If you send a measure he desires that they that take it may write on it which is the breast and which is the waist and the vest. He tells me that waistcoats are in fashion and they wear them very long but flowered silk is little worn but gold and silver striped is much worn and if you lace it before it must also be laced round the skirt and the slits also. As for the lining he says it will not be suitable to the rest if you line it with Persian taffeta but it should be a richer silk. Frost button is still in wear and gold or gold and silver upon sad-coloured cloth which is much worn as also dark greys are much in wear. The button that is in fashion is a pretty high button with ridges but they do not wear very well as I am informed but look handsome on a suit. I think a hat of the price you write of will be too mean for you; I think a beaver would do well and for £3 you may have a good one ...[109]

As we have seen, new fashions in silk fabrics were set each year by high-end mercers in Paris and London, as well as by the English East India Company. In 1677 Walter Roberts's new suit had incorporated a small amount of Persian flowered taffeta. By 1681 this would have been unfashionable: as Wightman's tailor advised, 'flowered silk is little worn but gold and silver striped is much worn'.[110] The choice of buttons was also important: frost buttons were 'still in wear' but the 'pretty high button with ridges' had become more fashionable. Which buttons were chosen for Jeake's new suit is not recorded but we do know that it was further embellished by a 'shoulder knot'.[111] For a hat Wightman recommended 'beaver', which was made from felted beaver fur and sheep's wool.[112] Wightman selected the hatband himself, advising Jeake that 'I am told a

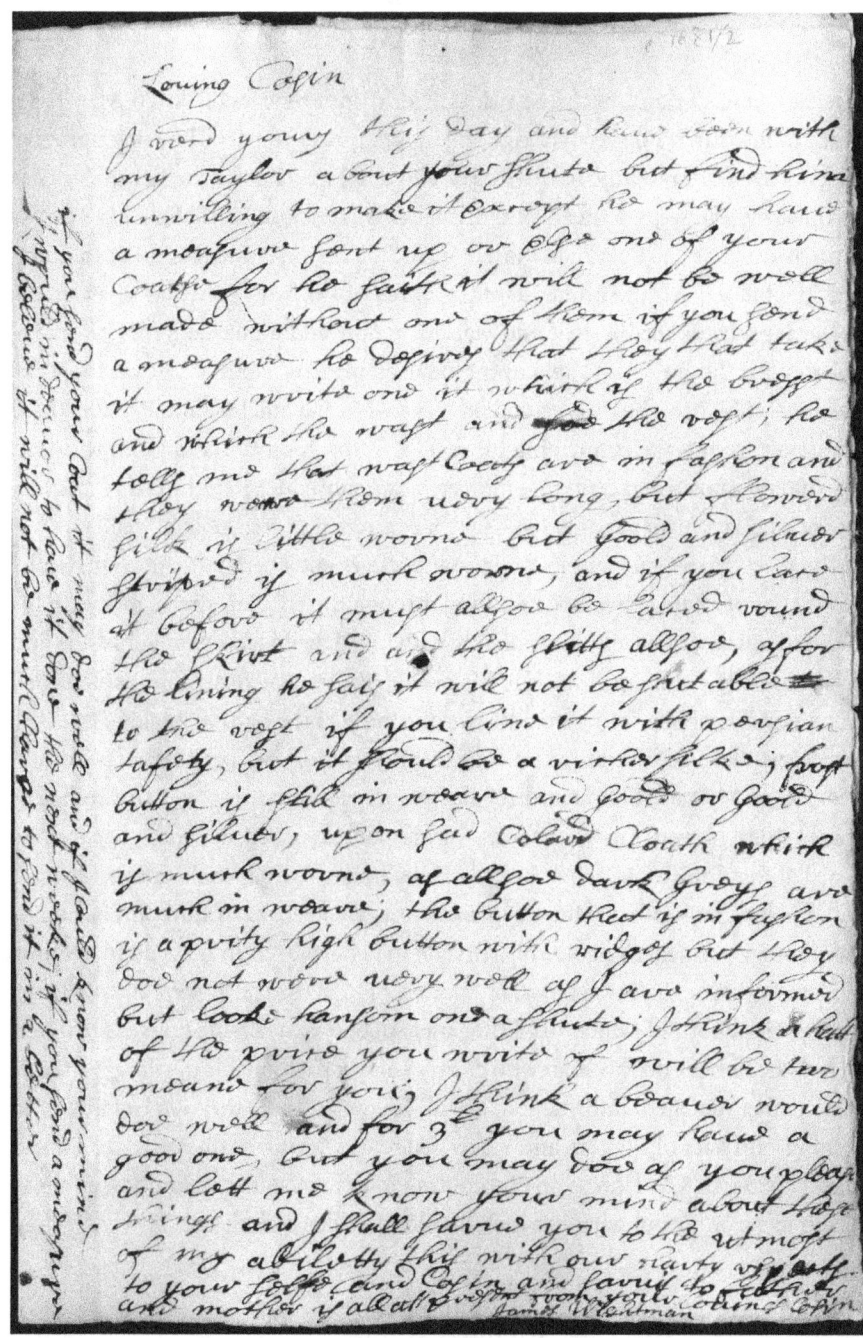

Figure 5.8 Letter from James Wightman to Samuel Jeake (undated, probably April 1681), East Sussex Record Office, Frewen 5047. Reproduced with the permission of East Sussex Record Office, copyright reserved.

ribbon [for the hat] the same of the shoulder knot is quite out of wear and this very fashionable'.[113]

Jeake's new suit and hat were dispatched to him by carrier on 28 May 1681, Wightman writing, 'I hope all things will fit and please you also, I having done my best endeavour. Pray let me have a line or two that I may know whether the suit fits for I have a great desire to hear'. With the letter was enclosed a bill for £21 7s 8d for all the items that Jeake had purchased, including his new watch and his wedding ring. The bill records the purchase of five yards of silk 'with gold and silver' at 12s the yard, probably for his coat and waistcoat, four and a quarter yards of taffeta, probably for the lining and two and a quarter yards of cloth at 15s 6d the yard, probably for his breeches. Also supplied was a white hat and hatband.[114] Sadly there is no letter from Jeake confirming his receipt of the goods or commenting on his new suit but a positive reception is indicated by a subsequent letter from Wightman in which he says 'I am very glad to hear that your suit fits reasonable well'.[115]

The story of the suit told in Wightman's letters ends here but the young Jeake must have cut a fine appearance walking through the cobbled streets of Rye in his gold-and-silver striped silk suit, possibly with his silver-hilted rapier at his side and his fashionable 'pendulum watch' in his pocket, the very picture of the aspirational and upwardly-mobile young man.[116] The one thing that is hard to imagine is Jeake's hair. As we have seen, it began to thin in his twenties. His personal expenditure accounts of 1674 to 1680 record regular payments for cutting and trimming his hair; in 1681 he was carrying combs in his pocket, which we know because he recorded that they broke when he fell off his horse.[117] This would suggest that he wore his own hair rather than a wig and there is no record of him purchasing or maintaining one. Jeake's choice of hairstyle may have been influenced by reading William Prynne's *The Unloveliness of Lovelocks* (1628) or Hall's *The Loathsomeness of Long Hair*, both of which his father owned, but such hirsutist austerity would perhaps be rather odd in a man who clearly enjoyed fashionable display.[118] There is little further detailed information about Jeake's clothes, the odd reference to clothing purchases in letters and a few references in his business ledger for the period 1680–1688. We know that he continued to buy clothes in London either in person or by proxy but what those clothes looked like is unknown.[119]

Richard Stapley

Richard Stapley recorded purchases of clothing and accessories in the margins and blank pages and spaces of a printed almanac which was small enough to carry around in his coat pocket. His clothing, as recorded, was relatively modest and supplied by local mercers, James Matthew of Twineham and Richard Smith and James Lintott both of nearby Bolney. He usually bought on credit, settling the account some months later. For example, on 9 May 1684 Stapley recorded that he bought a 'suit of clothes', a pair of shag breeches, two pairs of stockings and six and a half ells of cambric and thread 'for handkerchiefs' from mercer, Richard Smith, at a total cost of £7 7s 4d, all purchased on Smith's 'book' or on credit. A note in Smith's hand below Stapley's account records that the account was settled on 27 January 1685.[120] In May 1692 Twineham mercer, James Matthew, supplied Stapley with a serge coat and breeches, stockings and a new black hat, in July 1692 with a calamanco coat and breeches and a pair of stockings, in August 1692 with two fustian waistcoats, in October 1692 with a pair of shag breeches, in February 1693 with a coat and a waistcoat and in April 1693 with a periwig, costing a total of £9 19s, which Stapley paid in May 1693.[121] In January 1694 he bought four and a quarter yards of purple bays at 3s 6d a yard, which Matthew made up into a gown (probably a nightgown) for him and 2s for a pound of sweet powder, presumably to fragrance his wig.[122] The bays used in

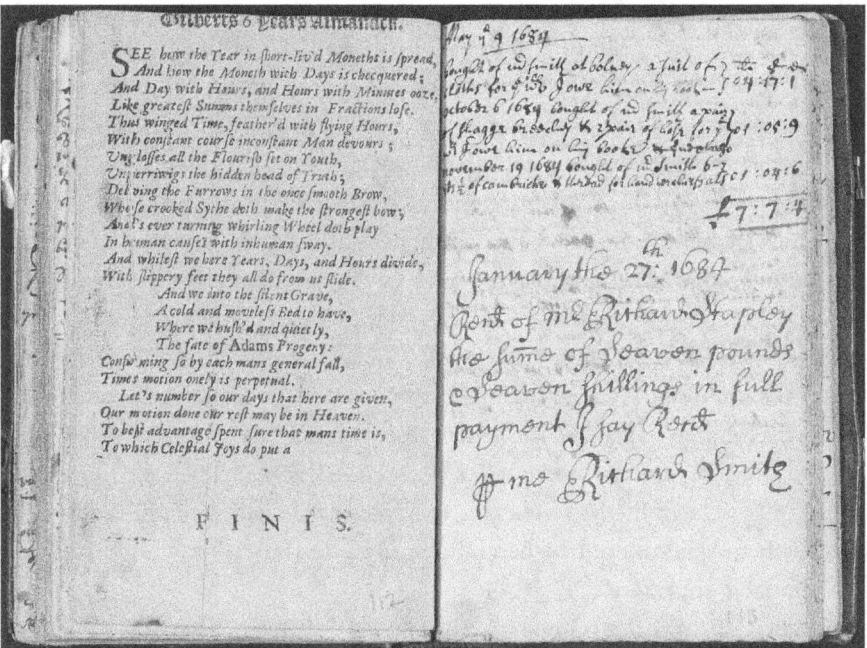

Figure 5.9 Pages from Richard Stapley's memorandum book showing entries for 1684–5, East Sussex Record Office, HIC 1166. Reproduced with the permission of East Sussex Record Office, copyright reserved.

Stapley's nightgown was a shilling a yard cheaper than that bought by Moore to make his purple nightgown in 1676.[123]

Like Moore's clothes, Stapley's were made of good quality, English, woollen cloth. There is no indication of style but presumably Stapley kept up with contemporary male fashion trends, even if his clothing was not especially fashionable. Possibly he was more concerned with practicality and durability than style; as we have seen, he seems to have spent all his time in rural Sussex. He records the purchase of four pairs of boots during the period covered by his memorandum book, but none of shoes (although he does record the purchase of shoe buckles in 1687).[124] In February 1693 he paid his brother-in-law, the tanner Walter Burt, 16s 6d for a stag's skin to 'make up' his breeches; in August 1697 he bought a sturdy pair of ram-skin gloves.[125]

However, whilst his clothes seem to have been quite utilitarian his accessories were often fashionable and exotic. Although bought locally, their provenance is likely to have been London. For example in 1694 Stapley bought a cane with an ivory-studded head and 'a purple and gold string to it' from James Matthew 'which cost in London 10s'.[126] Amongst the headwear that Stapley purchased were a black velvet cap 'turned up with fur' bought in 1692 from William Sheward, who had 'sent to London for it' and a fashionable Carolina hat bought in 1701 from Bolney mercer, James Lintott.[127] Other small, decorative, accessories that Stapley records are two tobacco boxes, one of silver and one of tortoise-shell, a silver snuff box and two pocket knives, one with a tortoise-shell handle and one with an agate handle.[128] The most extravagant accessory that Stapley bought was a silver-cased watch made by London watchmaker, Benjamin Hill (1617–1670), for which he paid £3 in 1687. The watch, bought locally in Hurstpierpoint and obviously second hand, showed 'the hour of the day, the day of the month, the months of the year, the age of the moon and the ebbing and flowing of the water and will go 30 hours without winding up'.[129] These small accessories were worn or carried out of view – the watch in a fob pocket at the top of the breeches, the snuff and tobacco boxes in coat pockets, the dagger in a sheath on the left hip – but they were nevertheless intended to be displayed. For Stapley, however, leading a relatively isolated life in Twineham, their value may have been in their tactile and aesthetic qualities rather than in their usefulness in helping him to achieve a fashionable appearance.

Other decorative items purchased by Stapley were a set of silver shirt buttons bought in Lewes in November 1683 for 4s 6d, which he subsequently exchanged for a new set in March 1693 and a pair of silver shoe buckles bought in January 1687 for 5s. It may have been the latter that he sold to his brother for 5s in 1693

Figure 5.10 Calendar watch made by Benjamin Hill (1650–60 with later alterations), British Museum, 1888,1201.175. The upper dial has an applied ring engraved 1–31 for the date. Within this is a revolving disc engraved with the months and the signs of the zodiac. The aperture to the left shows the days of the week with their ruling deities. The three apertures to the right show the age and phase of the moon and tidal indication. © The Trustees of the British Museum. All rights reserved.

to use at the knee buckles on his breeches; at the same time he sold Anthony a pair of silver buttons for 2s for the breeches' waistband.[130] There are a number of references in Stapley's memorandum book to wigs. In July 1697 he paid 43s for two wigs bought from John Wallis 'periwig maker' of Lewes, Wallis apparently delivering the wigs personally to Stapley since payment was made 'in Hickstead Hall'.[131] In January 1699 Stapley recorded that he had handed over his new periwigs in a paste-board box to Francis Alcock, innholder of the Royal Oak in Hurstpierpoint, 'to be sent John Wallis the periwig maker to be changed for a larger wig in the head and cowl'. Wallis had promised to take care of it in two or three weeks, which he did because Stapley noted that he received another wig approximately three weeks later delivered to him by Francis Alcock.[132]

Conclusion

As explained in the introduction, with the exception of Giles Moore the information available on the clothing of the men considered in this chapter is intermittent and incomplete. Nevertheless, a close reading of such evidence as does survive suggests a variety of sartorial practices amongst 'gentlemen' living in late seventeenth-century Sussex. Giles Moore emerges as the least fashionable man, apparently content to wear doublet and breeches until his death in 1679 rather than adopting the three-piece suit of long-line coat, waistcoat and close-fitting breeches. His other fashion choices – continuing to wear bands rather than a cravat and eschewing the wig – reinforce the image of Moore as a conservative and somewhat old-fashioned dresser. His clothing choices were no doubt influenced by his position as a clergyman, concerned to show his congregation that he was immune to 'the manners and fashions of this world'. Nevertheless, he wanted to make a respectable appearance and his suits were made out of good-quality English cloth. Whilst not averse to spending money (or, as discussed in Chapters Three and Four, shopping) Moore was always attentive to cost, as we see with his attempts to negotiate a fixed price for the shoes he bought from Thomas Stone.

The two men who appear to have the most in common sartorially, perhaps ironically given their difference in status, are Edward May and Samuel Jeake. In the early 1680s both were wearing fashionable, close-fitting three-piece suits, May's coat made out of pricey fine woollen cloth and Jeake's out of a flashier gold-and-silver striped silk. Their coats and waistcoat were embellished with fashionable buttons, 'frost' buttons in the case of May and perhaps 'pretty high buttons with ridges' in the case of Jeake. Both wore shoulder knots on their right shoulder, May's of the same colour as his hat band, Jeake, on Wightman's advice that such confluence was no longer fashionable, in a contrasting colour. Like any true gentleman, May and Jeake both wore rapiers at their sides. However, Jeake's suit may have been a one-off – or at least rare – sartorial event, intended to commemorate, or indeed celebrate, his wedding. On a day-to-day basis he is likely to have worn well-cut suits made of good quality woollen cloth, as described in his personal expenditure accounts of 1674 to 1680. Heath's bills suggest that May was wearing clothing of this quality on a more regular basis, consistent with a young gentleman of marriageable age about to come into a sizeable inheritance.

Clothing was undoubtedly important to the way these men constructed and maintained their social identities; but as this chapter has attempted to show, their clothing choices can also reveal something about their individual characters rather than just their social status. All of them dressed well, even if not all of them dressed especially fashionably, and each is likely to have made choices based on a complex range of factors, including affordability, lifestyle, age and self-image, which can only partly be revealed from the available evidence. As important as the clothes themselves, and essential to their status as 'gentlemen', were the small portable accessories that they carried with them – tobacco and snuff boxes, watches, rapiers and walking canes. Despite their differing social backgrounds, what appears to unite these men was a desire to use clothing to express some notion of 'gentility' although they may not have agreed on precisely what that meant.[133]

6

The Clothing of Provincial Gentlewomen

According to Richard Braithwaite the English gentlewoman should dress herself modestly in 'comely apparel' always remembering that 'the very habit of the mind may be best discerned and discovered by the state or carriage of the body'. As clothing was 'ordained by necessity' the gentlewoman should 'use it with Christian civility'.[1] This chapter looks at the clothes worn by a small number of women living in Sussex from the late 1630s through to the early 1700s. These women have already been encountered: middle-aged widow, Judith Morley, living in Chichester, Martha Mayhew, the young niece of Horsted Keynes' rector, Giles Moore, and Elizabeth Jeake, the wife of Rye merchant, Samuel Jeake. Broadly, these women were all members of the 'middle' or 'better' sort but there were clear differences in their social status. Martha's family background appears to have been relatively modest; possibly her father, Francis Mayhew, was a yeoman.[2] In taking Martha into his own household Moore sought to elevate her status to his own with a view to achieving an advantageous marriage for her. Judith was a member of the middle gentry, whose income came from estates in Lincolnshire and Fulham left to her by her first husband, Thomas Gresham. By the time we meet her in this chapter she has been widowed for a second time, after a disastrous marriage to William Morley, the younger brother of Sir John Morley of Halnaker.[3] As the wife of Samuel Jeake, Elizabeth was a member of Rye's urban elite: Jeake's penchant for dressing in the style of a 'gentleman' was discussed in the previous chapter and as we shall see in this chapter Elizabeth was also concerned to display her social position and her 'gentility' through expensive and fashionable clothes.

The same limitations in evidence occur as in the previous chapter: there is intermittent information about the clothing of Judith Morley and Elizabeth Jeake derived from letters sent to them from London; there is more consistent and detailed information about Martha Mayhew's clothing because of her uncle's detailed household and personal account book. The chapter is based on fewer case studies than the previous one as obtaining coherent information about the clothing of individual women living in Sussex has proved more difficult. This is partly down to the vagaries of the surviving documentary record but it must also reflect the fact that women's clothing was often accounted for separately from that of their husband's, and their own account books (where they were kept) have not survived. An example of this is Moore's wife, Susan (discussed below), whose clothing barely features in his account book and who presumably accounted for herself.

Women's dependent status is discussed in more detail below and it is suggested that their sartorial behaviour was subject to different constraints to that of their husbands or male relatives. As a minor Martha Mayhew would have had the least control over what she wore, with her clothing bought for her by her conservative and cost-conscious uncle. In theory at least, recently widowed Judith Morley should have had most independence but, as we shall see, her choices were constrained by her dependence on her son, James, to shop on her behalf, by a regular shortage of money and by the fact that social convention required her to dress in mourning.[4] It is possible that of the three women it was Elizabeth Jeake, the wife of upwardly mobile and fashion-conscious merchant, Samuel Jeake, who had the most sartorial independence although she too was largely dependent on her husband and friend to shop for her in London.

The style of women's clothes

Throughout the seventeenth century the basic items of female outerwear were the waistcoat and petticoat, which together made up a 'suit', and the gown, which could either be a one-piece or made up of two separate elements, the bodice (also described as a waistcoat) and the petticoat. Bodices were either closed with laces at the front or the back or could be worn with a 'V' shape gap at the front to display a decorative stomacher and they might be stiffened with narrow strips of whalebone to keep the fabric taut and shape the wearer's torso. Alternatively, a woman could wear a stiffened bodice, or 'a pair of bodies', as an undergarment over her smock.[5] Waistcoats could be sleeved or sleeveless; if sleeveless, they could be worn with separate sleeves attached to the waistcoat with ties or pins. Under petticoats were worn to provide additional warmth in winter; they could also be worn for show with the upper petticoat hitched up or opening at the front in a 'V' shape. Some women wore drawers – we know from Pepys's diary that his wife wore them, as did some of the women with whom he had sexual encounters – but their use is likely to have been limited.[6]

In the 1640s and 1650s fashionable women wore their bodices tightly laced, which narrowed the waist and pushed the breasts up. This fashion was condemned on medical grounds by John Bulwer who claimed that such 'straight-lacing' not only constricted their breathing making them vulnerable to 'consumptions' but could also lead to 'crookedness of the backbone'.[7] Others condemned the exposure of the neck and breasts on moral grounds: for Thomas Hall 'naked' breasts were 'temptations and known provocations to uncleanness' and a sign of a woman's immodesty, impudence and 'monstrous pride'.[8] Wearing a padded 'bum roll' or 'bum barrel' around the hips pushed the petticoat out at the back creating a bustle-like effect which further enhanced the appearance of a slender waist.[9] The main style of sleeve in the 1640s was a full, wide, sleeve ending below the elbow finished by a broad turned-up lace cuff or exposed smock sleeves. In the 1650s and 1660s sleeves were fuller, attached below the shoulders to a wider-necked bodice that displayed the upper chest and shoulders.[10] However, according to Randle Holme 'there is as much variety of fashion' in sleeves 'as days of the year'.[11]

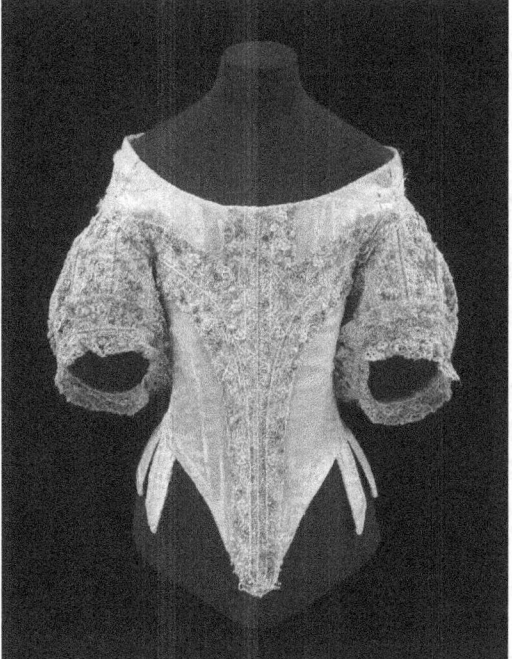

Figure 6.1 Ivory satin bodice trimmed with bobbin lace with parchment and coloured silk, stiffened with whalebone (1660–9), Victoria and Albert Museum, 429-1889. It would have been worn with a petticoat of matching satin with a padded roll or 'bum roll' underneath. © Victoria and Albert Museum, London.

Women also wore less structured loose-fitting gowns called nightgowns (also called morning gowns) and sacs (or saques), which could be worn at home without a tightly laced bodice or as an over-garment in public. Pepys noted that in March 1669 his wife had 'put on her first French gown, called a sac', suggesting that this was the first time she had worn one.[12] By the 1670s loose-fitting gowns were also known as 'mantuas', which in their early manifestation were kimono-like wraps. According to Randle Holme these could be knee or heel-length.[13] By the 1680s the mantua was often worn pinned or tied back at the hips giving it a more fitted appearance but kimono-style mantuas like the pink silk one worn by fashion doll, 'Lady Clapham' (*c.* 1690) were also still worn.[14]

The neck and chest could be partly or completely covered by a broad neck cloth or collar made out of fine linen and sometimes decorated with lace. A 'neckerchief' was a large linen square, folded diagonally and worn around the shoulders like a small shawl. The 'gorget' and the 'whisk', fashionable from the 1640s, were deep, circular, cape-like collars, which covered the upper chest and shoulders. It is not clear how they differed from each other and the terms were often used interchangeably.[15] In the 1680s and 1690s women also wore tippets which were elbow-length shoulder capes, sometimes with a short upper cape like a deep collar and in the 1690s 'steinkerks' or 'steenkirks' became fashionable, which as we saw in the previous chapter were long, loosely tied cravats initially worn by fashionable men.[16]

Women's head coverings from the 1640s to the 1670s were relatively simple. Less fashionable women continued to wear coifs beneath their hats; the more fashion conscious covered their hair with a loose-fitting hood tied under the chin or a plain gauze veil that hung down onto the shoulders.[17] From the 1680s headwear became increasingly elaborate with the fashion for 'top knots' or 'towers', made up of multiple layers of linen, lace and ribbon ascending a tiered wire frame known as a commode. As Angela McShane and Clare Backhouse have shown, these were much satirised in popular print.[18] A ballad of *c.* 1685 observed 'some misses wear as much ribbon a top/ in this their most gaudy attire/ as if their head were a milliner's shop' whilst another of *c.* 1690 told the story of a calf born with a top-knot-like structure on its head after its parents were frightened by a passing lady wearing 'top knots of ribbons full six stories high'.[19] These satires also found their way into the decorative arts: a tin-glazed earthenware dish from 1688 in the collection of the Fitzwilliam Museum, Cambridge, is inscribed with a ballad 'The À-la-mode Dress, or the Maiden's Mode Admired and Continued by the Ape, Owl and Mistress Puss'. It

Figure 6.2 'Lady Clapham' wears a pink silk damask mantua over a silk bodice and petticoat and a lawn and lace 'top knot' (c. 1690), Victoria and Albert Museum, T.846-1974. © Victoria and Albert Museum, London.

features a lion, an ape and an owl wearing top knots with pinners hanging down the side of their faces. The owl and the ape are also wearing short capes known as night rails. The ballad's message is clear: these fashions are associated with vanity, stupidity and sexual misconduct and as such should be eschewed by respectable women.[20]

Figure 6.3 Tin-glazed earthenware dish, 'The À-la-mode Dress or the Maiden's Mode Admired and Continued by the Ape, Owl and Mistress Puss' (1688), Fitzwilliam Museum, c.1443–1928. © Fitzwilliam Museum, Cambridge.

Like fabric patterns, fashions in women's accessories changed rapidly, something that Samuel Jeake found out to his cost when he tried to sell some 'jessamy' gloves and fans he had imported illegally from France in 1679 during a period when the import of French goods had been banned.[21] A delay in the delivery of his goods meant that he missed the start of the summer season: as his cousin, Anne Wightman, told him in May 'this is the best time for the sale of them because of Whitsun tide approaching [8 to 10 June] after which they will not be so valuable ...'[22] Having missed the London season he may have decided it was best to sell them in Rye but in January 1680 he still had a significant amount of stock on his hands. In March 1680 he sent some of it to Anne in London but by then, as she told him, the accessories were a year out of date. She decided that her best option was to try to sell them at some of London's street shops since they would 'not go off at the Change' but even this proved difficult because the gloves had lost their scent.[23] In the end she did manage to sell them but at a considerable loss.[24]

Cosmetics and artificial enhancements

Women had a range of cosmetics or artificial enhancements at their disposal.[25] 'Spanish paper', made from cochineal and available in leather or paper form, could be used to redden the lips or cheeks.[26] In a deeply unflattering pen portrait of his brother's new mistress, Katherine Williams, included in a letter to his mother in 1641 James Gresham described her as having a 'face of a harsh horse-like composure', 'overhanging eyebrows' and 'a rosy colour for which she is beholden to Spanish paper'.[27] Skin could be whitened and its wrinkles evened out using a white paste or 'fucus'. Hugh Plat included two recipes for 'fucus' in his *Delights for Ladies* (1602), the first using ground pig bones and the second using sublimate of mercury.[28] Sunken cheeks could be filled out using 'plumpers' described by the author of *Mundus Muliebris* (1690) as 'certain very thin, round, and light balls, to plump out and fill up the cavities of the cheeks, much used by old court countesses'.[29] Spots were covered with decorative face patches or 'mouches' 'cut out into little moons, suns, stars, castles, birds, beasts and fishes'.[30] Hair colour might be changed through hair dyes or the use of coloured hair pieces. Plat provided recipes for hair dyes that could 'colour a black hair presently into a chestnut colour' or 'make hair of a fair yellow or golden colour'.[31] Blonde hair was fashionable for most of the seventeenth century but by the end of the century dark, particularly black, hair was in fashion.[32] Hair pieces, sometimes wired to achieve fuller, more permanent, curls were also used to create fashionable hair styles or to bulk out thin, lank hair.[33]

Women could also make use of a wide range of washes and unguents to keep their skin white and freckle and spot free. Plat recommended the use of birch sap for the removal of spots and freckles and an exfoliator made of salt and lemon juice to 'help a face that is red or pimpled'. The importance of smelling sweet is reflected in the numerous recipes he provides for perfumes for the body and household linen.[34] Gloves, fans and handkerchiefs were frequently scented: the author of *Mundus Muliebris* mentions gloves fragranced with jonquil, tuberose, frangipane, orange, violet, narcissus, jasmine and amber and handkerchiefs fragranced with 'd'ange', orange, 'millefleur' and myrtle.[35] Pomander balls in decorative gold or silver-gilt filigree cases or 'bobs' could be suspended on a chain from the waist.[36] Despite the range of shop-bought and homemade perfumes available, some women were evidently less successful with their personal hygiene than others: according to Gresham, his brother's new mistress had a most unpleasant odour – 'there is such a perfume in a morning issuing out of her bed when she is therein that it would rather loath than invite a man to entrance' – and her linen smocks were patched under the arms where 'the nasty sweat rots them'.[37]

The use of cosmetics or artificial beauty enhancements attracted considerable moral condemnation as well as satirical comment. In his *Discourse against Painting and Tincturing of Women* (1616) Thomas Tuke argued that women who 'paint or dye their faces … are not able to clear themselves of pride and the practice of it … is a thing most odious to God and man'. Moreover, 'they that paint would have that which is artificial and borrowed taken to be natural and proper'.[38] For Thomas Hall the 'practice of artificial painting and colouring the body that people may seem that which indeed they are not is sinful and abominable'.[39] For both authors the use of cosmetics was a form of deceit, allowing women to trick others (especially men) into seeing them as something that they were not. Ribeiro has noted a shift in attitudes in the later seventeenth century with an increased acceptance that the judicious use of cosmetics could enhance and preserve a woman's appearance.[40] Indeed, the author of *Several Letters between Two Ladies Wherein the Lawfulness and Unlawfulness of Artificial Beauty in Point of Conscience are Nicely Debated* (1701) argued that the modest use of cosmetics to remedy the defects in a woman's 'natural beauty' was no more a sign of pride than the 'use of crutches or spectacles to those that are lame or dim-sighted'.[41] However, cosmetics and artificial enhancements continued to be represented as a type of trickery in comic and satirical literature. As we saw in Chapter Two, 'painted' women were often depicted as little better than prostitutes and ageing women who used cosmetics to try to maintain the illusion of youth were a common theme in popular literature and Restoration comedy.

Women's clothes and the law

Under common law a woman reached her majority at the age of twenty-one allowing her to take control for the duration of her spinsterhood of any real and personal property that had previously been under the control of her parent or guardian. Once married, a woman's legal identity was subsumed into that of her husband. In principle, a married woman lacked the capacity to own property in her own name and did not have the right to make a will unless she had her husband's permission. Any personal property she owned before marriage or acquired during marriage was vested in her husband who could do with it as he wanted. As the author of *The Law's Resolution of Women's Rights* (1632) explained,

> If before marriage the woman were possessed of horses, neat, sheep, corn, wool, money, plate and jewels, all manner of moveable substance is presently by conjunction the husband's to sell, keep or bequeath if he die ...

And

> The very goods which a man gives to his wife are still his own, her chain, her bracelets, her apparel, are all the good man's goods.[42]

In law the only way in which a woman could protect her personal property was if she entered into a legal settlement to create a 'separate estate' before marriage. As well as protecting her 'paraphernalia' (for example, her clothes, jewels, bed linen and plate) these settlements were used to specify the annual allowance or 'pin money' that the husband agreed to pay to his wife. 'Pin money' remained the wife's own personal property to spend as she saw fit on clothing and other personal items. However, legal settlements of this kind were not routinely used because of the expense of setting them up.[43] Since many women married before the age of twenty-one they might therefore not enjoy legal ownership of any of their personal possessions including their clothing unless, or until, they were widowed. However, in practice there appears to have been an assumption that a woman's personal possessions remained her own property to dispose of as she wished. This was certainly the view of clergyman, William Gouge. In his *Domestical Duties* (1622), he wrote that a wife had a right to dispose of goods that were 'proper and peculiar' to her, without her husband's consent. This included goods that she had before marriage as well as those her husband gave to her after marriage.[44]

Despite women's apparent *de facto* freedom to buy and dispose of clothing as they wished, in many cases their sartorial choices are likely to have been more constrained than those of their husbands or male relations. Whilst Gouge was clear that married women had the right of ownership of their personal goods, he was also clear that wives ought to dress modestly and in keeping with their husbands' status. A woman who dressed above her husband's status in 'costly and garish clothes' showed a lack of respect for him and damaged not only her own but also her husband's reputation.[45] Men could also control, or strongly influence, what their wives wore in other ways, for example by not giving them any money or by expressing disapproval of their clothing choices. As we saw in Chapter One, in December 1639 Judith Morley complained to her son, James, that her husband of eight months had not given her any money and that she was afraid of him.⁴⁶ In November 1666 Samuel Pepys argued with his wife, Elizabeth, over her low-cut neck cloth which, as he claimed, was 'down to her breasts almost' and which (in his opinion) she wore 'out of belief, but without reason, that it is the fashion'.⁴⁷ Moreover, he did not give her an allowance until 1669 which meant that she was forced to ask him for money for her own personal expenditure.⁴⁸ This was not about affordability, it was about control: as is well known, Pepys spent more money on his own clothes than on those of his wife.⁴⁹ His decision finally to give her an allowance seems to have been prompted by his guilt over his affair with his servant, Deb Willet, which Elizabeth had discovered the previous October.⁵⁰ Despite Pepys's controlling and sometimes censorious behaviour, he also took pride in Elizabeth's expensive and fashionable clothes, no doubt seeing in them affirmation of his own material and social success. Women's shopping opportunities were also more circumscribed than men's; in particular, provincial women had much less access to London and were more reliant on proxy shoppers to shop on their behalf.

The country gentlewoman

As we saw in Chapter Five, in the metropolitan view country fashions lagged years behind city fashions, and the fictional narrator of *The Spectator*, 'Mr Spectator' advised his country friends to avoid making themselves ridiculous by remaining 'fixed in one certain habit' in the expectation that at some point in time it would be in fashion again. In the same issue of the paper a fictional letter writer, 'a lawyer of the Middle Temple and a Cornish man by birth' who rode the Western Circuit, noted that he had observed that women's ability to keep up with fashion decreased the further they lived from London. The most fashionable woman he had met outside London was in Staines in Middlesex. Her commode was 'not half a foot high and her petticoat within some yards of a modish circumference'. But as he travelled further away he saw that 'the petticoat grew scantier and scantier' until 'about threescore miles from London' it was so unfashionable 'that a woman might walk in it without any manner of inconvenience'.⁵¹

However, whereas country gentlemen were typically presented as boorish, content with their country pursuits and rough country clothing, country gentlewomen were depicted as obsessed with fashion in the same way as their urban counterparts, but with less successful results. In Etherege's *The Man of Mode* (1676) London gentlewoman, Belinda, explains to her friend, Mrs Loveit, that she had not been around for the last couple of days because she had been stuck with 'two or three country gentlewomen' whose conversation had been 'more insufferable than a country fiddle'. They had, she said, asked her 'a thousand questions of the modes and intrigues of the town, and she had told them 'almost as many things for news that hardly were so when their gowns were in fashion'.[52] London's high fashion was not really suited to a rural milieu in any case. *The Spectator's* Middle Temple lawyer recounted a recent visit to a Cornish country church where the appearance of a fashionably dressed woman had caused some consternation amongst the parishioners:

> As we were in the midst of the service a lady who is the chief woman of the place and had passed the winter at London with her husband entered the congregation in a little headdress and a hooped petticoat. The people, who were wonderfully startled at such a sight, all of them rose up. Some stared at the prodigious bottom and some at the little top of this strange dress. In the meantime the lady of the manor filled the whole area of the church and walked up to her pew with an unspeakable satisfaction, amidst the whispers, conjectures and astonishments of the whole congregation.[53]

Whilst the butt of *The Spectator's* satire is the hoop petticoat, which had come into fashion in 1709 attracting much critical comment for its impracticality, the comedic value of the lawyer's comments comes from its play on the well-established contemporary trope of the incompatibility of the 'city' in the 'country' and vice versa.[54] According to the author of *The Grand Concern of England* (1673) country ladies would be perfectly happy with locally produced clothes 'provided they be kept from London'.[55]

Judith Morley

Information about what Judith Morley was wearing is mostly contained in a series of letters sent to her in Chichester between 1639 and 1643 by her son, James Gresham, who was living in London. At this time she was in her late fifties. There are also two suppliers' bills from this period dated 1639 and 1642.[56] Gresham's trials in commissioning a new gown for his mother from a London tailor called Pollard between November 1640 and February 1641 were explored in Chapter Four. Despite having Judith's pattern to work from, the waistcoat proved to be too small and had to be sent back to London to be altered. Gresham's letters provide some information about the gown's appearance: it was made out of velvet (probably black, although the colour is not recorded), the petticoat was bordered with black serge and the waistcoat sleeves lined with white calico.[57] Judith's scarf was used in the waistcoat skirts, sleeves and for 'facing the hands' or sleeve cuffs.[58] In terms of cut the tailor advised Gresham that 'the fashion for petticoats and waistcoats is without short hanging sleeves, longer-waisted and somewhat narrower in the shoulders'.[59] In line with contemporary fashion, her waistcoat (or bodice) is likely to have been tight fitting to the waist, with a relatively low round or square neckline and a square-tabbed skirt with a longer central tab ending in a rounded point. Its sleeves may have been relatively full, ending on the elbow, or above the wrist, with a turned-up cuff.[60] Judith seems to have belatedly decided that she wanted a 'bum roll' or 'barrel roll', which would have had the effect of pushing the petticoat out around her hips but the tailor advised that this would make it too short.[61] A bill dated 26 November 1642 from a tailor called John Stacey records the making up of another gown and petticoat made out of sixteen yards of black satin and 'laced' with forty-five yards of black bone lace. The gown skirt is likely to have opened in a 'V' at the front to display the under petticoat in contrast to the previous gown which probably had a closed skirt. The waistcoat, or bodice, was short sleeved and worn over a taffeta-lined stomacher.[62]

Judith would have worn a whisk or a gorget to cover up her neck and chest: a bill from an unidentified tradesman dated 1639 records the purchase of 'lace for a gorget'.[63] She may have worn on her head a cornet or 'shadow', which was a cap of linen or lawn, edged with lace.[64] It may be this type of cap that Gresham was referring to when he wrote to her in December 1641 telling her that he had bought her a 'lone cap of the best and newest fashion that money can procure but very dear as all French women's wares are'.[65] As we saw in Chapter Two, anything 'French' was sold at inflated prices because of the cachet associated with French goods.[66]

Gresham's letters also record his attempts to purchase a range of different accessories for her. As with the gown commission of 1640, these purchases were frequently problematic requiring him to relay advice to his mother about what was available or what was in fashion, or asking her to clarify what it was she wanted. For example, in a letter to her dated 25 October 1640 Gresham updated his mother on his progress in buying her a plush muff,

> Your plush muff I would have sent you now but that I thought good first to let you know that plush muffs be clean out of fashion and use and that although for the present you are not able to buy a fur one which are altogether worn yet before one plush one shall be worn out you may be able to purchase a fur muff

Figure 6.4 Cornelius Johnson, Portrait of Lady Coventry (*c.* 1635). Elizabeth Coventry (1583–1653), wife of Thomas Coventry, 1st Baron Coventry (1578–1640), was the same age as Judith Morley and the style of their dress is likely to have been broadly similar. She wears a 'gorget' or 'whisk' over her shoulders, covered by a neckerchief, both heavily embellished with lace, and a cap or 'shadow' on her head. Her hair is styled in fashionable curls. Black was an expensive and fashionable colour and was not just worn for mourning. © Museums Sheffield Collection.

> for as I would advise you to buy but enough for one and for that you must let me know how much will serve or I shall buy too much or too little.[67]

In his next letter to her dated 1 November 1640 Gresham told her that he had sent her the plush,

> but not shred plush for there is none in black but is so base and poor you would never have endured it so I bought this remnant at a broken (i.e. a bankrupt trader) for 7s which is not much more than thread would have cost and for the quantity I had the advice of a muff maker …

In the same parcel he also sent her four pairs of white gloves ('although you wrote for three pairs, yet I doubt not but the fourth pair may be useful'), four yards of black ribbon, an ounce of powder and a pair of sweet (i.e. scented)

Figure 6.5 Wenceslaus Hollar, Still life with muffs, gloves, fans, mask and kerchiefs (1647), The Metropolitan Museum of Art, 17.34.9.

gloves. He let her know that he had been unable to buy her the tortoise-shell rings and the damask powder (a rose-scented powder used to perfume the body or the hair) that she had asked him for, having forgotten about the former when he was 'in the Exchange' (probably the Royal or 'old' Exchange) and had received her request for the latter too late to add it to his purchases.[68] These items were sent to her a few days later.[69]

In his letter to his mother of 16 December 1640 Gresham mentions for the first time his mother's 'hair' being made for her by Mrs Pope who promised that he would have it to send to Judith 'by the post on Tuesday'.[70] How Judith intended to use this hair piece is not recorded. Fashionable women at this date wore their hair brushed back from the forehead and temples, coiled into a bun at the back of the head, with loose curls or ringlets covering their ears and descending in some cases as far as the shoulders.[71] Possibly Judith's hair was too thin to achieve this look and she relied on false hair to bulk it out; alternatively her 'hair' may have been a different colour to her own. Whatever she intended to do with it, the hair piece was to be designed according to 'patterns' which Judith had supplied: on 4 February 1641 Gresham reported to his mother that he had delivered her letter to Mrs Pope who had promised that her 'hair' would be made according to her instructions 'but that she desires you to excuse her for your first hair by reason her man has lost the patterns and if you will send new you shall not fail within two days after she receives them'.[72] Whether Judith's 'hair' was ever finished is not recorded; in a letter to his mother dated 19 December 1641 Gresham told his mother that he had 'sent my old hair too but I am afraid it is too short for your use'.[73]

Figure 6.6 Wenceslaus Hollar, Portrait of a young woman, showing the fashionable hairstyle of the 1640s (1642), The Metropolitan Museum of Art, 17.3.756-2261.

As a widow, Judith could exercise her own judgement about what she should or should not wear, choosing good quality, fashionably cut, but sombre garments in keeping with her age and status. However, her choices were constrained by her dependency on her son, not only to shop on her behalf but also to provide her with the money to make her purchases. Judith's income was principally derived from rents on lands in Lincolnshire and Middlesex left to her by her first husband, Thomas Gresham, and as we saw in Chapter One the family had some difficulty in collecting them. Moreover, the Lincolnshire lands were the subject of lengthy, and costly, legal disputes.[74] In consequence, as James's letters record, money was often tight.[75] In a letter dated 15 November 1640 Gresham advised his mother that the velvet she wanted for her new gown was so expensive that the £10 she had allowed for it would be short by £3 or £4. Conscious of Judith's 'want of a fit garment for Christmas' Gresham took out two bonds for her use, one for £15 intended to keep her going until her rents came in and the other for £10, which he recommended should be used only if absolutely necessary.[76] In the end, as we have seen, Gresham was able to buy the velvet at a cheaper price and so Judith's original £10 was sufficient.[77] In February 1641 Gresham was forced to substitute black satin ribbon for the gold ribbon that Judith had requested (and sent him a pattern for) because, as he told her, 'the price is beyond my reach'.[78] Like many seventeenth-century consumers, Judith's purchases were often made on credit. Gresham records two occasions on which Judith's tailor, Pollard, approached him for payment of his mother's bills; nevertheless, since she was a good customer, Pollard told Gresham that he was prepared to offer her £50 credit if she 'had occasion'.[79]

Martha Mayhew

As we have seen, Giles Moore's household and personal account book records the cost of his own clothing and that of his niece, Martha Mayhew (c. 1655–1727), who came to live with him in 1667. His wife, Susan, evidently bought her own clothing and accessories and accounted for them separately, paying for items from an annuity from her dead husband's estate or from an allowance given to her by Giles.[80] The separation of a wife's personal expenditure from that of her husband was not unusual. In early seventeenth-century Norfolk, Alice Le Strange managed the household accounts, which include expenditure on her husband's clothing, but her own personal spending is excluded, presumably recorded in a separate account book.[81] Similarly, in Sussex Mary Pelham (d. 1635), the first wife of Sir Thomas Pelham, was responsible for day-to-day household expenses as well as buying her own and their children's clothes. We know that Mary kept personal account books since they are referred to in Sir Thomas's own account book, but they do not survive.[82] Moore made the odd clothing-related purchase for his wife, a hat bought in London in 1657, a 'gorget or whisk' and a pair of gloves in 1660, another pair of gloves in 1672, another London-bought hat in 1674 and a London-bought lustring hood in 1676.[83] These appear to have been given to her as gifts. He also gave her the occasional 'fairing' to spend at Lindfield Fair.[84] Susan seems only to have accompanied her husband to London on two occasions, in 1662 and in 1670.[85] It is unlikely that she was travelling there on her own and so it is reasonable to assume that she shopped locally and used the same tailors as her husband and niece.

Martha, or Mat, was the daughter of Moore's sister and brother-in-law, Susan and Francis Mayhew who lived in Beyton in Suffolk.[86] Her date of birth is unknown but she was probably aged around eleven or twelve when she arrived in Horsted in 1667. She stayed with them until 1673 when, aged about seventeen or eighteen, she married John Citizen, rector of Streat.[87] Moore's meticulous record keeping of his expenditure on Martha means that we can reconstruct with reasonable detail what she was wearing during the six years and three months she lived with him. We can also get a glimpse her lifestyle and the expectations that might be placed on a girl that Moore sought to bring up to lesser gentry status. Moore was clearly fond of his young niece, referring to her as 'my little maid' and 'my daughter'.[88]

A conservative and money-conscious man, Moore is likely to have exercised a degree of control over the clothing choices of his wife and a greater level of control over the clothing purchased for his niece. In May 1674 he bought a copy of *The Ladies Calling* (1673, discussed briefly in Chapter Two), a conduct manual for women with advice tailored to the three 'distinct scenes in which a woman can be supposed regularly to be an actor', virginity, marriage and widowhood.[89] The author recommended that virgins be modest in their demeanour and avoid frivolity by occupying themselves in acquiring 'any of those ornamental improvements which become their quality as writing, needlework, languages, music or the like', as well as learning the 'proper feminine business' of 'economy and household management'.[90] They should avoid reading romances 'which seems now to be thought the peculiar and only becoming study of young ladies' because they set up unrealistic expectations of young love and, whilst he allowed for 'harmless and healthful recreations' such as 'mutual visits', young women should also be content to stay at home rather than 'always wandering', seeking out new entertainments.[91] He allowed for some vanity in dress, seeing it as a natural attribute in the young who had not yet fully abandoned the 'toys and gaiety' of childhood, as well as a necessary display for 'they who design marriage', but warned that excessive show was likely to put off the more prudent and sober suitor, especially the 'plain country gentleman' who looked on a modish woman as a 'gaudy idol' who would squander his wealth.[92] A wife had a duty to love her husband, protect his reputation and preserve his fortune.[93] If she was given the management of the household finances ('not ordinarily the wife's province') she was expected to administer them with caution and keep her own expenditure on clothes and household furnishings within her husband's financial means.[94] She should love her children (but not too much) and exercise an appropriate degree of discipline; she should treat her servants with respect and compassion whilst ensuring their diligence and instructing them in Christian behaviour.[95]

By the time Moore purchased this book Martha was already married but the details that can be recovered from his account book suggest that her upbringing largely conformed to its principles. As a well-educated and highly literate man it is unsurprising that Moore valued education and Martha was initially sent to school in September 1667 with John Breukes in Rotherfield for a period of 10 weeks 'to learn to write', suggesting perhaps that when she arrived in Horsted Keynes her literacy skills were limited. Given Moore's somewhat austere taste in literature it is unlikely that Martha would have had access to any 'romances' in her uncle's home. Moreover, the focus of much of her education is likely to have been on acquiring those other 'ornamental improvements' advised by the author of *The Ladies Calling* and a range of domestic skills. Back in Horsted in 1668, Martha was taught to embroider a sampler over a period of seven weeks by Goodwife Potter.[96] At this time she was probably also taught to spin by her aunt.[97] In March 1669 Moore recorded that he had 'bargained' with Mistress Elizabeth Challoner in nearby Cuckfield to take Martha 'at 12 pounds per annum board and schooling' and Martha began her schooling there the next month, staying with her intermittently for periods of between six weeks and four months for the next three years.[98] Under Challoner's tutelage she continued with her embroidery and also learnt lace making, sewing and possibly knitting; in April 1671 whilst at school she made Moore some shirts and neck bands.[99]

In June 1671, aged about fifteen or sixteen, her formal education seems to have ended. By this time Moore was trying to arrange a marriage for her, initially writing to a 'Mr Crayford, minister' to see whether he would agree to Martha's marriage to his son and setting out what he would offer as her settlement. This was a marriage to which Martha was expected to consent; as Moore noted in his letter to Crayford, she had no reason not to. In the event, nothing came of it and she remained in Horsted until her marriage to John Citizen in September 1673.[100]

Moore records expenditure on a fairly limited range of social events that Martha attended, mainly weddings and going to the local fairs, the bi-annual Lindfield Fair held on 1 May and 25 July and the Horsted Fair held on 1 September. For example in June 1669 she attended 'Batchelor's daughter's wedding' and Moore gave her 10s to give to the bride and groom and 1s to give to the fiddlers.[101] In June 1670 when she attended the wedding of Edmund Pelling and Elizabeth Pilbeam in Horsted she gave the bride a child's silver spoon monogrammed with 'MM', which Moore had bought in Lewes.[102] Other social events are suggested by Moore's record that he gave Martha 1s in March 1672 to 'spend at dancings'.[103] Whilst Moore was a regular visitor to London, usually going between one and three times a year and staying for two or three nights, Martha only visited London twice during her time in Horsted, in April 1669 and in September 1672, and in each case their activities appear to have been limited to shopping.[104]

Over the six years and three months that Martha lived with him Giles bought her nine complete new outfits, either 'suits' of waistcoats, petticoats and under petticoats or gowns and petticoats, together with an extensive range of accessories. Moore and his wife appear to have completely re-clothed Martha on her arrival with them: he noted in his account book that he spent £6 4s on 'habiting her' when he collected her from London in July 1667.[105] By late August she had a new 'suit' (a waistcoat and petticoat), made of paragon and a 'coat' (probably an under petticoat) made from penistone.[106] Martha was also provided with new aprons, handkerchiefs and coifs made of 'blue' linen, a new pair of shoes with red silk shoe strings, and a straw hat.[107] In October 1668 Moore purchased another complete outfit for Martha, including a pair of 'bodies' or bodice, a waistcoat and two petticoats. The outer petticoat and possibly the waistcoat were probably made from the five and a half yards of 'italany' (a type of worsted), the under petticoat from the two yards of shag.[108] Martha's clothes were clearly intended to be modest, practical and hardwearing, suitable for a country girl of 'middling' status. Like her uncle's, some of her stockings were home knitted, her working aprons were made of coarse 'blue' linen and she wore pattens to keep her shoes out of the mud.[109]

As she entered her teens her clothing began to display more decorative elements and is likely to have become more fashionable.[110] In April 1669 Moore took his 'little maid' with him to London so that he could 'habit' her for school. He bought her a new gown and petticoat, a new hood, gloves, two holland aprons, two neck handkerchiefs, two pocket handkerchiefs, two pairs of cuffs, two neck cloths and lace, two forehead cloths, a new pair of red worsted stockings, four yards of ribbon and silk laces to lace the gown with.[111] Moore also bought Martha a mask, probably a half mask that would have covered her brow, eyes and nose. Masks were fashionable accessories which enabled London ladies to conceal their identities whilst in a public place but they were also worn for practical reasons to protect the skin from the elements.[112] In February 1670 Martha had another new 'suit' of 'italany' made for her by Horsted Keynes tailor, Edward Waters. However, on this occasion her waistcoat sleeves were 'faced' with tabby and it was worn over a stomacher. Moore also bought her a new pair of green stockings and a new pair of bodies. A year later another of Moore's tailors, William Best, made Martha a gown of serge 'seraphick' with ribbon-decorated sleeves and a silver-lace trimmed serge under petticoat, a new pair of bodies and a stomacher, in all spending £3 9s. In December 1671 tailor, Thomas Pelling, made Martha a new suit, consisting of a 'rush drugget' upper petticoat, a striped silk under petticoat and a 'cloth' silver lace-trimmed waistcoat, in all spending

£2 14s 10d.[113] In September 1672 Martha accompanied her uncle to London for a second time. On this occasion he bought her a new riding suit, a new gown and 'coat', which cost him £3 10s. She bought herself a pair of bodies, two laces, a lawn whisk and a whisk box.[114] Moore spent £3 10s on a new gown and petticoat for Martha shortly before her marriage to John Citizen in September 1673, noting in his book that it was 'never worn by her until after her marriage'.[115]

The style of these gowns is likely to have followed fashionable lines with a tightly fitting bodice or waistcoat, ending in a deep point at the front, a low neckline with short straight sleeves. Martha's gown skirts would have opened in a 'V' at the front to display her decorative under petticoats. There is only one reference to the purchase of coifs in August 1667; thereafter Martha seems to have worn more fashionable hoods, usually made of linen but on occasion made of silk.[116] In May 1668 she bought (or had bought for her) a ducap hood for 4s and in May 1672 she bought a black silk hood for 4s 6d.[117] Around the house Martha is likely to have worn linen neckerchiefs covering her neck and shoulders

Figure 6.7 Peter Lely, Portrait of a young woman (*c*. 1662–3), British Museum, 1866,0714.34. Her hair, styled in fashionable curls and ringlets, is loosely covered by a scarf that ties under her chin. The identity of the sitter is unknown, but she is likely to have been of considerably higher status than Martha. © The Trustees of the British Museum. All rights reserved.

but she also wore fine lawn whisks, which as we have seen were circular, cape-like collars that covered the upper chest and shoulders.[118]

During the time Martha lived with him Moore bought her eighteen pairs of new shoes, averaging just under three pairs a year, at a cost of 2s 4d or 2s 6d a pair, and paid for old shoes to be mended on eight occasions. There is no information about what these shoes looked like and it is probable that most were relatively sturdy country shoes. Their cost was modest and in fact on a par with what the overseers of Rotherfield were paying for shoes for adult female paupers in the 1660s and 1670s (as discussed in Chapter Seven).[119] Some may have been more fashionable however: as we saw, Moore bought her a pair of red silk shoe strings in 1667 and in April 1670 Elizabeth Challoner bought Martha a pair of white shoes.[120]

The evidence from Moore's household account book suggests that Martha led a relatively circumscribed life, living with her aunt and uncle in rural Horsted Keynes or with her school teacher, Elizabeth Challoner, in nearby Cuckfield. Martha's clothes were made by the same tailors as Moore's; however, her ability to choose cloth and trimmings was more limited than his. Whereas Moore shopped for much of his cloth and haberdashery in person, either in Lewes or London, most of Martha's was supplied direct to the household by various tailors who then made up her clothes. The choice of what that garment would look like – at least when Martha was younger – was probably Susan's or, indeed, Giles's since he evidently took a close interest in quality and value for money. Much of her clothing was robust and practical, suitable for her country lifestyle. However, we can see an evolution in the style and quality of her clothes as she entered her teens: waistcoat sleeves 'faced' with tabby, a striped silk petticoat with a silver-laced trimmed waistcoat, possibly worn with her white shoes when she went to 'dancings'. As we have seen, the author of *The Ladies Calling* allowed for some vanity in dress at a point in a young woman's life when she was likely to be looking for a husband. Martha's marriage to John Citizen, arranged by her uncle, was hardly the stuff of 'romances'; she was in her late teens, he is likely to have been in his mid-thirties.[121] Her clothing was packed into a newly bought trunk and she left Horsted Keynes to begin her life as a clergyman's wife.[122]

Elizabeth Jeake

Elizabeth Jeake's social boundaries were largely determined by her residence in a small provincial town some seventy-five miles from London; her female friends and neighbours would for the most part have been the wives of merchants, mariners, tradesmen and artisans. Even so, she still sought to participate in London's vibrant consumer market and took a keen interest in London's fashions. We have already encountered her in Chapter Four shopping in London by proxy or in person and, like her husband, concerned to put in a fashionable appearance in late seventeenth-century Rye.

To a modern observer her marriage to Jeake in 1681 when she was just thirteen did not have the most promising start. She gave birth to her first child, a daughter, in December 1682 but 'being hurt in the birth in the right temple' the baby died eight days later.[123] Nevertheless, their letters to each other show that they had a happy, loving and cooperative marriage. Elizabeth went on to have five more children, four of whom survived to adulthood.[124] She was an affectionate and attentive parent, describing her children in her letters to her mother as 'my dear creatures', 'my little tribe' and 'the little cubs'.[125] For a provincial merchant's wife she was also well educated, with a high level of English literacy and some competence in Latin.[126]

As in Jeake's case the evidence for what Elizabeth was wearing is relatively limited.[127] There are odd references to clothing purchases that Jeake made for her whilst in London and a few references in her own letters to him or to her mother, Barbara Hartshorne. The most coherent account of what she was wearing is in letters written to her in late April and early May 1699 by her husband, Samuel, and her friend, Elizabeth Miller, the wife of Samuel's former business partner, Thomas Miller. At this date a fashionable woman would have been wearing a gown or mantua made up of a close-fitting bodice joined to a full pleated and trained upper petticoat, open to the front to reveal the under petticoat. Very long trains were fashionable for upper petticoats, which were often worn hitched up at the sides to create a bustle effect. Under petticoats were slightly shorter than the skirt of the gown and were trimmed with three or four tiers of horizontal lace or fringe, or with a single deep flounce at the hem. Sleeves were short, straight and ended just above the elbow, with 'ruffles' or lace or muslin frills forming cuffs. The bodice might be covered by a stomacher decorated with horizontal rows of ribbon loops and bows known as 'echelles'.[128] 'Steinkerks' with the ends twisted together and pinned to one side of the bodice had replaced tippets as fashionable neck-wear. Top knots were worn with the front hair arranged in curls and sometimes elevated by the use of a 'palisade' or wire support.[129]

We can see in Jeake's letters that he was dependent on Elizabeth Miller, with whom he was staying, for advice on women's fashions. In a letter to his wife

Figure 6.8 Nicolas Arnoult, 'The Iron Age' from his series 'The Four Ages of Man' (c. 1690), The Metropolitan Museum of Art, 54.510.9. Each woman wears a 'top knot' or 'tower' (here described as a 'fontange') and their mantuas are pinned back creating a bustle effect. The text at the bottom of the print translates as: 'This is an age woven through with the saddest of days/ which will overwhelm mortals with a thousand strange evils/ It can never finish its sad course/ until we see the end of the fashion for fontanges'.

dated 25 April 1699 Jeake told her, 'Madam Miller says that trains are worn still with women's upper petticoats but not so long as formerly. As for fringe [on the under petticoat] she says they wear them straight but she would not advise you to alter any for they are worn both ways'. Elizabeth had evidently also asked her husband to commission some painted silk for her because in the same letter he wrote:

> Madam Miller desires to know whether the silk you would have drawn with Indian sprigs be for a mantua or for a lining, for she says if it be for a mantua it will be so very tedious for you to work it that she would rather advise you to have it painted with lively flowers which shows exceeding well and may be done for about 15s and will wear very well provided it don't come too wet, which you will have no occasion to use it in.[130]

Jeake received Elizabeth's reply dated 27 April (which does not survive), which presumably confirmed that the painted silk was for a mantua.[131] In his next letter to her of 2 May he said 'your silk is put out to paint and will be done next week and with your mantua I intend to send your best petticoat being of most value'.[132] Other items that he had purchased for the Rye household – including new shoes, an oven door, hair powder, six wash balls, a pair of stockings, four pillow cases, one flannel petticoat, a pair of clogs, a cut-out frock or gown for Bab (Jeake's eleven-year-old niece, Barbara Hartshorne), a green girdle and 'other green ribbon' and three quarters of a yard of anterine – were put aboard a ship to be carried round the coast to Rye.[133] In a postscript to this letter Jeake advised: 'they begin to leave off trains from all their petticoats'.[134]

In an undated letter to Elizabeth, probably written in April 1699, Elizabeth Miller wrote:

> ...I hope your undercoat will please. It is very modish for this fashion has not been seen before this winter. It is the size they are all of; if too short the lining must eke it out at top. Those that would have them warm line [them] with flannel or serge, others with calico. Mr Jeake thought [you] might have something at home, old flannel or anything that will layer it out will do well; they are now of this fashion on purpose to be more without trimming. Pleat it backwards or gather it at top leaving a broad plain band on the belly... We see a variety of undercoats since the fashion is to pin up the uppermost like a pedlar which all do that walk the streets.

She also advised Elizabeth on the latest fashions in head and neckwear, commenting:

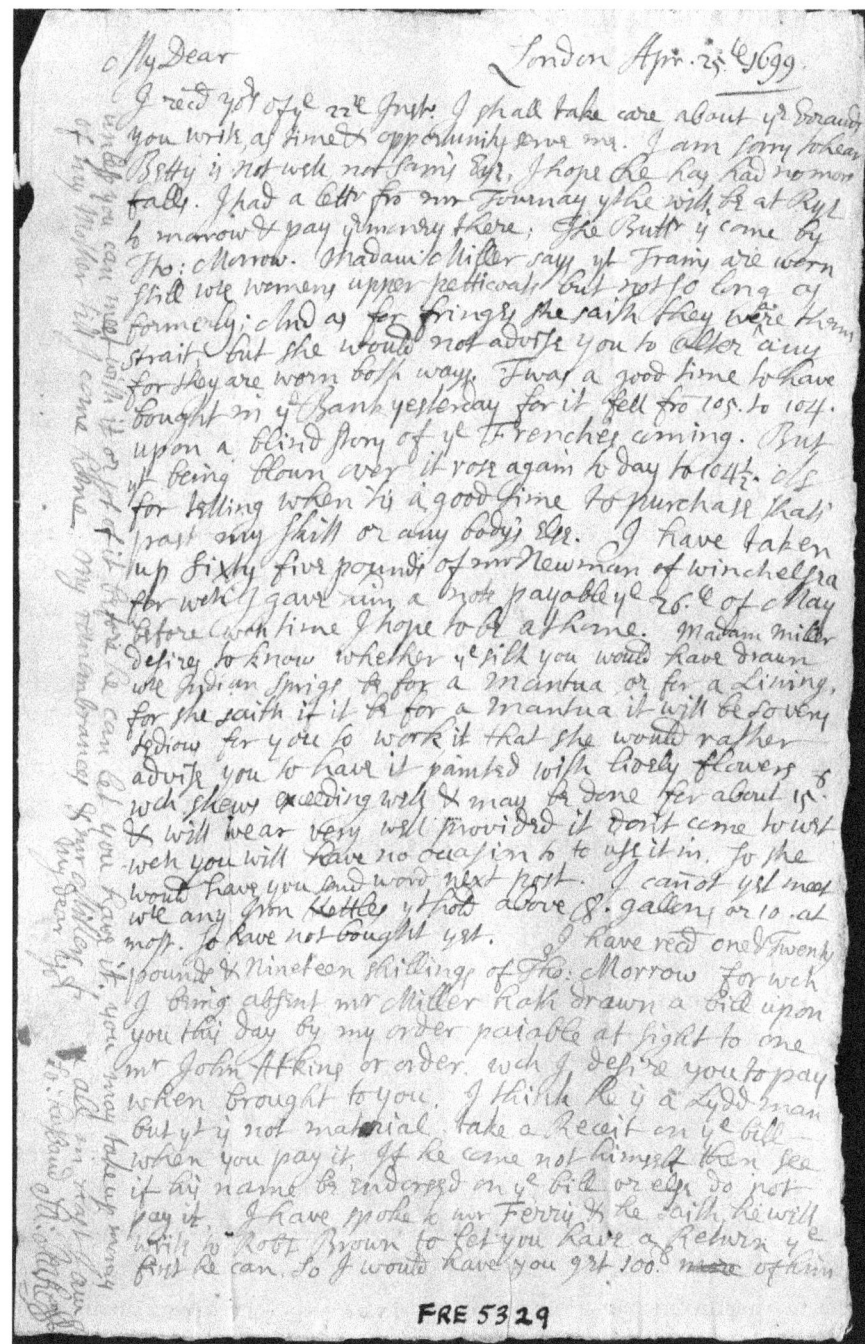

Figure 6.9 Letter from Samuel Jeake to Elizabeth Jeake (1699), East Sussex Record Office, Frewen 5329. Reproduced with the permission of East Sussex Record Office, copyright reserved.

... the pinner's headdresses remain still in the same fashion; there is a discourse of dressing them high and narrow as it was formerly but I have not seen it yet. Long muslin neck cloths like to men's to tie once about women's necks with a long scarf or without is now more fashionable than sable tippets ... .[135]

In the summer of 1699 Elizabeth would have been able to receive guests and make social visits in and around Rye confidant that she was wearing the latest London fashions. Assuming she had taken Elizabeth Miller's advice, her upper petticoat would have been pinned up 'like a pedlar' to show off her fringe-trimmed under petticoat and she would have worn it without a train. Perhaps she only wore her silk mantua indoors to avoid the risk of the hand-painted 'lively' flowers being ruined by the rain. Around her neck she wore a long muslin neck-cloth, maybe a fashionable steinkirk pinned to one side of her bodice. Her top knot may have remained relatively low, rather than 'high and narrow' since Elizabeth Miller had only been able to tell her that she had heard 'talk' of this fashion returning, rather than seeing it with her own eyes. We know that Elizabeth wore her front hair curled or 'frizzed' since she refers to it in a later letter (discussed below).[136] At her ears may have been a pair of diamond earrings, on her finger a diamond ring 'with the three stones and four sparks' and around her neck her pearl necklace, all items mentioned in her will of 1736.[137]

Whilst there is little other coherent information in the Jeake correspondence about Elizabeth's clothes we can see her dispensing London fashion advice to her seventeen-year-old daughter, Betty, during her two-month stay in London in 1701 via letters sent to her seventy-one-year-old mother, Barbara Hartshorne.[138] Betty's interest in her appearance had no doubt been heightened by the fact that she had an admirer, the thought of whom, as Elizabeth wrote to her mother, 'jostles other things quite out' of her head.[139] A propensity to gad about and spend money on fripperies (which the author of *The Ladies Calling* would no doubt have disapproved of) is reflected in Elizabeth's request that her mother tell Betty not to go out too much 'and especially on the Sabbath Day no more than to church and home again' and, 'above all', not to visit Mrs Shephard's shop.[140] At the age of seventeen Betty would have adopted a clothing style very similar to her mother's and in fact Elizabeth told her mother to pass on her own silk dust gown to Betty, because she could not find one 'so good' in London.[141] Her hair too was styled like her mother's: in a letter dated 24 May 1701 Elizabeth asked her mother to 'tell Betty her hair frizzed as mine used to be is the way'.[142] As a fashionable young woman Betty would have worn this style with a 'tower' or 'commode'. Elizabeth continued to take fashion advice from her friend, Elizabeth Miller, with whom she was staying, telling her mother, 'Madam Miller advises Betty to weave bone lace rather than point which is quite out of vogue'.[143] Giving fashion advice to a woman in her seventies was perhaps more difficult. In her letter of 24 May Elizabeth told her mother that she had bought her petticoats, 'but for head linen am at a loss, knowing you will not conform to high heads which young and old wear here'.[144]

The three generations of women – Barbara, Elizabeth and Betty – would all have been able to search out beauty treatments in Hugh Plat's *Delights for Ladies*, which formed part of Samuel Jeake senior's extensive library, perhaps making his 'excellent pomatum to clear the skin' or one of his 'sweet water' perfumes.[145] His recipe for removing chilblains from hands and feet may also have been useful for frozen fingers and toes: in a letter to her husband written in January 1686 Elizabeth apologised for her poor handwriting telling him that her fingers were very cold.[146] As we have seen, Jeake senior also owned Hall's *Loathsomeness of Long Hair* (1654) with its appendix, *Against Painting, Spots, Naked Breasts Etc.* They might have taken note of Hall's warning that 'painting' caused wrinkles, poisoned the skin and damaged the eyesight but by the late seventeenth century his vitriolic denunciation of cosmetics may have seemed curiously old fashioned, at least to the two younger women.[147]

Conclusion

It was suggested in the introduction that of the three women who feature most fully in this chapter – Judith Morley, Martha Mayhew and Elizabeth Jeake – it was the last who may have had the most sartorial independence. She appears to have had an equitable and companionable marriage and both husband and wife enjoyed fashionable and conspicuous consumption. When Samuel died in 1699 Elizabeth was still a relatively young woman of thirty two. Her letters to her mother from London in the summer of 1701 suggest that she adjusted to her new status as a widow with relative ease. It was the first time in her life that she had had any real autonomy. She continued to engage in fashionable consumption and shared her fashion knowledge, as well as some of her clothing, with her teenage daughter, Betty.

Despite her relative independence as a widow and her middle gentry status Judith Morley's consumer choices were restricted by her reliance on her son as her proxy shopper, by a constant shortage of money and by the social conventions of mourning. As an older woman, she was perhaps also conscious of the need to dress in an age-appropriate way. Nevertheless, we see that she still aspired to a fashionable appearance, taking advice from her son on the latest London trends and making use of a hair piece (or pieces) to bulk out or to allow her to restyle her natural hair.

Martha's own views about her clothing are impossible to discern. There is limited evidence in her uncle's account book that she was making small purchases for herself, for example the bodice, laces, whisk and whisk box she bought for herself whilst in London with her uncle in 1672 but final decisions on more substantial clothing purchases are more likely to have been made by her aunt and uncle. Like many young women of the middle or better sort, Martha married whilst still in her teens. In the years immediately preceding her marriage her clothing became more decorative and fashionable, reflecting her growing maturity and her availability for marriage.

7

The Clothing of the Poor

The previous two chapters have explored the clothing of men and women belonging to the 'middle' and 'better' sort. In contrast, this chapter focuses on the clothing of the Sussex poor. The use of the word 'poor' is intended to cover that large, shifting and seemingly amorphous group that contemporary commentators labelled the 'poorer' or 'meaner' sort (to distinguish them from the 'better' or 'best' sort and the 'middle' sort). This group was expanding in the early seventeenth century as a growing population began to outstrip the demand for labour and the economy entered a period of long-term inflation that saw the cost of rents and consumables rising rapidly whilst wages remained low. It has been estimated that whilst those on relief constituted perhaps five per cent of a parish population, a further twenty per cent or more may have been 'in need': in other words, they were living at or below subsistence some or all of the time.[1] Using contemporary socio-economic descriptors, those belonging to this group included poorer husbandmen, tradesmen and craftsmen, labourers, the parish poor (those in receipt of parish relief) and vagrants.[2] In Sussex, the words 'husbandman' and 'labourer' were frequently interchangeable, reflecting the reality that many of those described as 'husbandmen' had little or no land and were at least partly wage-dependent; they might also be involved in some trade or craft activity.[3] Both 'husbandmen' and 'labourers' might find themselves in need of parish support at some point in their lives or, indeed, might be forced out onto the road through economic necessity.[4]

The apparent instability and fluidity of the lives of many of the men and women who appear in contemporary records should not obscure the fact that there were marked social, economic and material gradations between them, which would have been immediately obvious to the poor, even if they are only partially visible to the historian.[5] Such gradations were frequently made visible through dress, with those able to clothe themselves adequately differentiating themselves socially and morally from those who could not. In the 'rural life' ballads discussed in Chapter Two the clothing of the rural poor was a material sign of social stability and contented and deferential poverty.[6] However, in reality clothing could be indicative of social flux and grinding and humiliating poverty.[7]

Clothing and 'counterfeit' vagrants

For the middling and better sort, the poor were profoundly problematic. There was widespread acceptance that the most vulnerable members of society, typically the elderly, the infirm and the very young, could not be held responsible for their own penury and must therefore be supported. There was less consensus about, and more hostility towards, the able-bodied poor; their apparent inability to find, or continue in, work, or otherwise to 'make shift' for themselves, was viewed with suspicion and linked to a range of behavioural and moral failings.[8] The greatest opprobrium, however, was reserved for vagrants whose itinerant and mendicant lifestyles threatened the nation's economic and social fabric.[9] The 1598 Act for the Punishment of Rogues, Vagabonds and Sturdy Beggars required that vagabonds be whipped by order of a JP or parish officers and sent with a passport to their place of birth or last dwelling for a year. Those encompassed by the Act included 'all idle persons going about any county either begging or using a subtle craft or unlawful games and plays or saying themselves to have knowledge in physiognomy, palmistry or other like crafty science' or pretending to be fortune tellers, common players and minstrels, jugglers, tinkers, pedlars and petty chapmen, 'all wandering persons and common labourers being persons able in body' who refused to work for 'reasonable wages' and those 'pretending themselves to be Egyptians or wandering in the habit, form or attire of counterfeit Egyptians'.[10] The use of the word 'counterfeit' here reflects a widespread suspicion

Figure 7.1 Jacques Callot, Beggars (1630), The Metropolitan Museum of Art, 17.50.15-341.

that vagrants were not what they seemed; they were shams who transformed their appearance in order to trick and deceive.[11]

Contemporary estimates of the numbers of vagrants in England varied widely and none can be relied on. In 1678 Richard Haines confidently asserted that there were 'above 100,000 beggars or others that want a lawful employment in this kingdom'; Gregory King's estimate in 1688 was a considerably more modest 30,000.[12] Whilst vagrants presented a threat to ordered society throughout the seventeenth century, periods of severe economic and social distress exacerbated their numbers and made the need to find a way of dealing with them more acute.[13] However, vagrancy was not necessarily a permanent condition: for many of those wandering the Sussex countryside sleeping under hedges, in barns or in furnace houses it was likely to be a temporary phase brought on by a significant life event such as loss of employment or spousal abandonment.[14] Young servants and apprentices were especially likely to find themselves temporarily homeless. Many servants moved on to a different employer at the end of their year's term but others left mid-term either of their own volition or because they were forced out by their master or mistress.[15] In 1698 Cuckfield lawyer, Timothy Burrell, fired his footman, Thomas Goldsmith, for theft; he subsequently took him back into his service after he returned from 'a ramble to London, being almost starved'.[16] Apprenticeship in theory provided a more secure form of employment but relationships between masters and apprentices frequently broke down or the circumstances of one of the parties changed making it impossible for the apprenticeship to continue. Nine-year-old Henry Barker was found filthy and begging in Slindon in 1608 after he ran away from his master, John Mancell, a glover in Havant, some twenty miles away.[17] In 1650 apprentice, Francis Button, ended up begging after his master, Drew Miles, became unable to support him.[18]

In the rogue literature of the late sixteenth and early seventeenth century such as Thomas Dekker's *The Bellman of London* (1608) there was a clearly defined hierarchy of rogues with each category having its own behavioural, physical and sartorial characteristics.[19] In this literature, begging and thieving were inextricably linked, with the former merely operating as a pretext to achieve the latter. Whilst these literary rogues typically worked on their own or in pairs on a day-to-day basis, they nevertheless formed part of a fraternity, or company, with its own behavioural rules and a unique language of 'cant' or 'pedlar's French'. 'Anglers', for example, dressed in 'frieze, jerkins and gallyslops', begged from house to house during the day 'not so much for relief as to spy what lies fit for their nets'.[20] They then returned at night, using a pole with a hook on its end to steal clothing and bed linen from open windows. The 'rogue' pretended to be crippled, dragging himself along the street with a staff. His head was bound with foul linen 'as filthy in colour as the complexion of his face'; he was shirtless and what clothing he did wear was ragged. His lack of clothing, however, was mere pretence intended to provoke pity and when he was given better clothes he sold them on to other members of his fraternity. The 'palliard'[21] travelled with a 'mort'[22] at his side begging alms door to door or in the street. He wore an old cloak 'made of as many pieces patched together as there be villainies in him'.[23] In each of these cases the rogue's clothing was part of a disguise or 'counterfeit', an 'attire fitting to their trade of living'; according to Dekker, when they gathered together for their quarterly fraternity feasts each rogue wore 'handsome clean linen'.[24] None of these literary rogues was actually in need; instead their vagrancy was presented as a lifestyle choice from which they accrued considerable material benefits.

Gypsies or 'Egyptians' were different to other types of rogue since they were rarely associated with begging, earning their living through fortune telling and sleight-of-hand tricks, and as horse dealers, blacksmiths, tinkers and scrap dealers. Nevertheless, like other fictive rogues they were described as having a distinctive style of dress. In *Lantern and Candlelight* (1608) Thomas Dekker described their clothing as

> odd and fantastic, though it be never so full of rents: the men wear scarves of calico, or any other base stuff having their bodies like morris dancers with bells and other toys to entice the country people to flock about them and to wonder at their fooleries or rather rank knaveries. The women as ridiculously attire themselves and (like one that plays the rogue on a stage) wear rags and patched filthy mantles uppermost, when the undergarments are handsome and in fashion.[25]

Moreover, according to Dekker, they applied paint to their faces giving their skin a tawny or yellowish-brown appearance as if 'they had all the yellow jaundice'.[26]

Despite Dekker's claims to authenticity, his were works of fiction that played on popular fears and prejudices about vagrants and their association with criminal behaviour. This is not to say that they had no basis in reality: as we saw in Chapter Three, in Sussex vagrants tended to congregate in the furnace houses attached to iron works because they were warm. It appears to have been common knowledge, both amongst vagrants and the local population, that these were places where stolen goods could be taken for sale or barter.[27] However, whilst some of these vagrants clearly knew each other, many were strangers.[28] Moreover, as Beier has observed, the majority of vagrant crime was 'protean' rather than

Figure 7.2 Jacques Callot, Marching gypsies (1621–31), The Metropolitan Museum of Art, 2012.136.260.

specialised and lacked any coherent organisation.[29] Nor is there much evidence of 'professional' vagrants adopting particular clothing disguises. In 1615 and 1616 the magistrates in Hampshire rounded up a motley group of vagrant men and women accused of being fraudsters and petty criminals and imprisoned them in Winchester gaol. Giving evidence against some of his fellow prisoners Thomas Hall, 'otherwise called Horsefaced Hall', 'a notable rogue ... of an ancient standing' described their appearance. John Clapham, for example, was a 'tall man with a yellow beard'; Thomas Floyd was 'of a small stature and black complexion [with] a pearl in his right eye'. Only one of the men he described, Ned Beadle, 'a little fellow of black complexion' with a turned up 'beard' or moustache, wore clothing that was distinctive enough to be mentioned; according to Hall he dressed 'in the habit of a Jew'. Walter Hindes, who had been arrested in the company of 'counterfeit Egyptians', provided no information at all about their physical appearance and dress. If they were dressed in 'odd and fantastic' clothes as Dekker suggests he clearly did not think it worth mentioning to the court.[30]

The amount and variety of clothing owned by the poor

The majority of poor men and women of course led more settled lives in the sense that they had a roof over their head. This section assembles evidence from a variety of different sources – wills, inventories, coroners' inquests and depositions surviving amongst quarter session records – to assess the range of clothing that was worn by the poor, or 'poorer sort'. The assumption here is that for the most part this was clothing that the poor had provided for themselves. The clothing provided to the parish poor is considered separately later in the chapter.

Trying to provide any kind of 'average' for the number of garments owned by the poor is impossible. There is, for example, no way of telling what proportion of testators' clothes is recorded in their wills and in any case the men and women who made wills represented the wealthier among the poorer sort. However, to get an idea of the amount and variety of clothing that might be owned by poor men and women we can look at a few examples from different sources where the total clothing stock of an individual appears to be listed. A coroner's inquest into the suicide of William Duke of Mayfield (who was servant to a wealthy widow, Katherine Aynscombe, and therefore probably a young man) in 1629 recorded that at the time of his death he had 7s 6d in his purse, a bible (worth 4s), two pairs of breeches, one doublet, one jerkin, one cloth coat, one hat (20s), a box, three handkerchiefs, one pair of gloves and one dozen points (worth 2s 6d). In addition, Aynscombe owed him 40s for half a year's wages.[31] In a case heard in quarter sessions in 1658 witnesses were examined about the disappearance of a young male servant or labourer called James Farnden from Lodsworth some ten years previously. According to witnesses, at the time of his disappearance, Farnden only had 'one suit of apparel', consisting of a pair of canvas breeches, a ragged stuff doublet, a 'canvas coat called a frock' and a little black cap. The discovery of these clothes hidden in a hop garden ('amongst the hop hills') had led to suspicions that Farnden had been murdered.[32] The 1619 probate inventory of Jane Smith, a spinster living in Chidham, recorded that at the time of her death her 'apparel' was made up of four old petticoats and two old waistcoats valued at 14s 6d, 'green say aprons with all her wearing linen' valued at 5s and a felt hat with a 'ciperis' (i.e. 'cypress') band valued at 2s. The rest of her possessions were meagre: a new tick bolster, a small old kettle, one small skillet, a small old coffer and two old blankets. Her total estate was valued at £11 11s 4d but £10 of this was a debt owing to her.[33] Duke, Farnden and Smith are all likely to have been young adults living dependent or semi-dependent lives. Clothing no doubt made up most if not all of a young person's personal possessions until such time as she or he set up an independent household. When servants appearing as witnesses in cases heard in the archdeaconry court of Chichester were asked by the court to state their financial worth they usually replied that they were worth little or nothing besides the clothes they stood up in.[34]

As we saw in Chapter Three, parish overseers usually sold off the goods of parish paupers in order to recoup some of their expenditure. The rather sparse clothing collection of Widow Terry, sold by the parish overseers of Lindfield in 1656, has already been described.[35] Even more limited was the clothing owned by widow, Mary Jones, sold off by the overseers of the parish of St Nicholas in Arundel in May 1681, which included 'changes and small linen', her 'manto' (or mantua) and 'coats' (probably petticoats).[36] It is possible that these women had been forced to sell items of clothing before their deaths in order to survive; alternatively some of their remaining clothing may have been too threadbare to sell.[37] Perhaps more typical was the range of clothing owned by widow, Joan Hawkins of Hamsey, who committed suicide in 1606. The coroner's inquest recorded that at the time of her death she had goods and chattels worth 30s, which comprised a petticoat (valued at 10s), a gown (2s), a russet petticoat (12d), a hat (2s), a safeguard (6d), two neck cloths (18d), two cross cloths (12d), one blue apron (8d), another apron (4d), one pair of shoes (no value), one pair of stockings (6d) and 10s 6d in money.[38] Joan had no other personal possessions and appears to have been living at or near destitution; nevertheless she owned a range of garments of variable quality. These examples show that there was considerable variation in the amount of clothing owned by those who can collectively be categorised as 'poor'.

The clothing of poorer men and women was usually made out of relatively coarse, locally produced, woollen cloth.[39] The type of cloth that appears most frequently in testamentary clothing bequests is russet, which, as we saw in Chapter Three, could be used for almost any outerwear as well as for blankets.[40] Other types of cloth recorded in wills, probate inventories and quarter session records are 'homemade', blanket, thickset, kersey, frieze, serge and cotton.[41] Linsey-woolsey and fustian were also used for a variety of outerwear.[42] Coarse linen cloth like canvas, linsey and lockram was used for head and neckwear, smocks, shirts and aprons, and sometimes for outerwear. Finer linen, like holland and lawn, where it is recorded, was used for women's head and neckwear and occasionally their aprons. Men's working clothes (their doublets and breeches) were often made of canvas or leather or cloth breeches had detachable leather linings, reflecting the more arduous nature of their work.[43]

Despite the coarseness of many of these fabrics, women endeavoured to present as colourful an appearance as possible: the most popular colour for petticoats was red although some were green or blue; stockings are described as 'grass green', blue or yellow; aprons could be coloured or striped.[44] Poorer women could also achieve an element of social display by wearing fine linen head and neckwear trimmed with bone lace (which Margaret Spufford described as 'the most straightforward index of cheap luxury').[45] Coloured ribbon, which, like

Figure 7.3 Charles Beale, Portrait of an elderly woman, possibly a household servant (1680), British Museum, Gg,5.12. © The Trustees of the British Museum. All rights reserved.

bone lace, was widely sold by mercers and itinerant traders, was used for a variety of decorative purposes such as apron and shoe strings, hat bands and fastenings for neckwear. In 1658, fourteen-year-old Margaret Godden was accused of stealing a 'pretty broad green ribbon about the quantity of ten yards' from the shop of William Hale of Westbourne. In her examination she said that she cut off enough of the ribbon to make a pair of apron strings which she gave to Mary Bickley and gave the rest to Elizabeth Tomes.[46] Better-off women might own a gold wedding ring or a silver pin, the latter probably used as a front-fastening for neck cloths.[47] Men's working clothes were often drab – where colours are recorded they were typically 'buff', 'grey' or 'ash-coloured'. But men also wore bright colours when they were able to and, like women, could enhance their appearance with fine linen neckwear, decorative hatbands and coloured handkerchiefs. Even children's clothing could be personalised by the addition of decorative trim. In 1614 Katherine Furlonger was accused of stealing a dozen yards of bone lace from a chapman at Green fair. According to Elizabeth

Michelborne, Furlonger, who claimed to have bought the lace at the fair from a woman selling small wares, gave her three yards of lace to edge 'a band, a coif, a cap and other small wearing linen for her child' and kept the rest for herself.[48]

As we saw in Chapter Three, testators sometimes described clothes as 'work days' or 'holidays', indicating that they made a distinction between working clothes and 'best'.[49] For example, in her will of 1606 widow Agnes Slater of Sompting bequeathed (amongst other things) her 'best gown', her 'second gown with a red petticoat', her husband's 'best cloak', her 'holy days neckerchief' and 'one other for the working days'.[50] The distinction that men and women made between 'work days' and 'holidays' clothing is a subtle one and on the whole seems to have come down to how old and worn a garment was. There are some obvious exceptions to this: it is hardly likely that a woman would wear a lace-edged lawn coif or a holland apron to milk a cow but she probably would wear them to go to church. But in terms of colour, bright, as well as drab clothing was worn for work as can be seen in some of the clothing descriptions in cases from quarter sessions. A female testator describing a red petticoat as 'my best' is making a clear statement that it was not for daily wear; but a red petticoat described as 'my old' had obviously seen better days and been reassigned from 'holidays' to 'work days' wear.[51]

The endless repetition of petticoats, waistcoats, gowns and aprons in women's wills and breeches, doublets, waistcoats and coats in men's wills made of a limited variety of fabrics and dyed in plain colours suggests a uniformity in clothing – and therefore appearance – which belies the reality. For a start, the range of colours produced by natural dyes varied considerably. The red petticoats favoured by women would have been dyed using the roots of the madder plant, producing shades of 'red' ranging from a dark, russet brown, through true red, to soft apricot. Weld produced a range of yellows from dark gold, through true yellow, to lemon yellow, and woad could produce blues ranging from sky blue through to dark navy.[52] Moreover, frequent wear and the effects of sun and rain would have faded these colours over time, so a bright blue might end up looking grey and a bright yellow might fade to beige. Some of the ways in which women were able to customise their clothing have already been suggested – the quality of the linen used for neck and headwear, lace and ribbon trimmings. The ability to identify a piece of stolen clothing could be crucial in securing a conviction. In 1671 Mary West told the court of quarter sessions that she could identify the linsey-woolsey petticoat allegedly stolen from her by Dorothy Burgess 'by the strings and the gathering of it' and that 'there was a red bordering to the petticoat which is pulled off since she lost it'. She claimed that the reason it was a different colour from the one she had lost was because Burgess had 'new dyed it'.[53]

Figure 7.4 Randle Holme's original drawings of working men for his *Academy of Armory* (Chester, 1688), British Library, Harley 2027, f.244ᵛ. © British Library Board.

The distinctiveness of clothing is suggested by the fact that deponents at quarter sessions described alleged wrongdoers by what they were wearing rather than what they looked like. Implicit in these descriptions was the expectation that the perpetrator would be wearing the same or similar clothing when he or she was brought before the court, thus ensuring successful identification and adding authenticity to the witnesses' accounts. Whilst Joanne Steele's description of the man who allegedly robbed her in December 1637 as 'a tall lusty fellow in grey clothes with a black hat' who she thought was 'one Roger who dwelt sometime with William Coot of Binsted' might seem rather vague to us, it led to the indictment of a labourer called Roger Cotman.[54] More plausibly, perpetrators could be identified through the pattern of wear and repair of their clothes. In 1626 Francis Terry was identified as the thief who had stolen wheat out of a barn because the sole of his right shoe had 'three nails towards the middle' which matched the footprint discovered at the scene of the crime.[55] In 1638 Joanne Lewes could identify an old hat 'with a little hole in the crown and cut in the brim' found at the scene of a crime as belonging to Edward Lee because whilst he had been working at her house some two weeks previously her child had played with the hat 'putting a stick through the said hole'.[56] The type of clothing that was worn and its arrangement on the body could also be indicative of criminal activity. In 1605 Elizabeth Homeley gave evidence in an alleged sexual assault case. She said that when she saw Alice Vaughan, the victim of the alleged attack, her hair had been 'somewhat tousled' and her kerchief was set 'more backward than women usually wear them'.[57] At the time of his alleged theft of a pig and some gold coins in 1627 John Burt was described as 'very meanly apparelled and had only a blue jerkin and a pair of canvas breeches' whereas since the theft he wore a 'suit of red cloth' and had bought himself a 'horseman's coat' for £3.[58] As we saw in the Chapter One, Mary Watts's guilt was supposedly proven by the fact that she had exchanged her 'very mean clothes' for those that were 'not fit for a woman of her quality to wear'.[59]

Clothing the parish poor

The implementation of the poor laws in early seventeenth-century Sussex was slow and piecemeal. However, by the 1630s it is likely that most parishes were setting annual rates of taxation and had established policies for allocating relief to their poorest residents.[60] Parishes had considerable discretion within the framework of the poor law legislation to decide who to relieve and what form that relief should take. Typically parishes paid weekly cash pensions to a small number of resident paupers, some of whom also received ad hoc help with house rent and medical expenses, as well as occasional in-kind payments of fuel, working tools and clothing. Other resident paupers who were not in receipt of a pension might also receive ad hoc help with living expenses, either as cash or in-kind payments. As we have seen, it has been estimated that those on relief constituted approximately five per cent of a parish population.[61]

Analysis of overseers' accounts shows that parishes adopted different policies when it came to clothing their parish poor. We can take the parish of St Nicholas's in Arundel as an example. In 1676 its population was about 550.[62] The overseers' account book covering the period 1678 to 1704 records that the parish was paying regular weekly pensions to between ten and twelve paupers (about two per cent of its population), including orphan children.[63] A small and varying number of other paupers received occasional relief, perhaps a bundle of faggots or help with their house rent. Bearing in mind that at least twenty per cent of the town's population are likely to have been living in poverty some or all of the time, the parish's welfare policy was clearly highly restrictive. Some of Arundel's neediest residents are likely to have benefited from intermittent charitable relief distributed by the parish either in money or in kind but the majority of the town's poor must have had to make shift for themselves.[64]

When it came to the provision of clothing, further restrictions applied. Typically, the parish only supplied clothing to pauper children, usually orphans; very occasionally they supplied some clothing to elderly and infirm paupers. Where children were being clothed they appear to have had complete sets of clothing bought for them with items replaced or renewed as need arose. For example, in 1679 the parish began providing clothing for nine-year-old Luke Wareham after the death of his mother.[65] Together with another boy, Luke was supplied with a new 'cloth' suit, 'changes' (or shirts), coarse linen neck cloths and a pair of stockings.[66] At the same time the parish paid for his shoes to be mended. The cost of outfitting the two boys was just under £2 15s. One or both boys was evidently at school because the overseers also spent 4d on a horn book and a primer.[67] In the same year the overseers paid for Luke's shoes to be repaired again and spent 4d on hobnails for them, they bought him two new pairs of stockings and had a pair of kersey breeches with knee buckles and three new shirts made for him.[68] In 1680 he received three shirts, two pairs of stockings, a pair of drawers and two pairs of shoes. In 1681 his shoes were re-soled and repaired twice, he was provided with two new pairs of stockings, a hat and a pair of 'linings' (probably leather linings for his breeches). In 1682 he was provided with two new pairs of shoes, a pair of drawers, a hat and two pairs of stockings. He also had a new coat, waistcoat and breeches and two shirts made for him. His new suit was probably made in anticipation of his being put out as an apprentice: in the same year the overseers paid 2s for 'his indentures and signing them' and £3 10s to Thomas Burgess for taking him as an apprentice.[69]

Where adults were provided with clothing it was on an ad hoc and highly restricted basis. 'Old' John Barber was one of the only adult paupers the overseers deemed sufficiently destitute to be clothed at their expense. Barber did not receive a parish pension himself; instead a weekly sum of 3s to 4s was paid to Nathaniel Holcomb for his board. In addition to being elderly, he was also infirm: the accounts record regular payments of 1s 6d to Goody Michener for looking after him and tending his leg, in 1679 they paid 'Old Barber's surgeon' 4s and in 1680 Mrs Whittington was paid 6s for 'looking to Old Barber's leg six weeks'. In 1678 the parish spent 18s 10½d on a new set of clothes for 'Old Barber' and for mending his old clothes. In 1679 they bought him a bolster and a pair of drawers, an ounce of thread and a pair of shoes. Barber died in late May or early June 1680 and was buried at the parish's expense.[70]

Clothing provision to pauper families was also very restricted, as can be seen in the case of the Selden family. John and Joan Selden and their two children, Thomas and Joan, were clearly troublesome for the overseers. In July 1678 they paid John Coot 10s 'for carrying Selden's wife and children to Portsmouth'. Thomas was aged six and Joan was about a month old.[71] Either Selden had absconded to Portsmouth or found work there but at some point the family all returned to Arundel. By June 1680 John Selden had become seriously unwell and was unable to work. Over the next seven months the parish lent him small sums of money of between 2s and 4s to tide him over until he recovered as well as paying Widow Michener for tending his arm.[72] By now the family must have been in dire financial straits and in December 1680 the parish spent 3s 'for making Thomas and Joan Selden's clothes'. In January 1681 the parish began to pay John a weekly pension of 3s, no doubt recognising that he was not going to get better. He died in February 1681 and the parish spent 11s 4d on laying him out, providing him with a shroud and coffin and for digging his grave and ringing his knell.[73] The parish continued to pay a weekly pension of 3s to his widow, Joan. In March 1681 the parish spent 9d making young Joan a coat and two shifts.[74] Selden's widow was now seriously ill and the parish spent 18s 8d on her care over a seven-week period. She recovered, only to have to face the death of her two-year-old daughter.[75] The parish spent 3s on her coffin and digging her grave. Later that year the parish spent 1s on a pair of shoes for Thomas Selden,

5s 6d for making his indentures and £7 for putting him out as an apprentice. At this point the boy, then aged eight or nine, disappears from the records. His mother continued to receive a small weekly pension of 1s 6d, the reduced sum reflecting the fact that she no longer had any dependents. The desperation of her poverty and the stringency of the overseers' welfare policy is suggested by the fact that in 1682 she was given 6d 'towards a pair of bodies'.[76]

The clothing policies of other parishes were more generous. In Ticehurst, for example, complete sets of clothing were provided for a number of their adult paupers. Between 1663 and 1666 John Gynt was receiving a parish pension of 4s a month.[77] The parish appears to have provided all, or at least a substantial amount, of his clothing. In 1663 they spent £2 5s 11½d on a new woollen suit for him, a change, a pair of stockings and two pairs of shoes.[78] The parish also bought him a new canvas sheet, as well as a pair of shoes for his son, John, apprenticed the same year, and a pair of 'cards' (to card wool) for his daughter, Mildred. The following year the parish spent a further £2 15s 4d on another new suit for him, two pairs of shoes, a pair of stockings and two changes, along with another new sheet, an axe and a pair of cards for 'her' (presumably his wife).[79] Gynt was provided with new suits in each of the two subsequent years, along with new shoes, stockings, changes and drawers. In contrast to the relatively generous provision of clothing to Gynt, his wife received nothing. His daughter, Mildred, who from 1664 was accounted for separately, was provided with new shoes in 1664 and 1665 but no other clothing was provided for her.[80] Whilst Ticehurst may have been more generous than Arundel in clothing its adult paupers the amount they paid in cash pensions was comparatively lower. Gynt, like John Selden, had three dependents – a wife and two young children – but he was receiving a monthly pension of 4s in comparison to the 3s a week that was being paid to John Selden and subsequently to his widow, Joan. This suggests that it was a deliberate policy in Ticehurst to keep cash pensions low and to make more payments in kind.[81]

Whilst careful reading of overseers' accounts can reveal parishes' policies for clothing their paupers, they disguise the processes of negotiation that took place between parish officials and individual paupers. For a later period paupers explained their reasons for asking their home parishes for clothing in letters written to parish overseers. In his analysis of some of the pauper letters that survive for the late eighteenth and early nineteenth centuries, Peter Jones has shown that they frequently used the motif of 'nakedness' when negotiating with parish authorities for additional clothing. This was not intended to mean that they were literally naked; instead, nakedness was used as a rhetorical device to convey their extreme material distress and their inability to preserve basic standards of sartorial decency.[82] This is perhaps the argument that Joan Selden used when negotiating with the Arundel overseers over the purchase of a new bodice in 1682. However, the 6d the overseers gave her would not have gone far since the price of even a second-hand bodice or 'pair of bodies' is likely to have been in excess of 3s.[83]

Another argument put forward by late eighteenth and early nineteenth-century pauper letter writers was that lack of suitable clothing undermined their ability to secure work either for themselves or for their children. Here, the argument was more pragmatic since regular employment would remove, or at least reduce, the pauper's need for parish relief.[84] It is possible that John Gynt was in work at least some of the time because in January 1666, 'in his sickness', he received a higher monthly pension of 6s 6d.[85] Ticehurst appears to have offered its paupers relief on condition that they work if they were able and the overseers may therefore have seen the clothing they provided him with, like the axe they bought him in 1664, as essential to ensuring that insofar as possible he made shift for himself.[86] Jones has termed this kind of parish policy 'compassionate pragmatism'.[87] In the case of someone like John Gynt this description is reasonable. But as we have seen, parish overseers were especially likely to be generous in their clothing provision to children that they were about to bind out as apprentices. Given the extreme youth of many of them it is difficult to see where compassion came in. To give another example, in December 1642 the overseers of the parish of Cowfold spent £2 8s 7d on two new suits, two hats, two pairs of shoes, a shirt and two pairs of stockings for John, or Jonathan, Mote in anticipation of his being bound out as an apprentice.[88] Jonathan was just six years old.[89] Once a pauper child had been apprenticed it is unlikely that parish officials took any further interest in his or her welfare and, as Steve Hindle has shown, these children were often placed out against their parents', and indeed their own, wishes.[90]

For the eighteenth century John Styles has tried to assess the equivalence between clothing provided to the parish poor and that worn by the working poor. His conclusion was that it is 'hard to believe that either the standard to which the adult poor were clothed by their parishes or the rate at which the parishes clothed them did more than barely match, let alone surpass, most non-pauper adults'.[91] Broadly, this may have been true for the seventeenth century too. However, as we have seen, clothing policies varied from parish to parish, which means that the sartorial experiences of the parish poor in one area may have been very different to those of the parish poor in another. It should also be

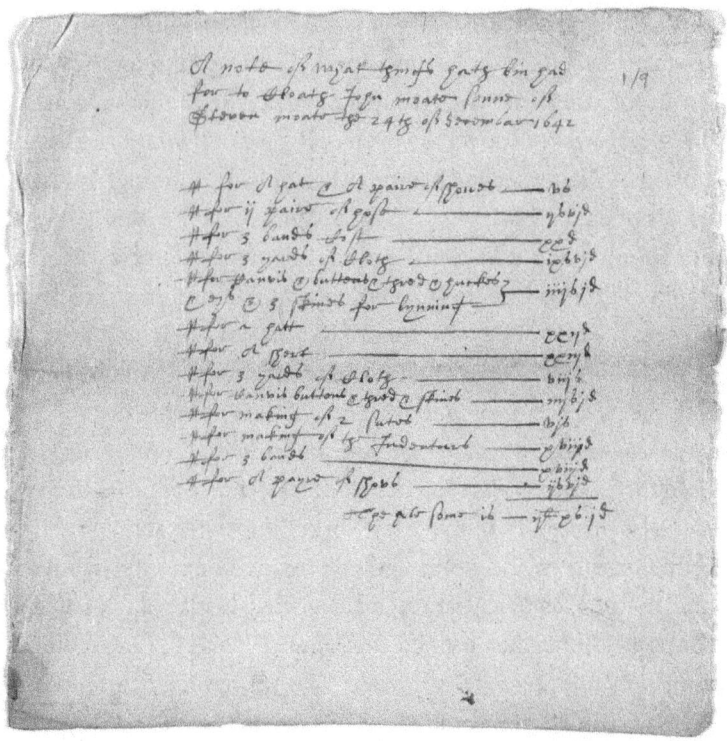

Figure 7.5 Cowfold overseers' account for the cost of clothing Jonathan Mote (1642), West Sussex Record Office, Par 59/31/1, f.1/9. Reproduced with the permission of West Sussex Record Office.

borne in mind that many of the poorest inhabitants of seventeenth-century Sussex received little or no relief from their parishes. For them, the provision of adequate clothing must have been a constant struggle; as we have seen, some poor men and women owned little more than the clothing they stood up in. Where parish clothing was provided it was robust and practical. Jonathan Mote's suits were made out of woollen cloth and his breeches were lined with leather to make them more hard wearing and weather resistant; John Gynt's coats and breeches were made of kersey, his waistcoats of cotton.[92] Paupers who were being regularly clothed by the parish might expect at least one new pair of shoes a year and over the course of the year the parish would also meet the cost of repairing and resoling them.[93] The price that overseers paid for shoes suggests that they were good quality. In the parish of Rotherfield in the 1660s and 1670s the overseers typically paid between 2s 4d and 3s 10d for a pair of shoes for an adult female pauper and about 4s a pair for an adult male pauper; those provided for

John Gynt in Ticehurst in the 1660s cost between 3s 6d and 4s a pair.[94] In comparison, the shoes Giles Moore bought for his niece, Martha, between 1667 and 1673 cost between 2s 4d and 2s 6d a pair and Giles's own shoes cost between 3s 10d and 4s 6d a pair.[95] It is also the case that parishes were providing their parish poor with new, rather than second-hand, clothing and footwear.[96] In this respect, those fortunate enough to receive a regular supply of clothing from their parish may have been considerably better clothed than many of their poor, but non-dependent, neighbours.

'Clothes to go handsome in': the clothing culture of the poor

> Yet with that and such like work I made shift to buy me some clothes, and then I went to church on Sunday, which I never could do before for want of clothes to go handsome in. My father being poor and in debt could not provide us with clothes fitting to go to church in (so we could not go to church) unless we would go in rags, which was not seemly.[97]

This passage is taken from the autobiographical writings of Edward Barlow, the son of an impoverished husbandman, born in Prestwich in Lancashire in 1642. Written retrospectively when Barlow was a thirty-one-year-old seaman (and had learned to read and write), it describes the period leading up to his first departure from home aged twelve or thirteen.[98] Since his father could not afford to indenture him as an apprentice Barlow worked for his neighbours, harvesting and haymaking and carting coal from the local coal pits, for which he received 'but small wages' of about two or three pence a day.[99] By making 'shift' he was able to buy himself some clothes to 'go handsome in' to replace the 'rags' that he had worn before. The significance of these new clothes in Barlow's account is that they allow him to attend church, something he could not do before 'unless [he] would go in rags, which was not seemly'. His description of his clothing as 'rags' may be an exaggeration but it enables Barlow to express his sense of shame at having nothing decent to wear to church. However, Barlow does not want just any clothes: he wants clothes 'to go handsome in'. In other words, he wants to look good.

The distinction between 'ordinary' and 'best' is reflected in Barlow's account of the day he left home for the second time in 1657, now aged fourteen and heading for London,

I went up into the chamber where I lay, and putting on my best clothes, which were but ordinary in the country ... So coming down the stairs, my mother and one of my sisters being in the house and not knowing my intent, marvelled to see me put on my clothes that day.[100]

For his mother and sister, his appearance in his 'best' clothes on a working day is a surprise; it signified something unusual. However, Barlow acknowledges (presumably with the benefit of hindsight) that what he and his family regarded as his 'best' clothes were really only 'ordinary'.

The ballads discussed in Chapter Two drew attention to pecuniary differences amongst the fictionalised rural poor: some were poorer than others.[101] These differences are manifest in their clothing. We can compare, for example, the husbandman of 'God Speed the Plough and Bless the Corn Mow' with his 'good strong russet coat' with the poor man in 'Ragged Torn and True' whose cloak was 'threadbare', his doublet 'rent in the sleeves' and his jerkin 'worn and bare'.[102]

Figure 7.6 Edward Barlow's drawing of himself leaving home aged fourteen (1673), National Maritime Museum, JOD/4. 'By and by when I was gotten almost out of call my mother coming out and seeing that I did intend to go she calling to me and in this manner as you see here drawn beckoning her hand to come again and willed me not to go'. © National Maritime Museum, Greenwich, London.

Despite his poverty the poor man was able to live 'wondrous well' and rather than being embarrassed by his threadbare clothing he celebrated it as a sign of his honest and virtuous life. The same pecuniary differences can be perceived in the way the actual poor articulate their own clothing needs or describe the clothing needs of others but rather than being a source of pride, inadequate clothing was a source of shame.

Moreover, an individual's lack of decent clothing could be interpreted by others as a sign of a dishonest, immoral and 'beggarly' life. As Alexandra Shepard has shown, it was not unusual for deponents to be asked if they were appearing in court in their own clothes and litigants sometimes drew attention to the shabbiness of a witness's clothes in order to discredit their testimony.[103] Frequently, those making this assessment were relatively poor themselves but it is clear that they viewed clothing insufficiency and, by extension, extreme poverty, as an indication of the personal and moral failings of the individual. In other words, their views reflected those of wider society that pauperism was to an extent a matter of personal choice. We can see this in the case of Alice Hayward who appeared as a witness on behalf of Margaret Grevett in a defamation case heard in the archdeaconry court of Chichester in March 1614.[104]

Witnesses on behalf of Mercy Lock, who had brought the case, claimed that Grevett had lent Hayward clothes 'for the better countenancing of herself when she was produced and sworn as witness in this court on behalf of the said Margaret'.[105] Henry Oley (a 'nailer') deposed that on the day Alice went to give evidence her husband, who lived by 'making or mending of bellows', had come into his shop.[106] Oley asked him 'whither his wife went she was so fine' to which Hayward had replied that she was going to be Grevett's witness. Oley, 'knowing her life to be lewd and herself of small credit' then said to Hayward 'she ... would be a good witness no doubt' (meaning, as he said, the contrary) to which Hayward answered 'what cares she what she says or swears so long she may have meat, drink and apparel'. Oley further deposed that he 'did see a hat upon the said Alice Hayward's head which he has also seen the said Margaret Grevett wear before that time and that at the same time the said Alice Hayward did also wear other apparel which this deponent does verily believe was none of her own for he had never seen her wear it before nor since'. Concluding his evidence Oley told the court that Alice had worn borrowed clothes when she went to her brother's wedding, adding that 'it is well known that she is so poor and indigent that she has not of her own neither is she able to buy such by reason of her poverty'.[107]

Oley's description of Hayward's sartorial need is about her lack of *suitable* clothing to wear in public. Like Barlow's description of his own clothing Oley is articulating a view that decent clothing and respectability are closely related and that the latter cannot be achieved without the former. Borrowed clothes could not bestow respectability. Whilst the church court officials would not know that Alice was wearing borrowed clothes her neighbours in the small rural parish where she lived identified her sartorial transformation immediately: as Oley deposed 'he had never seen her wear it [i.e. the apparel] before or since'. Hayward's indigence is given material expression by her lack of decent clothing. But the various witnesses called on behalf of Mercy Lock also attribute to her a range of moral failings that are presented as if they were both a result and a cause of her poverty. According to Christopher Tidy, she was 'an idle woman, a common liar and a tale bearer, a reporter of untruths and false tales and a very poor and needy body'. Tidy's wife, Margaret, deposed that 'she is so poor and indigent that no man will trust her' and accused Alice of stealing a piece of fustian, a pie and some roast beef whilst attending the wedding dinner of John Pratt.[108] These witnesses were poor themselves. Tidy, a tailor, told the court that he was worth, 'every man paid', 40s, a sum that Shepard has identified as a marker of church court deponents' relative poverty in the early seventeenth century.[109] Like the 'statements of worth' analysed by Shepard, cases like this one reveal 'the many gradations at the lower end of the social hierarchy' that enabled some members of the rural poor to claim a social, moral and material superiority over others. Shepard observes a 'critical dividing line' amongst the poor between those in need of charitable relief (either from the parish or well-meaning neighbours) and those who were able to support themselves.[110] However, there is nothing in the deponents' statements to indicate that either Alice or her husband were in receipt of alms. In fact, their depositions suggest that they 'made shift' for themselves.[111] What Alice thought about her own clothes, her penury or her neighbours' ruthless assessment of her is not recorded.

We can see the same interplay of moral and material failings in witnesses' discrediting of Richard Hall's testimony in a matrimonial contract dispute heard in the archdeaconry court in 1622. Hall had been called as a witness to give evidence for the plaintiff, John Atwood, who maintained that the defendant, Katherine Puttock, had entered into a legal contract of marriage with him, which she had subsequently reneged on. Hall told the court that he knew that Puttock had agreed to the marriage because he had been working as a servant in her father's household at the time and had heard her promise marriage to Atwood 'in a most faithful and serious manner'; he had also witnessed the two parties exchange gifts. However, his testimony was discredited by two other witnesses,

John Grafton and John Richbell. Husbandman, Grafton, claimed that Hall had worked for him as a household servant for a period of between nine and ten weeks before he had run away. According to Grafton, during this time Hall 'did so much accustom himself to lying, swearing and forswearing of himself that neither [he] nor any of his household could believe him in anything that he said nor trust him to do any business that he was appointed to do'. Moreover, Hall never attended church and was 'a very poor, needy and beggarly fellow, not having shoes to wear until this deponent gave him a pair'. In Grafton's analysis, therefore, Hall's inability to provide himself with shoes was material evidence of his social and moral failings. Weaver, John Richbell, corroborated Grafton's assessment, adding that Hall was 'descended of a very poor and mean parentage and his father was first taken in by one Henry Fayre late of Rudgwick...of a poor wandering beggar boy and so has continued ever since very poor and needy being little worth himself'.[112]

In the case of Alice Hayward and Richard Hall, their lack of suitable clothing is used as evidence that they are socially inferior to their neighbours. But clothing could also be used by the poor to express a view that they were as good as their social superiors and that it was merely their outward appearance that made them inferior. In 1630 Thomas Newland found himself in the Chichester archdeaconry court for allegedly verbally and physically abusing a local minister, Robert Johnson. Newland was alleged to have called the minister a 'boy priest and jackanapes' and claimed that he (i.e. Newland) was 'as good a man as...Mr Johnson...excepting his cloth and place in the church'.[113] In 1636, Joanne Chart, a young servant, gave evidence to the court of quarter sessions against a labourer called John Phillips whom she accused of stealing hemp cloth from her master. Chart recounted how after she had given her information to the local justice of the peace, Sir Henry Compton, she had encountered Phillips at Compton's gate and that he had said to her 'if he had his best clothes on...he would show the constable a pair of heels'. What precisely Phillips meant by this is unclear but it is apparent that he thought that putting on his 'best clothes' would give him a social advantage.[114] The comments of both Newland and Phillips point to an underlying resentment of their social and material inferiority, which is here expressed through the medium of clothing.

Conclusion

Clothing clearly mattered to the poor; it could be a source of pride but it could also be a source of shame. Edward Barlow's account of his childhood poverty and his shame at the state of his clothing provides poignant evidence of the social embarrassment that inadequate clothing could cause to the poorest members of seventeenth-century society. Unlike the fictional poor man of the ballad 'Ragged, Torn but True' Barlow took no pride in his shabby appearance. Moreover, as the cases of Alice Hayward and Richard Hall show, the poor themselves could judge harshly those who could not maintain a decent appearance. As we have seen, the sartorial failings of Hayward and Hall were linked by their detractors to a series of moral, social, economic and personal failings, which they saw as the root cause of their poverty. In making these judgements they were expressing a common view that individuals could be responsible for their own indigence.

Providing, and maintaining, decent clothing must have been a constant battle for the poor. The amount of clothing that poor men and women owned varied widely; some owned nothing more than the clothes they stood up in, others had the luxury of 'work day' and 'holiday' clothing. But even those who were able to provide themselves with a spare set of clothing for 'best' would have had to wear the same set of 'work day' clothing six days a week. The heavy woollen cloth used to make outerwear would easily have become sodden with rain and it cannot have been unusual for men and women to go to work in damp clothes. Linen underwear, shirts and smocks, although changed more regularly than outerwear, would have become sodden with sweat. The provision of adequate footwear must have been even more challenging: the frequency with which parish overseers were repairing and replacing paupers' shoes is an indication of the kind of wear and tear they endured.

Parish policies for clothing their paupers varied. The case studies presented in this chapter show that in some parishes clothing provision was relatively restricted whilst in others it was relatively generous. The quality of the clothing provided, however, appears to have been good and it has been suggested that those who were receiving regular clothing from their parishes would have been better clothed than many of their poor but non-dependent neighbours. This is likely to have been especially the case with parish children who must have stood out from some of their peers by the fact that they were wearing completely new sets of presumably quite well-fitting clothing. Many children of non-dependent poor households must have been used to hand-me-downs from older children or indeed the occasional roughly-altered garment of their parent.

The type of coarse woollen cloth worn by the poor reflected the limitations of their budgets but also the need for functionality. Clothing had to be robust enough to withstand the rigours of outdoor work as well as to protect the wearer from inclement weather. Despite this, the poor were not immune to sartorial display. If functionality had been the poor's sole criterion when choosing clothing then they would not have been interested in colour but as we have seen colourful clothing was fairly typical, particularly for women. Moreover, a 'cypress' band on a felt hat or a 'pretty' green ribbon trim on an apron could lift an item of clothing above the purely utilitarian and marked the garment out as the wearer's own. The desire for display was shared by men as well as women – the first thing John Burt did on receiving his 'windfall' of a pig and some gold coins in 1627 was to exchange his 'mean apparel' for a suit of red cloth and a 'horseman's coat'. Women were not only concerned with their own appearance, but with that of their children – think of Elizabeth Michelborne edging her child's 'small wearing linen' with bone lace in 1614. The poor, then, were aspirational in their clothing choices in the sense that they aspired to look as good as possible, at least when wearing their 'holiday' clothes.

Conclusion

On 18 December 1639 Judith Morley wrote to her son, James, from Chichester, telling him that her anxiety in not hearing from him had caused her to dream that he was dead:

> My imagination is full and my thoughts press and throng for utterance yet will I [hold] them back till I have made you acquainted with that which last afflicted me although it was but a dream. On Thursday last at night lying in my bed troubled much in mind what should be the reason I could not hear from you after many hours I fell asleep. No sooner had sleep closed my eyes but I dreamed you were dead which soon awaked me. I lay waking many hours in a great passion, yet at length I turned to the other side and fell asleep again which so soon as my eyes were closed I dreamed the same. Then I was more affrighted, awaking called Nan and charging her that she knew of it long before, blaming her that she would abuse me so in suffering me to write so many letters when she knew I could not be answered, but she vowed she never heard so much. After a violent weeping I lay still and then I dreamed I went to Fulham myself to find you out and coming to your brother's house standing at the door I met with him desiring him to satisfy me what was become of you but he would not answer but prayed me to come in but I replied no, that I would never come within his door till I did see you. Then suddenly you appeared before me, you threw yourself flat upon the ground at my feet and cried 'Oh mother what a miserable man am I to be the cause of your so much affliction'. You were in a suit of cloth of the colour of the earth laced with gold lace. I fell upon you, wept and waked and then concluded this did as much foretell your death as the other, interpreting the colour of the cloth to be the earth you were laid in and the gold to the glory I hoped you were in, and so I have continued mourning ever since . . .

A couple of days later her 'disturbed thoughts' and 'trembling joints' were calmed when she received a letter from him but she remained angry that his failure to reply to her letters promptly had caused her so much suffering.[1]

In his reply dated 3 January 1640 James told her that he had not received her letters because he had been out of London and that he could not afford the 12d that it would cost him to send a man especially to collect her letters to him and send his own. He told her that he would 'earnestly and cheerfully embrace the earth-coloured cloth suit' when God called him, 'so it be adorned with the gold lace of glory'. Nevertheless, his understanding was that dreams usually meant the 'contrary' of what they appeared to foretell; rather than being a portent of death and posthumous glory the earth-coloured suit and gold lace could therefore be interpreted as a promise of wealth, health, honour and 'all earthly felicity'. Such wealth had yet to materialise for James, however. Returning to more mundane matters, he told his mother that he had managed to get hold of £12 of his £40 annual allowance from his brother but that his debts and 'extreme want of linen' had 'already quite ravished [it] from my almost starved pockets'. As a consequence of his impoverishment he wrote that he had no hope at all of buying a new suit, despite the apparent promise of one offered by her dream.[2]

On 17 January 1660, aged seventy-six and now living in Haslemere in Surrey, Judith wrote an informal will, apparently addressed to James, in which she made a series of small bequests and gave instructions about the care and placement of her body after death. Her official will, made in 1641, had left her entire estate, including all her personal possessions, to James whom she had appointed her executor but now she wished to make some final, and more intimate, bequests from the money she still had at her disposal.[3] Conscious of her limited means she expressed reluctance to make bequests that would burden her son financially but reminded him that he had promised her £10 for this purpose. In addition to small charitable bequests, Judith gave small sums of money and death's head rings to her granddaughters, Anne, Fines and Elizabeth, the daughters of her son, James. These were to be inscribed with the words 'not the gift but the giver' and her initials ('JG') marked out in black enamel. Death's head rings were also left to her granddaughter, Judith Joyce, the daughter of her long-dead son, John, and her husband, inscribed with the words 'I live to die eternally' and her initials, marked out again with black enamel. She asked her son, James, to wear one too, 'never parting with it till you die' so that he would remember her 'continually'.

Judith requested that her body be taken back to Dorney in Buckinghamshire and buried in the tomb erected by her father, Sir William Garrard.[4] She stipulated that rather than using household sheets to wrap her body in she would instead buy some new linen cloth 'as soon as I have money', which she would keep in a box ready for that purpose. Having asked God to strengthen her faith in this final part of her life and said 'farewell to all the world' Judith added a postscript:

> Let not anybody come to strip me but my own maid to put me on a clean smock and waistcoat with night clothes on my head and my jaws tied up then let the sheet be put about my shoulders and tied with a knot at my feet.

At the end of her life, therefore, sartorial concerns, here linked to concerns about bodily intimacy and decency, remained prominent in Judith's mind. Her corpse was to go to the grave dressed in clean linen clothes and wrapped in a linen sheet especially bought for that purpose. Her ability to make purchases for herself continued to be circumscribed by her lack of means: as she said, she intended to buy linen cloth for her shroud 'as soon as I have money'.

When we first encountered Judith in 1639 she was at a low point in her life, married to a man who refused to give her any money and of whom she was afraid, living in a small provincial city she did not know and separated from her beloved son, James. Even after William Morley's death in 1640 her disposable income remained restricted which, together with her dependence on James as her proxy shopper in London, put considerable constraints on her consumer choice. Nevertheless, as we have seen, she still placed considerable value on London-made clothing and despite her relatively advanced age retained an interest in her appearance, wearing gowns made out of velvet and satin that were cut in fashionable styles.

Despite the challenges of proxy shopping Judith preferred to have her clothing made for her by a London tailor who was familiar with contemporary fashion trends. London was 'the heart of the nation, through which the trade and commodities of it circulate, like the blood through the heart'.[5] It had an unassailable position as the consumer capital, offering the buyer almost unlimited choice. It was also the nation's fashion capital. However, like all women and men living in the provinces, Judith also made use of local shops and tailors; in his letter to her of 27 January 1641 James suggested that she get the final alterations done to her new gown by 'one of your tailors there' (i.e. in Chichester).[6] This pattern of local and metropolitan clothing consumption can be seen in the behaviour of the other men and women we have encountered in this book. For example, we know that in 1672 Walter Roberts had a new coat made for him by Ticehurst mercer, Thomas Nash, but that much of his clothing, as well as that of his two sons and young ward, was being made by London tailor or mercer, John Heath.[7] We have been able to explore Giles Moore's local and metropolitan clothing consumption in some detail thanks to the meticulous nature of his record keeping. Moore acquired much of his clothing locally, from local mercer, James Holford, and from Lewes mercers, William Marshall, Hercules Courtney and Edmund Middleton, and it was made up for him by local tailors, including Richard Harland and Edward Waters. But he still liked to shop in London for cloth and clothing accessories, taking his Sussex tailor with him to help him choose.[8] Although poorer provincial men and women had little direct access to London's extensive range of shops, they may nevertheless have participated in metropolitan clothing markets. As we have seen, by the late seventeenth century an increasing amount of ready-made clothing was being manufactured in London and distributed to the provinces. Ready-made clothing was coming in through Sussex's ports and it can also be found in the probate inventories of Sussex mercers like Michael Woodgate of Horsham.[9]

There were also strong overlaps in the way that provincial men and women of varying social statuses engaged with local clothing and textile markets. All rural households were involved with some aspects of textile production, growing flax and hemp in their gardens and spinning linen and woollen yarn. They were dependent on the same weavers to weave their cloth, used the same tailors and seamstresses to make their clothes and the same shoemakers to make their shoes. Alongside shopping in fixed retail units in Lewes and London, Giles Moore, like his poorer neighbours, also participated in other, more mobile, consumer markets, buying from pedlars who showed up at his door and visiting his local fairs where shopping was combined with lively entertainment.[10] The shop stock of Sussex mercers shows that they tried to appeal to a range of customers from the relatively wealthy to the relatively poor; they could not afford to be exclusive. Goods were often sold on credit, which meant that even someone with relatively limited means might be able to obtain the odd small 'luxury', perhaps a 'pretty broad green ribbon', a 'cypress' hat band or some bone lace, and to have their debt recorded in the shop book.[11] There was, then, a common provincial clothing culture, created through overlapping spheres of production, distribution and consumption.

In the early modern world, clothing and status were of course inextricably linked. For Judith Morley, James's gold-trimmed, earth-coloured cloth suit symbolised his death and ultimate resurrection. Within the more prosaic and this-worldly context of the clothes encountered in this book we can observe that at least he was meeting his maker wearing good-quality clothes, consistent with his status as a young gentleman.[12] But in the absence of any legal sumptuary restraints the 'status' that clothing embodied was far from straightforward. As we have seen, non-conformist merchant, Samuel Jeake, shared common sartorial ground with the young Ticehurst gentleman, Edward May, whose family were established members of the middle gentry, both dressing in fashionable 'three-piece' suits adorned with shoulder knots and carrying decorative rapiers at their sides. Jeake's purchase of a gold and silver striped silk suit was undoubtedly an expression of a new social and material confidence engendered by his recent, lucrative, marriage to the young Elizabeth Hartshorne and in that sense it can be seen as aspirational. It was also 'emulative' in the sense that he wanted to be in fashion; but this was not a straightforward vertical emulation of the type envisaged by the author of *England's Vanity* where 'each pitiful fellow' aspired to dress like a lord and 'every mechanic's wife' aspired to dress like a lady.[13] Instead, the sartorial standards Samuel Jeake and Edward May both looked to were those set by London's fast-paced fashion culture. In this respect, 'fashion' created a shared sartorial group that can be described as 'supra-status', accessible to anyone with the means and inclination to join it. However, as the contributors to *The Spectator* were keen to point out, the wearer's ability to pull off à-la-mode styles diminished the further they lived from the capital. From the perspective of the fashionable London set, the provincial 'gentleman' and 'gentlewoman' could never really be in fashion.[14]

Of course not everyone wanted to dress fashionably. Giles Moore, for example, stuck to his old-fashioned doublet, waistcoat and breeches until his death in 1679; he continued to wear neck bands rather than cravats and eschewed what by the 1670s had become the essential male accessory, the wig. His sartorial choices were undoubtedly influenced by his profession; clergymen were expected to dress soberly and were discouraged from participating in 'the manners and fashions of this world'.[15] But Moore was also a conservative and money-conscious man; when shopping for new clothes (something he did with considerable regularity) he wanted good-quality, reasonably priced clothing, suitable for his profession and country lifestyle, but which nevertheless displayed his status as a gentleman. Richard Stapley, too, appears to have adopted a relatively conservative style of dress; his suits were made out of good-quality, English, woollen cloth and were probably cut in line with contemporary male fashion trends without being especially fashionable. He did, however, have a penchant for fashionable and exotic accessories like his ivory-topped cane, his tortoise-shell tobacco box and his agate-handled pocket knife – the materials used to manufacture them speaking of global trade networks, which contrast starkly with the circumscribed provincial milieu in which Stapley lived.

Women's ability to participate in fashion was often more restricted. Provincial women were less likely to travel to London to shop and in consequence were more heavily dependent on proxy shoppers. Women's sartorial behaviour was also more likely to be constrained by male control – spousal or parental – whether restricting the amount of money they had at their disposal or refusing to allow them to adopt a contemporary fashion trend because it contravened male notions of female decency. In contemporary literature men and women were criticised in equal measure for their obsession with clothes and their foolish fashions but caricatures of fashionable women – 'town misses' – linked fashion excess with sexual availability. We recall here Pepys's fury at his wife's low-cut neck cloth, 'down to her breasts almost' which in his opinion she wore 'out of a belief, but without reason, that it is the fashion'.[16] As Martha Mayhew entered her teens her conservative and moralising uncle, Giles Moore, is likely to have exercised a high level of supervision of what she wore whilst also ensuring that her clothes were consistent with her status as a young gentlewoman of marriageable age. This 'parental' control no doubt continued after her marriage to John Citizen, a man whom she barely knew and who was some fifteen or twenty years her senior. Women's use of cosmetics and artificial beauty enhancements also attracted male opprobrium: James Gresham's savage attack on his brother's 'mistress', Katherine Williams, made reference to her 'rosy colour for which she is beholden to Spanish paper', a clear sign, in his eyes, of her sexual availability – 'she is my brother's whore'.[17]

For most men and women living in seventeenth-century Sussex, of course, London-set fashion was completely out of reach; there was little chance that the Sussex poor (using that term as it was defined in Chapter Seven) could ever really engage with a process of vertical emulation, which is not to say that they were not concerned about their appearance. Women in particular enjoyed wearing colourful clothing, including the ubiquitous 'red' petticoats; they wore head and neckwear made out of fine, imported linen and trimmed with bone lace; 'best' aprons might be made out of fine linen, coloured or striped, and trimmed with lace or ribbon.[18] Men too dressed to impress when they were able: as soon as he came into some money in 1627 John Burt exchanged his 'mean' apparel for a 'suit of red cloth' and a 'horseman's coat'.[19] With limited wardrobes poor men and women made clear distinctions between 'work days' and 'holidays' clothing – the latter kept for best, worn to church on Sundays and 'holy days', to weddings and perhaps on outings to local fairs. However, for a sizeable proportion of the Sussex population – some twenty-five per cent or more – the provision of *adequate* clothing must have been a constant struggle.[20] The lack of suitable clothing caused shame and social embarrassment: as Edward Barlow recorded in his memoir, in his youth his father's inability to provide him and his siblings with decent clothing meant that they had been unable to attend church 'unless we would go in rags, which was not seemly'.[21] Barlow was well aware that his 'rags' would be scrutinised by his neighbours in church and no doubt understood that both his and his family's respectability and social standing would be impugned as a consequence. Whilst the overseers of the poor in some Sussex parishes, like Ticehurst, were relatively generous in the clothing provision they made to their paupers, others were less so. In the parish of Arundel Joan Selden, desperately poor and bereft of her family, was given a mere 6d 'towards a pair of bodies'.[22]

There were, then, very clear demarcations in dress within Sussex. Whilst the basic elements of men and women's clothes may have been the same, the range of clothing they owned and its style and appearance varied enormously. These variations were likely to have been most evident when parishioners assembled to attend church on Sunday. In the late 1660s Walter Roberts and his two young sons may have encountered parish pauper, John Gynt, in his parish-bought clothing whilst entering or leaving the church of St Mary's in Ticehurst. Once seated, their view would have been limited to their more affluent neighbours sitting in private pews nearby whilst Gynt and other members of the 'meaner' sort, dressed in whatever passed for their Sunday best, sat on benches or stood at the back.[23] Whilst this social stratification of dress no doubt pleased contemporary moralists like Richard Braithwaite or the author of the *Coma Berenices*, it might be a source of resentment for the poor themselves – a reminder of their social and material inferiority. Contrary to the views of the fictional rural poor dressed in their 'poor felt and frieze' that we encounter in contemporary ballads, poor men and women were not all contented with their lot and many would have been only too happy to exchange their 'country fashion' for something else.[24]

Notes

Chapter 1

1 WSRO: QR/W56, ff.42/57.
2 For an introduction to the use of the 'language of sorts' in early modern England see Jonathan Barry, 'Introduction', and Keith Wrightson, '"Sorts of People" in Tudor and Stuart England' *in* Jonathan Barry and Christopher Brooks (eds.), *The Middling Sort of People: Culture, Society and Politics in England, 1550–1800* (Basingstoke: Macmillan, 1994): pp. 1–27; 28–51. A more detailed analysis of those forming the 'poorer' sort can be found in Chapter Seven below.
3 For an analysis of the provincial 'middle sort' see Henry R. French, *The Middle Sort of People in Provincial England 1600–1750* (Oxford: Oxford University Press, 2007).
4 These views are discussed in more detail in Chapter Two. For an introduction to debates about morality and consumption see Nancy Cox, '"Beggary of the Nation": Moral, Economic and Political Attitudes to the Retail Sector in the Early Modern Period' *in* John Benson and Laura Ugolini (eds.), *A Nation of Shopkeepers: Five Centuries of British Retailing* (London: I. B. Tauris, 2003): pp. 26–51.
5 There is an extensive literature on the history of early modern consumption, much of it focusing on the eighteenth century. Books that cover the seventeenth century include Joan Thirsk, *Economic Policy and Projects: The Development of a Consumer Society in Early Modern England* (Oxford: Clarendon Press, 1978); Laura Weatherill, *Consumer Behaviour and Material Culture in Britain 1660–1760* (London: Routledge, 1996); Mark Overton, Jane Whittle, Darron Dean and Andrew Hann, *Production and Consumption in English Households, 1600–1750* (Abingdon: Routledge, 2004); Woodruff D. Smith, *Consumption and the Making of Respectability* (London: Routledge, 2002); Linda Levy Peck, *Consuming Splendor: Society and Culture in Seventeenth-Century England* (Cambridge: Cambridge University Press, 2005); Jane Whittle and Elizabeth Griffiths, *Consumption and Gender in the Early Seventeenth-Century Household* (Oxford: Oxford University Press, 2012); Jon Stobart, *Sugar and Spice: Grocers and Groceries in Provincial England, 1650–1830* (Oxford: Oxford University Press, 2013).
6 This was of course the explanation offered by Neil McKendrick for why there was a 'consumer boom' or 'consumer revolution' in eighteenth-century England (see McKendrick, 'The Consumer Revolution of Eighteenth-Century England' *in* Neil McKendrick, John Brewer and John H. Plumb, *The Birth of a Consumer Society:*

The Commercialization of Eighteenth-Century England (London: Europa Publications, 1982): pp. 9–33.

7   For a nuanced and insightful analysis of early modern consumer behaviour see Smith, *Consumption and the Making of Respectability*; see also Stobart, *Sugar and Spice*, pp. 1–17, for a useful overview of the historiography of consumption.

8   John Styles, *The Dress of the People: Everyday Fashion in Eighteenth-Century England* (New Haven and London: Yale University Press, 2007): p. 247.

9   Nancy Cox and Karin Dannehl, *Perceptions of Retailing in Early Modern England* (Aldershot: Routledge, 2007): p. 146.

10 Nancy Cox, *The Complete Tradesman: A Study of Retailing, 1550–1820* (Aldershot, Routledge 2000); Cox and Dannehl, *Perceptions of Retailing*; Claire Walsh, 'Social Meaning and Social Space in the Shopping Galleries of Early Modern London' in Benson and Ugolini (eds.), *A Nation of Shopkeepers*, pp. 2–79; Levy Peck, *Consuming Splendor*, pp. 25–72.

11 Bruno Blondé, Peter Stabel, Jon Stobart and Ilja Van Damme (eds.), *Retail Circuits and Practices in Medieval and Early Modern Europe* (Turnhout: Brepols, 2006). See also Evelyn Welch, *Shopping in the Renaissance: Consumer Culture in Italy 1400–1600* (New Haven and London: Yale University Press, 2005).

12 Cox and Dannehl, *Perceptions of Retailing*, pp. 151–153.

13 Whittle and Griffiths, *Consumption and Gender*, pp. 9–10. As Whittle and Griffiths note, 'in the early seventeenth century it is evident that much, probably most, pleasurable shopping was done by elite men as such shopping required a trip to London, something men undertook more often than women' (p. 9). The restrictions placed on women's consumer choice by their limited access to London and heavier reliance on proxy shoppers is discussed below, pp. 85, 96–97, 98, 138, 143.

14 Aileen Ribeiro, *Fashion and Fiction: Dress in Art and Literature in Stuart England* (New Haven and London: Yale University Press, 2005); Susan Vincent, *Dressing the Elite: Clothes in Early Modern England* (Oxford: Berg, 2003).

15 Margaret Spufford, *The Great Reclothing of Rural England: Petty Chapmen and Their Wares in the Seventeenth Century* (London: The Hambledon Press, 1984).

16 Anne Buck, *Dress in Eighteenth-century England* (London: B T Batsford, 1979); Styles, *Dress of the People*.

17 Margaret Spufford and Susan Mee, *The Clothing of the Common Sort, 1570–1700* (Oxford: Oxford University Press, 2017). This draws on earlier work undertaken by the authors, including Spufford, 'The Cost of Apparel in Seventeenth-Century England, and the Accuracy of Gregory King', *Economic History Review* 53:4 (2000): pp. 677–705; *idem*, 'Fabric for Seventeenth-Century Children and Adolescents' Clothes', *Textile History* 34:1 (2003): pp. 47–63; Mee, 'The Clothing of the Common Sort, 1570 to 1700: A Study Based on Evidence from Probate Accounts and Poor Relief Records' (unpublished PhD thesis, University of Roehampton, 2005).

18 One pictorial source for non-elite dress is the woodcuts found in contemporary ballads, which are the subject of a recent monograph by Clare Backhouse, *Fashion and Popular Print in Early Modern England* (London: I. B. Tauris, 2017).
19 During the sessional weeks of Epiphany, Easter and Michaelmas, one court convened on Mondays and Tuesdays for the western part in Arundel, Chichester or Petworth, and another met on Thursdays and Fridays for the eastern part in Lewes. Midsummer sessions for both divisions were held jointly in Lewes until 1686; thereafter they were held separately. Although a single Commission of the Peace empowered local justices to preside at all meetings, most magistrates attended only the sessions closest to home. Records for the courts of quarter sessions include order books and indictment books (covering both divisions and held by ESRO) and session rolls (covering eastern and western divisions and held by ESRO and WSRO respectively). Session rolls contain indictments, presentments, petitions, recognisances, depositions, jury lists, writs and rates of servants (B. C. Redwood (ed.), 'Quarter Sessions Order Book, 1642–1649', *SRS* 54 (1954): pp. vii–xxi).
20 Membership of this group is discussed in more detail in Chapter Seven.
21 R. F. Hunnisett (ed.), *Sussex Coroners' Inquests 1603–1688* (Kew: PRO Publications, 1998). Seventy-three suicides were recorded during the period covered by this volume; sixty-eight of these were judged to be felonious rather than the acts of those of unsound mind (see p. xxi).
22 Deposition books for the Archdeaconry courts of Chichester and Lewes were surveyed for this study.
23 For an explanation of the probate process see Tom Arkell, 'The Probate Process' in Tom Arkell, Nesta Evans and Nigel Goose (eds.), *When Death Do Us Part: Understanding and Interpreting the Probate Records of Early Modern England* (Oxford: Leopard's Head Press, 2000): pp. 3–13.
24 Spufford, 'Cost of Apparel', p. 677. For an example of a study of late sixteenth-century clothing using wills see Jane E. Huggett, 'Rural Costume in Elizabethan Essex: A Study Based on the Evidence from Wills', *Costume* 33 (1999): pp. 74–88.
25 As is discussed in more detail in Chapter Six, in law any personal property a woman owned before marriage or acquired during marriage, including her clothes, was vested in her husband. However, in practice there appears to have been an assumption that a woman's personal possessions remained her own property to dispose of as she wished.
26 Here taken from the 1647 probate inventory of glover, Thomas Fielding, of Midhurst (WSRO: EP I/29/138/47). For a brief analysis of clothing and textiles recorded in early seventeenth-century Bedfordshire inventories see Anne Buck, 'Clothing and Textiles in Bedfordshire Inventories, 1617–1620', *Costume* 34 (2000): pp. 26–38.
27 See Amy Erikson, 'Using Probate Accounts' *in* Arkell *et al*, *When Death Do Us Part*, pp. 103–119.

28 The former problem can be resolved by locating the baptism dates in the parish register but even with a small sample of accounts not all baptism dates can be identified successfully.
29 See for example Styles, *Dress of the People*, pp. 257–275; Steven King, 'Reclothing the English Poor, 1750–1840', *Textile History* 33:1 (2002): pp. 37–47; Peter Jones, 'Clothing the Poor in Early Nineteenth-Century England', *Textile History* 37:1 (2006): pp. 17–37. But see Anne S. Saunders, 'Provision of Apparel for the Poor in London, 1630–1680', *Costume* 40 (2006): pp. 21–27 for a short discussion of the pauper clothing strategies in a number of London parishes and more recently Spufford and Mee, *Clothing of the Common Sort*, pp. 43–65.
30 Steve Hindle, *On the Parish? The Micro-Politics of Poor Relief in Rural England, c1550–1750* (Oxford: Oxford University Press, 2004): pp. 270–271.
31 Hindle, *On the Parish*, p. 270.
32 See Chapter Seven.
33 The Gresham family archive forms part of the Loseley Manuscripts held at the Surrey History Centre.
34 SHC: LM/1087/6/431, 436.
35 SHC: LM/COR/7/25.
36 Garrard was the son of Sir William Garrard, a wealthy London haberdasher, merchant tailor and mayor of London in 1555–1556; he served as High Sheriff of Buckinghamshire in 1598 and was knighted in 1603. Judith was the eighth of fifteen children (see Helen Miller, 'Garrard (Garrett), Sir William (by 1518–71), of London and Dorney, Bucks' in S. T. Bindoff (ed.), *The History of Parliament: The House of Commons 1509–1558* (Woodbridge, 1982) [https://www.historyofparliamentonline.org/volume/1509-1558/member/garrard-%28garrett%29-sir-william-1518-71 (accessed 2 October 2017)] and [https://www.dorney-history-group.org.uk/the-garrard-monument-st-james-the-less-dorney/ (accessed 2 October 2017)].
37 For Thomas Gresham's will and inquisition post mortem see Granville Leveson Gower, *Genealogy of the Family of Gresham* (London: Mitchell and Hughes, 1883): pp. 102–105; 138–139. Some of the land in Fulham was copyhold. John Gresham was aged nine years and nine months at the time of his father's death on 6 July 1620. Judith was granted wardship in 1621 (see SHC: LM/1083/35).
38 See SHC: LM/COR/7, LM/1083 and LM/1228–1232 for documents relating to the family's estates and their various legal wranglings.
39 SHC: LM/COR/7/21, 22, 23; LM/COR/7/13.
40 Leveson Gower, *Genealogy of the Gresham Family*, p. 18. This is possibly Martin Williams who is referred to in a couple of James Gresham's letters (SHC: LM/COR/7/56, 70).
41 Morley married (1) Cicely Ryman in 1605 (d. 1628) (2) Susan Earnley in 1633; Alan Davidson, 'Morley, Sir John (1572–1622), of Halnaker, Boxgrove, Sussex and

Aldersgate, London' in A. Thrush and J. P. Ferris (eds.), *History of Parliament: The House of Commons 1604–1629* (Cambridge: Cambridge University Press, 2010) [http://www.historyofparliamentonline.org/volume/1604-1629/member/morley-sir-john-1572-1622, accessed 12 October 2016]; Anthony Fletcher, *Sussex 1600–1660: A Community in Peace and War* (Chichester: Phillimore, 1975): pp. 258–263.
42 SHC: LM/COR/7/55.
43 SHC: LM/COR/7/63.
44 SHC: LM/COR/7/25.
45 The date of his death is unknown; a letter from James to his mother dated 17 October 1640 refers to 'when Morley lived' suggesting he was already dead. Judith refers to herself as a widow in her will dated 13 June 1641 (SHC: LM/1083/57); letter from George Garrard dated 12 September 1641 (SHC: LM/COR/7/19).
46 SHC: LM/COR/7/94.
47 SHC: LM/COR/7/99.
48 SHC: LM/COR/7/25.
49 SHC: LM/COR/7/67.
50 SHC: LM/COR/7/53.
51 SHC: LM/COR/7/98.
52 See James Gresham's will for a lengthy statement of his belief in, and commitment to, the King and the Church of England (TNA: PROB 11/395/383).
53 SHC: LM/COR/7/25; LM/1083/57; LM/1083/83. The first will, dated 13 June 1641, is her legal will; the second will, dated 17 January 1660, is an informal will.
54 J. S. Crossette, 'Gresham, James (*c.* 1617–89), of Haslemere, Surr.' in B. D. Henning (ed.), *The History of Parliament: the House of Commons 1660–1690* (Woodbridge: Boydell and Brewer, 1983) [http://www.historyofparliamentonline.org/volume/1660-1690/member/gresham-james-1617-89 (accessed 16 August 2017)]; TNA: PROB 11/395/383.
55 WSRO: Par 384/6/1.
56 Ruth Bird (ed.), 'The Journal of Giles Moore', *SRS* 68 (1971) (hereafter 'Journal').
57 This supposition is based on a memorandum in Moore's 'Journal' that he had been taken prisoner by parliamentary forces at Saltash in Cornwall in 1644 ('Journal', p. vii).
58 'Journal', pp. vii–viii; 'Giles Moore (CCED Person ID 64575), The Clergy of the Church of England Database 1540–1835 [http://www.theclergydatabase.org.uk (accessed 25 April 2015)].
59 Her date of birth and the date of her marriage to Moore are unknown. She was the widow of George Brett of Lindfield. During her marriage to Brett she had eight sons; only two survived to adulthood ('Journal', p. viii).
60 'Journal', p. 355. The full quote is: 'No peace at home with such a wife, or in the realm with such a despot. Only when I am laid in earth shall I at last find peace. I have

been your faithful spouse, I have been made to submit to domination; and it is thus that you will have been the only portion allotted to me in life'.
61 This is discussed below in more detail p. 144.
62 They were buried on 22 September and 3 October respectively ('Journal', p. ix).
63 WSRO: Ep/II/17/192.
64 'Journal', p. ix.
65 'Journal', p. 83.
66 'Journal', p. 83; TNA: PROB 11/361/89; PROB 4/18013. The figure of £1678 15s includes 'monies upon bond' (i.e. money owing to Moore) of £1160 and £40 in unpaid tithes. If these sums are excluded the total value of his moveable estate is £478 15s.
67 'Journal', pp. 116, 181, 183; the martyrologies are, Lambert Wood, *The Life and Reign of King Charles From his Birth to his Death* (London, 1659), William Langley, *The Death of Charles the First Lamented* (London, 1660).
68 'Journal', pp. 141, 183, 189, 190, 192.
69 'Journal', p. 192. This play is discussed below pp. 36–37, 109.
70 These have been translated and collated by Bird ('Journal', pp. 354–356).
71 'Journal', pp. 354–355.
72 'Journal', p. 356.
73 Father and son moved into the house in August 1680; the marriage took place in March 1681 (Michael Hunter and Annabel Gregory (eds.), *An Astrological Diary of the Seventeenth-Century: Samuel Jeake of Rye 1652–1699* (Oxford: Clarendon Press, 1988): pp. 153, 154 (hereafter *Diary*)).
74 For a Jeake family tree see T. W. W. Smart, 'A Biographical Sketch of Samuel Jeake Senior of Rye', SAC, 13 (1861): pp. 78–79. Jeake had two other children who died in infancy: Elizabeth (b. 1682; d. 1682) and Manasseh (b. 1688; d. 1690).
75 TNA: PROB 11/662/135 (Joseph Tucker, 1733); TNA: PROB 11/678/209 (Elizabeth Tucker, 1736).
76 The original diary is in the William Andrews Clark Memorial Library, University of California. The following section draws on the extensive introduction to the published edition which was written by Michael Hunter.
77 Hunter describes Jeake's astrology as a kind of 'secularized providentialism' (*Diary*, p. 19).
78 The correspondence (FRE 4814–5358) forms part of the Frewen archive held at ESRO; Jeake's business ledger covering the period 1680–1688 (RYE 145/11) is in the Rye municipal archive (also held at ESRO); Jeake's personal accounts covering the period 1674–1680 (RYEYT: N39.40) form part of the Selmes archive held at Rye Castle Museum.
79 An edited collection of the Jeake letters has recently been published by Anne Murphy: Anne L. Murphy (ed.), *The Worlds of the Jeake Family of Rye, 1640–1736* (Oxford: Oxford University Press, 2018).

80 John Spurr, 'From Puritanism to Dissent, 1660–1700' *in* Christopher Durston and Jaqueline Eales (eds.), *The Culture of English Puritanism, 1560–1700* (Basingstoke: Palgrave Macmillan, 1996): pp. 234–265.
81 *Diary*, p. 9.
82 *Diary*, pp. 10–11.
83 Miller was born in 1644 (RCM: RYEYT INV 17.71).
84 In 1678 all French imports were banned in anticipation of war with France; initially intended to last three years, the ban was not repealed until 1685.
85 *Diary*, pp. 58–73. The Million Adventure was a project to raise £1,000,000 from subscriptions in multiples of £10 in return for guaranteed basic annuities and the chance of winning supplementary ones (*Diary*, p. 70).
86 *Diary*, pp. 150, 158.
87 *Diary*, p. 34.
88 Jon Stobart, 'Who were the Urban Gentry? Social Elites in an English Provincial Town, c.1680–1760', *Continuity and Change* 26:1 (2011): pp. 89–112. This group has also been described as the 'pseudo-gentry' – see Alan Everitt, 'Social Mobility in Early Modern England', *Past and Present* 33 (1966): 70–72.
89 See *Diary*, p. 117 for Jeake's audit of his learning aged nineteen. For a discussion of Jeake's intellectual development see *Diary*, pp. 40–50.
90 *Diary*, p. 37; ESRO: FRE 5308, 5356. Elizabeth seems to have been trying to sell the collection of 'rareties' that her husband had inherited from his father (described by Jeake as 'several curious fishes, shells, stones and other rarities' (*Diary*, p. 120)).
91 Anne L. Murphy, '"You Do Manage It So Well That I Cannot Do Better": The Working Life of Elizabeth Jeake of Rye (1667–1736)', *Women's History Review* 27:7 (2018): 1190–1208.
92 *Diary*, p. 153.
93 Michael Hunter, Giles Mandelbrote, Richard Ovenden and Nigel Smith (eds.), *A Radical's Books: The Library Catalogue of Samuel Jeake of Rye, 1623–1690* (Woodbridge: D. S. Brewer, 1999). This is an analysis and transcription of Jeake's 'register' or library catalogue held at the Rye Castle Museum (RYEYT: Jeake MS 4/1). The library itself is now almost entirely lost.
94 Pietro Bertelli, *Diversarum Nationum Habitus*, 3 volumes (Padua, 1589, 1594, 1596). Jeake's copy of volume two survives amongst the Frewen archive (ESRO: FRE 612). Hugh Plat, *Delights for Ladies. To Adorn their Persons, Tables, Closets and Distillatories* (London, 1617). This work is discussed below pp. 135, 155.
95 For the family's background see Robert Tittler (ed.), 'Accounts of the Roberts Family of Boarzell, Sussex c1568–1582', *SRS*, 71 (1977–1979).
96 For their property holding see the list of property deeds held by ESRO (DUN 1–14); for the farming activities of the Roberts family in the sixteenth century see Tittler (ed.), 'Accounts of the Roberts Family'.

97 ESRO: DUN 49/22.
98 L. F. Salzman (ed), *A History of the County of Sussex: Volume 9* (Oxford: Oxford University Press, 1937): pp. 245–255.
99 M. W. Helms and B. M. Crook, 'Courthope, George (1616–85) of Whiligh, Ticehurst, Suss.' in Henning (ed.), *History of Parliament: the House of Commons 1660–1690* [http://www.historyofparliamentonline.org/volume/1660-1690/member/courthope-george-1616-85 (accessed 31 August 2017]; Fletcher, *Sussex*, p. 354; [http://www.westsussexlieutenancy.org.uk/west-sussex-lieutenancy-1540-high-sheriff-1086-1974.html (accessed 31 August 2017)]. For Anthony May's will see TNA: PROB 11/171/483; TNA: C231/7.
100 This all forms part of the DUNN archive held at ESRO.
101 Walter's wife, Mary (née Busbridge) had died in childbirth in 1666 and he did not remarry (ESRO: DUN 52/26, LIB/500874).
102 Edward May was baptised on 7 April 1664 and buried on 10 November 1685 (ESRO: LIB/500866, LIB/500874). His brother was buried on 7 April 1674 (LIB/500874). For Thomas May's will see TNA: PROB 11/344/553. For Edward May's will see TNA: PROB 11/ 383/199. May continued to live at Pashley with his widowed mother, Ann, who submitted quarterly bills to Roberts for his board and some household expenditure. From 1682 these included the cost of keeping one male servant (see ESRO: DUN 50/6/77-80); by the first half of 1684 May had two male servants (ESRO: DUN 50/6/99).
103 For Walter Robert's will see TNA: PROB 11/399/318. For Anna Farnden's will see TNA: PROB 11/483/349.
104 ESRO: DUN 37/9.
105 ESRO: DUN 52/13.
106 See for example the probate inventory of Walter Roberts junior, dated 27 March 1700 (TNA: PROB 4/12601). No books are listed and the house had no study.
107 ESRO: DUN 50/6/22, 30, 31, 42.
108 Trevor Cliffe, *Puritan Gentry Besieged, 1650–1700* (London and New York: Routledge, 1993).
109 Anthony Stapley senior had five sons, the eldest of whom was John Stapley. By 1670 three of the sons, including John, were dead leaving Anthony junior and Richard as his principal heirs. He also had two daughters, Ann and Elizabeth. His widow, Jane, retained possession of Hickstead Place until her death (see TNA: C5/632/33 and PROB 11/325/393). See also L. F. Salzman (ed.), *A History of the County of Sussex: Volume 7* (Oxford: Oxford University Press, 1940): pp. 186–191.
110 See family tree in Edward Turner, 'Extracts from the Diary of Richard Stapley, Gent, of Hickstead Place in Twineham, from 1682 to 1724', *SAC* 2 (1849): p. 107.
111 Samuel Gilbert, *An Almanac for Six Years* (London, 1697); ESRO: HIC 1166, pp. 20, 77. See also Turner, 'Extracts from the Diary of Richard Stapley', pp. 102–119.

112 Adam Smyth, 'Almanacs, Annotators and Life-Writing in Early Modern England', *English Literary Renaissance* 38:2 (2008): pp. 200–244.
113 He was in London in 1684 because he and his mother were involved in a tithe dispute with the rector of Twineham which was heard in the Court of Exchequer (ESRO: HIC 1166, pp. 7, 83; TNA: E134/35&36Chas2/Hil6; E134/36Chas2/East6).
114 William Sheward (CCEd Person ID 65755), *The Clergy of the Church of England Database 1540–1835* [http://www.theclergydatabase.org.uk (accessed 16 August 2017)].
115 Edward Turner, 'The Stapley Diary', *SAC* 18 (1866): p. 155. This article includes extracts from memoranda books kept by Anthony Stapley and his son, John Stapley (1677–1743). Two of these survive (ESRO: HIC 467, 472) but Turner evidently had access to at least one further memorandum book which is now missing. The reference to Richard's illness is from the missing book.
116 Turner, 'Stapley Diary', p. 154. He could still write, however. The last entry in his hand in his memorandum book is dated 14 January 1724, three months before his death (ESRO: HIC 1166, p. 168).
117 ESRO: HIC 1106.
118 ESRO: HIC 1166, p. 78.
119 ESRO: HIC 1166, p. 13. The *Companion to the Temple and the Closet* is a commentary on the Book of Common Prayer.
120 ESRO: HIC 1106. £900 of this was described as held 'on good security and interest'; £757 7s 'on doubtful securities and interests'.
121 Turner, 'Stapley Diary', p. 155.
122 Turner, 'Stapley Diary', p. 155; Wyn K. Ford (ed.), 'Chichester Diocesan Surveys 1686 and 1724', *SRS* 78 (1992): p. 155.
123 Cynthia Herrup, *The Common Peace: Participation and the Criminal Law in Seventeenth-Century England* (Cambridge: Cambridge University Press, 1987): pp. 11–12; Fletcher, *Sussex*, p. 146.
124 Joan Thirsk, 'The Farming Regions of England' *in* Thirsk (ed.), *The Agrarian History of England and Wales: Vol. IV 1500–1640* (Cambridge: Cambridge University Press, 1967): pp. 55–64; Herrup, *Common Peace*, pp. 11–22; Fletcher, *Sussex*, pp. 3–21; Colin Brent, 'Rural Employment and Population in Sussex between 1550 and 1640 (part one)', *SAC* 114 (1976): pp. 27–48; *idem* 'Rural Employment and Population in Sussex between 1550 and 1640 (part two)', *SAC* 116 (1978): pp. 41–55.
125 Alan Everitt lists twenty market towns in Sussex in the sixteenth and early seventeenth centuries (Everitt, 'The Marketing of Agricultural Produce' *in* Thirsk (ed), *Agrarian History IV*, pp. 467–480); fifteen market towns are included in Anon., *The English Chapman's and Traveller's Almanac* (London, 1697) for Sussex including 'Stevington' (probably Storrington) and 'Coxfield' (Cuckfield).
126 Fletcher, *Sussex*, pp. 3–21; Everitt, 'Marketing of Agricultural Produce', pp. 467–480.

127 ESRO: DUN 51/60.
128 Daniel Defoe, *A Tour through the Whole Island of Great Britain* ([1724] Harmondsworth: Penguin Books, 1971): p. 144.
129 Fletcher, *Sussex*, pp. 7–8.
130 Brent, 'Rural Employment and Population (part one)', p. 27; Fletcher, *Sussex*, p. 7.
131 J. H. Andrews, 'The Port of Chichester and the Grain Trade', *SAC* 92 (1954): pp. 93–105.
132 TNA: E190/775/12.
133 Fletcher, *Sussex*, p. 8.
134 Roy Morgan identified 288 merchants (including mercers) operating in Chichester in the seventeenth century (Roy Morgan, *Chichester: A Documentary History* (Chichester: Phillimore, 1992): p. 43).
135 WSRO: Chicity/AH/11. According to Morgan, cloth remained a major industry in Chichester until the mid-seventeenth century when a combination of foreign wars, tariffs and trade protectionism led to a crisis, with exports declining by one third in the 1620s (Morgan, *Chichester*, p. 42).
136 Charles Thomas-Stanford, *Sussex in the Great War and the Interregnum* (London: Chiswick Press, 1910): pp. 47–48; Morgan, *Chichester*, p. 49.
137 Morgan, *Chichester*, pp. 47–48.
138 WSRO: Chicity/AH/12.
139 TNA: PROB 4/9733. For his will see PROB 11/372/186. Some of Godfrey's stock was in his warehouse.
140 L. F. Salzman (ed.), *A History of the County of Sussex: Volume 3* (Oxford: Oxford University Press, 1935): p. 98.
141 John Ogilby, *Britannia, or, The Kingdom of England and Dominion of Wales Actually Surveyed* (London, 1675): p. 58.
142 Herrup, *Common Peace*, p. 17.
143 Colin Brent, *Pre-Georgian Lewes c890–1714: The Emergence of a County Town* (King's Lynn: Colin Brent Books, 2004): pp. 256–257.
144 Brent, *Pre-Georgian Lewes*, pp. 319–323.
145 For a discussion of Moore's Lewes shopping see below pp. 60–61, and Danae Tankard, 'Giles Moore's Clothes: The Clothing of a Sussex Rector, 1656–1679', *Costume* 49:1 (2015): pp. 39–40. For his medical expenses see 'Journal', pp. 136–143.
146 Brent, *Pre-Georgian Lewes*, p. 231.
147 Brent, *Pre-Georgian Lewes*, pp. 252, 269, 270–271.
148 TNA: E190/772/12.
149 Defoe, *Tour Through the Whole Island*, pp. 144–150.
150 Christopher Morris (ed.), *The Illustrated Journeys of Celia Fiennes 1685–c1712* (London: Macdonald & Co, 1982): p. 62.
151 Quoted in Fletcher, *Sussex*, p. 5.

Chapter 2

1. WSRO: QR/W56, ff.42/57. See above p. 1.
2. Some of these themes have been considered by Aileen Ribeiro in *Dress and Morality* (London: B. T. Batsford, 1986): pp. 74–94 and *idem*, *Fashion and Fiction*, and Susan Vincent in *Dressing the Elite* and *idem*, *The Anatomy of Fashion: Dressing the Body from the Renaissance to Today* (Oxford: Berg, 2009).
3. Francis Boyle, *Discourses Useful for the Vain Modish Ladies and their Gallants* (London, 1696): p. 144.
4. Richard Braithwaite, *The English Gentlewoman* (London, 1631): pp. 1–25.
5. Anon., *Coma Berenices or the Hairy Comet* (London, 1676): p. 4.
6. Negley B. Harte, 'State Control of Dress and Social Change in Pre-industrial England' in D. C. Coleman and A. H. John (eds.), *Trade, Government and Economy in Pre-Industrial England* (London: Littlehampton Book Services, 1976): pp. 148–149. See also Vincent, *Dressing the Elite*, pp. 118–119.
7. Some of these are discussed in Harte, 'State Control of Dress', pp. 148–153.
8. Anon., *England's Vanity or the Voice of God Against the Monstrous Sin of Pride in Dress and Apparel* (London, 1683): p. 31
9. Joan Thirsk and J. P. Cooper (eds.), *Seventeenth-Century Economic Documents* (Oxford: Oxford University Press, 1972): p. 215. [My italics].
10. Henry Peacham, *The Complete Gentleman* (London, 1634): p. 220.
11. *Journal of the House of Commons: Volume 1, 1547–1629* (London, 1802), British History Online [https://www.british-history.ac.uk/commons-jrnl/vol1/pp463-464 (accessed 20 November 2017)]. The full text of his speech does not survive. For a brief discussion of Brooke's sumptuary bills see Harte, 'State Control of Dress', p. 149. For Brooke's background and parliamentary activity see J. P. Ferris and S. Healey, 'Brooke, Christopher (*c*. 1570–1628) of York, Yorkshire, and Lincoln's Inn, London; Later of Drury Lane, Westminster' in A. Thrush and J. P. Ferris (eds.), *The History of Parliament: The House of Commons 1604–1629* (Cambridge: Cambridge University Press, 2010) [http://www.historyofparliamentonline.org/volume/1604-1629/member/brooke-christopher-1570-1628 (accessed 19 March 2017)].
12. Braithwaite, *English Gentlewoman*, p. 20.
13. Ibid., pp. 14–15.
14. *Journal of the House of Commons: Volume 1, 1547–1629* (London, 1802), British History Online [https://www.british-history.ac.uk/commons-jrnl/vol1/pp523-525 (accessed 20 November 2017)]. The full text of Brooke's speech does not survive.
15. Randle Holme, *Academy of Armory* (Chester, 1688), Book III, Ch. V, p. 234.
16. Braithwaite, *English Gentlewomen*, pp. 6–7.
17. Anon., *New Additions to Youth's Behaviour* (London, 1663): p. 61.

18 Richard Braithwaite, *The English Gentleman* (London, 1631): pp. 17–18. Numa Pompilius was the legendary second king of Rome, ruling from 715 to 673 BC.
19 Anon., *New Additions*, p. 61.
20 Anon., *New Additions*, p. 61; Braithwaite, *English Gentleman*, pp. 16–17.
21 Harte, 'State Control of Dress', pp. 151–152; for France see Daniel Roche, *The Culture of Clothing: Dress and Fashion in the Ancien Regime* (Cambridge: Cambridge University Press, 1996): pp. 39–40, 49–51.
22 As Ruth Hentschell has observed it was 'a stock emblem for representing the absurd sartorial habits of the English' (Ruth Hentschell, 'A Question of Nation: Foreign Clothes on the English Subject' in Catherine Richardson (ed.), *Clothing Culture, 1350–1650* (Aldershot: Ashgate, 2004): p. 55.). However, it was not unique to England. As Ulinka Rublack has shown, other countries represented their own inhabitants in the same way (Ulinka Rublack, *Dressing Up: Cultural Identity in Renaissance Europe* (Oxford: Oxford University Press, 2010): pp. 144–145).
23 Andrew Boorde, *Introduction to Knowledge* (London, 1542): f. Aiii^v.
24 Anon., *England's Vanity*, p. 132.
25 See Sara Warneke, 'A Taste for Newfangledness: The Destructive Potential of Novelty in Early Modern England', *The Sixteenth Century Journal*, 26:4 (1995): pp. 881–896.
26 Anon., *New Additions*, p. 54.
27 Anon., *England's Vanity*, p. 130.
28 Thomas Dekker, *The Seven Deadly Sins* (London, 1606): p. 32.
29 For a discussion of 'Gallomania' in Restoration England see Gesa Stedman, *Cultural Exchange in Seventeenth-Century France and England* (Farnham: Routledge, 2013).
30 Anon., *A Satire against the French* (London, 1691): p. 6.
31 John Evelyn, *Tyrannus, or, the Mode in a Discourse of Sumptuary Laws* (London, 1661): p. 8.
32 Francis Boyle, *Several Discourses and Characters Addressed to the Ladies of the Age* (London, 1689): p. 148.
33 Evelyn, *Tyrannus*, p. 12.
34 Anon., *Grand Concern of England Explained* (London, 1673): pp. 49–50. See Maria Hayward, '"We Have Better Materials for Clothes, They, Better Taylors": The Influence of La Mode on the Clothes of Charles II and James II', in Tony Clayton and Charles-Edouard Levillain (eds.), *Louis XIV Outside In: Images of the Sun King Beyond France, 1661–1715* (Abingdon: Routledge, 2015), pp. 72–74, for a longer discussion of contemporary English attitudes to French Fashion.
35 Braithwaite, *English Gentleman*, p. 2.
36 Andrew Wear, *Knowledge and Practice in English Medicine, 1550–1680* (Cambridge: Cambridge University Press, 2000): pp. 168–169.

37 Braithwaite, *English Gentleman*, p. 2. For a longer discussion of contemporary ideas of youth and age see Alexandra Shepard, *Meanings of Manhood in Early Modern England* (Oxford: Clarendon Press, 2003): pp. 21–46; 54–69.
38 Medical divisions of the ages of man varied from as few as three to as many as twelve although four-part and seven-part schemes were especially popular (see Shepard, *Meanings of Manhood*, pp. 54–55).
39 William Vaughan, *Directions for Health, Natural and Artificial* (London, 1626): p. 121.
40 John Strype, *Lessons Moral and Christian for Youth and Old Age* (London, 1699): pp. 7–8.
41 MC: Pepys 4.363.
42 Richard Allestree [attributed], *The Ladies Calling in Two Parts by the Author of the Whole Duty of Man* (Oxford, 1673): p. 154.
43 Vaughan, *Directions for Health*, p. 121.
44 Strype, *Lessons Moral and Christian*, pp. 65, 67.
45 Richard Ames, *The Folly of Love, or, An Essay upon Satire against Women* (London, 1691): p. 6.
46 BL: Roxburghe 2.379 (c. 1681–1684).
47 Anon., *Coma Berenices*, p. 18.
48 Dekker, *Seven Deadly Sins*, p. 31.
49 Anon., *Coma Berenices*, pp. 29–30.
50 Anon., *New Additions*, p. 56.
51 See Backhouse, *Fashion and Popular Print*, pp. 144–145, for a short discussion of this theme.
52 BL: Roxburghe 1.476–477.
53 NLS: Crawford 744.
54 MC: Pepys 5.432.
55 MC: Pepys 4.363.
56 Mark Dawson, *Gentility and the Comic Theatre in Late Stuart London* (Cambridge: Cambridge University Press, 2005): pp. 145–163. See also Philip Carter, 'Men about Town: Representations of Foppery and Masculinity in Early Eighteenth-Century Urban Society', in Helen Barker and Elaine Chalus (eds.), *Gender in Eighteenth-Century England: Roles, Representations and Responsibilities* (Harlow: Routledge, 1997): pp. 31–57 and Philip Carter, *Men and the Emergence of Polite Society, 1660–1800* (Abingdon: Routledge, 2014): pp. 124–162.
57 John Vanbrugh, *The Relapse or Virtue in Danger* (London, 1697): pp. 9–10.
58 Ibid., pp. 12–13, 26.
59 Anon., *The Character of the Beaux* (London, 1696): pp. 11–18.
60 Anon., *The Character of a Town Miss* (London, 1680): p. 1.

61 Ibid., p. 1.
62 Thomas Crowne, *The Country Wit* (London, 1675): p. 46.
63 BL: Roxburghe 2.379.
64 Anon., *New Additions*, p. 55.
65 Quote from *New Additions*, p. 54.
66 Braithwaite, *English Gentlewoman*, pp. 4, 9.
67 Anon., *New Additions*, pp. 54–55.
68 Nicholas Barbon, *Discourse of Trade* (London, 1690): pp. 14–15. The term 'conspicuous consumption' was coined by the American economist and sociologist, Thornstein Veblen, in his seminal work, *The Theory of the Leisure Class: An Economic Study of Institutions,* first published in 1889.
69 Barbon, *Discourse of Trade*, p. 16.
70 Anon., *England's Vanity*, p. 31
71 Anon., *Coma Berenices*, pp. 3–4.
72 Nicholas Barbon, *Discourse showing the Great Advantages that New Buildings and the Enlarging of Towns and Cities Do Bring to a Nation* (London, 1678): pp. 5–6.
73 Braithwaite, *English Gentlewoman*, p. 12.
74 Ibid., p. 10.
75 *House of Commons Journal*, vol. 1, pp. 523–525.
76 Thomas Mun, *England's Treasure by Foreign Trade* (London, 1664): pp. 16–17; P. Gauci, 'Mun, Thomas (*bap.* 1571–*d.*1641)', *Oxford Dictionary of National Biography*, Oxford University Press, 2004; online edn. Jan 2008. [http://www.oxforddnb.com/view/article/19527 (accessed 7 March 2017)]
77 Thomas Shadwell, *Epsom Wells* (London, 1673), p. 56. A 'kickshaw', from the French word, *quelquechose*, can refer to a fancy (usually French) dish or to a trifling object or knick-knack.
78 Shadwell, *Epsom Wells*, p. 57.
79 Ibid., p. 56; Anon., *Grand Concern*, p. 54.
80 Ibid., *Epsom Wells*, p. 70. See Margaret Priestley, 'Anglo-French Trade and the "Unfavourable Balance" Controversy, 1660–1685', *Economic History Review* 4:1 (1951): pp. 37–52.
81 For a discussion of John Houghton and Nicholas Barbon, see Paul Slack, 'The Politics of Consumption and England's Happiness in the Later Seventeenth Century', *English Historical Review* 122: 497 (2007): pp. 609–631.
82 A. McConnell, 'Houghton, John (1645–1705)', *Oxford Dictionary of National Biography*, Oxford University Press, 2004 [http://www.oxforddnb.com/view/article/13868 (accessed 1 March 2017)].
83 John Houghton, *England's Great Happiness, or a Dialogue between Content and Complaint* (London, 1677): pp. 5–8 [quote from p. 8].
84 Ibid., pp. 6, 18.

85   R. D. Sheldon, 'Barbon, Nicholas (1637/1640–1698/1699)', *Oxford Dictionary of National Biography*, Oxford University Press, 2004; online edn, Jan 2008 [http://www.oxforddnb.com/view/article/1334 (accessed 28 May 2015)].
86   Barbon, *Discourse [on] New Buildings*, p. 5.
87   Barbon, *Discourse of Trade*, p. 65.
88   Ibid., p. 66.
89   Peter Millard (ed.), *Notes of Me: The Autobiography of Roger North* (Toronto: University of Toronto Press, 2000): pp. 125–126. For a discussion of Barbon's building activities see Elizabeth McKellar, *The Birth of Modern London: The Development and Design of the City 1660–1720* (Manchester: Manchester University Press, 1999), especially pp. 38–56.
90   Barbon, *Discourse of Trade*, pp. 62–63.
91   Anon., *Coma Berenices*, p. 3.
92   MC: Pepys 4.153.
93   Anon., *Grand Concern*, p. 5.
94   See Tim Reinke-Williams, 'Women's Clothes and Female Honour in Early Modern London', *Continuity and Change* 26:1 (2011), pp. 69–88, for a discussion of concerns about female clothing.
95   Anon., *Grand Concern*, p. 50, 51.
96   It has been suggested that many of the 8,000-odd migrants arriving in London each year would have been in their late teens or early twenties (E. A. Wrigley, 'A Simple Model of London's Importance in Changing English Society and Economy, 1650–1750', *Past and Present* 37:1 (1967): pp. 44–70).
97   Anon., *Grand Concern*, p. 6.
98   Ibid., pp. 6–7.
99   Ibid., p. 29.
100 Ibid., pp. 5–7.
101 Henry Peacham, *The Art of Living in London* (London, 1642): title page.
102 Peacham, *Art of Living*, p. A2^r.
103 Ibid., p. A2^r-A4^r.
104 Crowne, *Country Wit*, pp. 3–4, 72.
105 Anon., *Character of the Beaux*, pp. 22–27. A 'bully' or 'hector' beau is described as 'one, who having no estate to subsist on, is forced to live by his wits, yet is a man of mode and strives to be soon in every fashion' (pp. 18–19). For a longer discussion of these themes see Danae Tankard, '"Buttons no Bigger than Nutmegs": The Clothing of Country Gentlemen, c1660–1715', *Cultural and Social History* 14:1 (2017): pp. 1–16. Permission to reuse some of the content of this article here and elsewhere in this book has been given by Taylor & Francis Ltd [https://www.tandfonline.com] on behalf of The Social History Society.
106 NLS: Crawford 549.

107 Anon., *Grand Concern*, p. 30.
108 'Mock-Beggars Hall, with his Situation in the Spacious Country called Anywhere', *c.* 1640 (BL: Roxburghe 3.218–219).
109 Braithwaite, *English Gentlewoman*, pp. 6–7.
110 NLS: Crawford 1244.
111 NLS: Crawford 458. The ballad is undated but possibly *c.* 1700–1720.
112 BL: Roxburghe I 252, 253.
113 See Backhouse, *Fashion and Popular Print*, pp. 152–154, for a discussion of 'prodigal son' ballads.
114 For a longer discussion of this theme see Danae Tankard, '"I Think Myself Honestly Decked": Attitudes to the Clothing of the Rural Poor in Seventeenth-century England', *Rural History* 26:1 (2015): pp. 17–33. Permission to reuse some of the content of this article here and elsewhere in this book has been given by the editor of *Rural History* on behalf of Cambridge University Press.
115 BL: Roxburghe 2.117.
116 MC: Pepys 4.272.
117 MC: Pepys 3.255.
118 BL: Roxburghe 1.160–161.
119 BL: Roxburghe 1.352–353.
120 MC: Pepys 1.268.
121 'The Innocent Country Maids' Delight', 1685–1688 (BL: Roxburghe 2.230). See also 'The Milkmaid's Life', *c.* 1633–1669 (BL: Roxburghe 1.244–245).
122 BL: Roxburghe 2.117; MC: Pepys 4.279, 1685–1688.
123 'The Country Lass', *c.* 1628 (BL: Roxburge 1.52–53).
124 'The Map of Mock-Beggar's Hall', *c.* 1640 (BL: Roxburghe 1.252–253).
125 'The Countryman's Delight', 1681–1684 (MC: Pepys 4.349)
126 'homely, adj.', *OED Online*, Oxford University Press, 2013 [http://www.oed.com/view/entry/87905 (accessed 5 April 2013)].
127 He bought a copy of *The Complete Gentleman* in 1658, a copy of *Epsom Wells* in 1673 and a copy of *The Ladies Calling* in 1674 ('Journal', pp. 116, 181, 192).

Chapter 3

1 This chapter draws on two previously published articles, '"A Pair of Grass-Green Woollen Stockings": The Clothing of the Rural Poor in Seventeenth-Century Sussex', *Textile History* 43:1 (2012): 5–22 and 'Giles Moore's Clothes'. Permission to reuse some of the content of the first article here and elsewhere in this book has been given by Taylor & Francis Ltd [https://www.tandfonline.com] on behalf of the

Pasold Research Fund Ltd. Permission to reuse some of the content of the second article has been given by Edinburgh University Press.
2. Some years ago Negley Harte proposed a 'simple model' of the clothing market based on 'market' and 'non-market' sectors. His model works up to a point if we divide the market into those with retail premises (including those who sold from their workshops, like tailors) and those without, such as itinerant traders or the many women who dealt in linen cloth and 'small ware', but it is too reductive. Harte's accompanying table is very confusing because he includes tailors, seamstresses, dressmakers, shoemakers and hatters in the 'market' sector but drapers, haberdashers and mercers in the 'non-market' sector (Negley B. Harte, 'The Economics of Clothing in the Late Seventeenth Century', *Textile History* 22:2 (1991): pp. 286–287).
3. For an analysis of provincial clothing production and supply networks, see also Spufford and Mee, *Clothing of the Common Sort*, pp. 219–254.
4. TNA: PROB 11/184/257.
5. See above p. 19.
6. Brent, 'Rural Employment and Population in Sussex (Part One)', pp. 33–34, 45–46. For example, in 1657 John Everenden of Sedlescombe sold his annual clip to a 'Mr Carter of London' (cited in Brent, p. 46). See also Brent, 'Rural Employment and Population in Sussex (Part Two)', p. 41.
7. See will of Eme Smyth of Harting, 1602 (WSRO: STC I/15/150r).
8. WSRO: STC I/15/301r, 321v.
9. WSRO: STC I/15/153r.
10. ESRO: QR/E9, f. 110.
11. ESRO: QR/E85, f. 67.
12. 'Journal', pp. 154–155.
13. Broadcloth is a fine woollen cloth with a plain weave. Serge is a woollen fabric with a warp of worsted and a weft of wool.
14. For a description of the processes involved in woollen cloth production and the housewife's involvement with it, see Gervase Markham, *The English Housewife*, ed., Michael R. Best (Montreal: McGill-Queen's University Press, 1986): pp. 146–152.
15. See probate inventory of Richard Hamper of Washington, husbandman, 1639 (WSRO: EP I/29/205/21) which includes 'one pair of stock cards, one old woollen turn'.
16. WSRO: STC I/15/233r-v; STC I/15/278r.
17. ESRO: QR/E91, f.62.
18. WSRO: QR/W213, ff. 4142.
19. ESRO: QR/E117, f. 35.
20. See Donald C. Coleman, 'An Innovation and its Diffusion: The "New Draperies"', *Economic History Review* 22:3 (1969), pp. 417–429, for a discussion of 'old' and 'new' draperies. For mercers' probate inventories see Anthony Mutton of Rusper, 1632

(WSRO: EP I/29/163/6), Walter Deane of Rudgwick, 1661 (WSRO: EP I/29/160/50), William Silverlock of Westbourne, 1678 (WSRO: EP I/29/206/162).

21 ESRO: PAR 465/6/1; 'Journal', p. 73.
22 'Journal', pp. 119–135. Moore preferred to buy his broadcloth in London.
23 'Journal', p. 124.
24 'Journal', pp. 70–80.
25 'Journal', pp. 26, 27, 47, 48.
26 'Journal', pp. 120–122.
27 'Journal, p. 71.
28 'Journal', p. 122.
29 There is only one further reference to Moore using Harland: in October 1669 he paid him 3s for making a cassock ('Journal', p. 124).
30 Dishonest tailors were a popular theme in ballads – see for example 'True Blue Ploughman' (BL: Roxburghe 2.471, 1685). For a discussion of the representation of tailors in ballads see Backhouse, *Fashion and Popular Print*, pp. 68–72.
31 WSRO: Shillinglee ACC 454, bundle No. 5, part 2 (unnumbered bills).
32 WSRO: QR/W82, f. 53.
33 The overseers of the parish of Rotherfield were using at least three different tailors to make up their paupers' clothing in the 1660s, Abraham Alchorne, Thomas Hosmer and Richard Wilson (ESRO: PAR 465/6/1).
34 'Journal', p. 114.
35 See for example 'Journal', pp. 110, 115.
36 'Summer' hemp refers to the male plants, which are harvested after fertilising the female plants. The female plants ('winter' hemp) are left to grow so that their seeds ripen before harvesting. See 'Hemp' in R. P. Wright (ed.), *The Standard Cyclopedia of Modern Agriculture and Rural Economy* (London: Gresham, 1910).
37 'Journal', p. 115.
38 Markham claims that it is best to soak flax and hemp in a running stream but because it is toxic to fish it is not advisable unless you live near 'some broad and swift stream' (Markham, *English Housewife*, p. 155).
39 These processes are described by Markham, *English Housewife*, pp. 158–160.
40 'Journal', pp. 110, 111, 115.
41 Craig Muldrew has estimated that a married woman could spin one pound of linen or hemp yarn a day (Craig Muldrew, '"Th'Ancient Distaff" and "Whirling Spindle": Measuring the Contribution of Spinning to Household Earnings and the National Economy in England, 1550–1770', *Economic History Review* 65:2 (2012): 519.
42 'Journal', pp. 112, 114.
43 See Markham, *English Housewife*, pp. 164–165.
44 'Journal', pp. 109, 110.

45 'Journal', pp. 74, 175.
46 'Journal', pp. 14–16, 27, 72, 73.
47 'Journal', pp. 47, 74, 75, 132, 135.
48 'Journal', p. 72.
49 'Journal', pp. 26, 27.
50 'Journal', pp. 14, 15.
51 ESRO: PAR 465/6/1.
52 The clothing of the poor is considered in Chapter Seven.
53 'Journal', p. 72.
54 In 1637 Joan Daniel was assaulted whilst doing her laundry at the New Conduit in Rye (see Hunnisett (ed.), *Sussex Coroners' Inquests*, no. 358).
55 WSRO: QR/W213, ff. 41–42.
56 ESRO: QR/E44, f. 60.
57 See probate inventory of Anthony Mutton of Rusper, 1632 (WSRO: EP I/29/163/6).
58 WSRO: EP I/29/106/165 (1679). Hambrow is a fine linen cloth originating in Germany. 'Genting' is a middle-weight linen cloth originating in Ghent.
59 See Spufford, *Great Reclothing*, for a discussion of the stock-in-trade of itinerant traders, pp. 85–105.
60 WSRO: EP I/29/149/224. Osnaburg is from Germany; silesia and garlicks (corruption of 'Görlitz') from the Silesia region of central Europe.
61 Spufford, *Great Reclothing*, p. 91.
62 TNA: E190/773/9; *Diary*, p. 128.
63 French imports were banned in anticipation of war with France; initially intended to last three years, the ban was not repealed until 1685.
64 ESRO: RYE 145/11; Jeake was appointed overseer of Barham's will when he died in 1692 (see *Diary*, pp. 217–218).
65 WSRO: EP I/29/160/50; EP I/29/98/95; EP I/29/149/224.
66 For a discussion of the use of cotton see Spufford, *Great Reclothing*, pp. 108–109, 121–122.
67 WSRO: EP I/29/149/224.
68 Audrey W. Douglas, 'Cotton Textiles in England: The East India Company's Attempt to Exploit Developments in Fashion, 1660–1721', *Journal of British Studies* 8:2 (1969): pp. 40–43.
69 For a discussion of cloth, haberdashery and clothing accessories stocked by provincial shopkeepers including mercers, see Susan North, '"Galloon, Incle and Points": Fashionable Dress and Accessories in Rural England, 1552–1665', in Richard Jones and Christopher Dyer (eds.), *Farmers, Consumers, Innovators: The World of Joan Thirsk* (Hatfield: University of Hertfordshire Press, 2016): pp. 104–123.
70 WSRO: EP I/33/1611.

71 For a discussion of the general stock of provincial shopkeepers see Jon Stobart, 'The Village Shop, 1660–1760: Innovation and Tradition' in Jones and Dyer (eds.), *Farmers, Consumers, Innovators*, pp. 89–102.
72 WSRO: EP I/29/160/50.
73 WSRO: EP I/29/106/165.
74 WSRO: QR/W64, f. 79.
75 'Journal', pp. 19, 154, 255, 259, 299.
76 'Journal', pp. 14, 19, 20, 47, 136, 144, 145, 299.
77 WSRO: EP I/29/163/6. See probate inventory of Thomas Puttock of Slinfold, tailor, 1639 (WSRO: EP I/29/176/21), which included two pairs of shears and two pressing irons.
78 David Vaisey (ed.), *The Diary of Thomas Turner* 1754–1765 (Oxford: Oxford University Press, 1985), pp. 9, 11, 212, 317, 330.
79 'Journal', pp. 16–17, 18, 20, 54, 128, 248–249, 267–268, 269.
80 'Journal', pp. 71, 100.
81 'Journal', p. 119. This is a cryptic entry since it implies that the trousers were ready-made, which may have been the case, but given the price it seems unlikely.
82 'Journal', pp. 20, 22, 27, 265, 304.
83 'Journal', pp. 268–272.
84 Brent, *Pre-Georgian Lewes*, pp. 319–361.
85 'Journal', pp. 124–125.
86 'Journal', p. 122.
87 'Journal', pp. 132, 133, 134.
88 'Journal', p. 134.
89 Brent, *Pre-Georgian Lewes*, pp. 289–361.
90 See also Spufford and Mee, *Clothing of the Common Sort*, pp. 233, 239–240, for a short discussion of shopping at fairs.
91 Samantha Letters, *Online Gazetteer of Markets and Fairs in England and Wales to 1516* [http://www.history.ac.uk/cmh/gaz/gazweb2.html] [Sussex] (Centre for Metropolitan History, Institute of Historical Research: last updated 16 December 2013) [accessed 3 December 2018].
92 'Journal', pp. 68, 29.
93 'Journal', pp. 26, 47, 48.
94 'Journal', pp. 72, 77, 78, 79.
95 'Journal', pp. 174, 177, 179, 315, 322.
96 WSRO: QR/W122, f. 52–54.
97 WSRO: QR/W156, f. 56.
98 WSRO: QR/W8, f. 6/53; QR/E19, f. 89.
99 Jonathan Fryer (ed.), *George Fox and the Children of Light* (London: Kyle Cathie, 1991): pp. 24–25.

100 'Journal', p. 301.
101 *Diary*, p. 238.
102 For quarter sessions cases involving purses being cut at fairs, see WSRO: QR/W90, f. 98 and ESRO: QR/E11, f. 7A/52.
103 Spufford, *Great Reclothing*, p. 94.
104 'Journal', pp. 25, 133, 134.
105 WSRO: EP I/29/149/224.
106 WSRO: QR/W110, f.38. This case involves the settlement of Mary Pierce. Since her last place of permanent residence had been Rogate, the court ordered the overseers of the poor for Rogate to find her and her two children a 'convenient habitation'.
107 ESRO: QR/E63, ff.63-64.
108 Spufford, *Great Reclothing*, pp. 12-14.
109 TNA: AO 3/370. All of the licensees were men, except for Jane Vain of Mayfield who purchased a licence along with her husband, William Vain, and an unnamed woman who was included in the licence of her husband, William Coney of Warbleton. See Spufford, *Great Reclothing*, pp. 6-16, for a discussion of licensing schemes.
110 Spufford, *Great Reclothing*, pp. 14-20; see also Cox and Dannehl, *Perceptions of Retailing*, pp. 49-54 for shopkeepers' hostility to itinerant traders, and authorities' attempts to regulate their activities.
111 Beverly Lemire, 'Consumerism in Preindustrial and Early Industrial England: The Trade in Secondhand Clothes', *The Journal of British Studies* 27:1 (1988): pp. 1-24; *idem*, 'Shifting Currency: The Culture and Economy of the Second Hand Trade in England, *c.* 1600-1850' *in* Alexandra Palmer and Hazel Clark (eds.), *Old Clothes, New Clothes: Second Hand Fashion* (Oxford: Berg, 2005): pp. 29-47.
112 Henry Morley (ed.), *A Survey of London Written in the year 1598 by John Stow* (Stroud: Alan Sutton Publishing, 1994), p. 151; Ann R. Jones and Peter Stallybrass, *Renaissance Clothing and the Materials of Memory* (Cambridge: Cambridge University Press, 2000): pp. 30-31; both cited in Lemire, 'Shifting Currency', pp. 32, 36.
113 Lemire, 'Consumerism', p. 1. See also Spufford and Mee, *Clothing of the Common Sort*, pp. 114-122, for a discussion of the second-hand clothing market in London and the limited evidence for its operation in the provinces.
114 See probate account for Richard Barker of Arundel (1611) WSRO: EP I/33/1611 'paid for striking up the drum to give notice of a sale to be made'. See also ESRO: QR/E123 (April 1659) deposition of Katherine Gravely of Bolney about a port sale held in Slaugham.
115 See probate account for Thomas Kewell of Lyminster (1648) WSRO: EP I/33/1648 'for bread and drink for the sale'; George Mersher of Birdham (1682) WSRO: EP I/33/1682 'for beer at the sale of the goods'.

116 WSRO: EP I/11/15, f. 275r.
117 WSRO: Par 416/37/2.
118 ESRO: FRE 4831. In fact, Jeake senior managed to sell it for 9s, telling his son that it 'was the most I could get' (FRE 4826).
119 WSRO: QR/W213, f. 42.
120 ESRO: QR/E44, f. 58.
121 WSRO: QR/W13, f. 13/71.
122 WSRO: QR/W53, f. 54/37.
123 ESRO: QR/E168, ff. 63, 66.
124 'Journal', pp. 173, 326.
125 Anne Key was the wife of Rye mariner, William Key. Key already had four daughters at the time of their marriage. Anne and William had three daughters together. Anne died in childbirth on 21 September 1665. William Key died on 20 December 1666. The five younger daughters then became the wards of Samuel Jeake the elder. He kept accounts of his expenditure on the girls from December 1666 until October 1679 (RCM: RYEYT N39.6.1).
126 See for example wills of Avice Bartholomew of Treyford, 1606 (WSRO: STC I/15/233r-v), Agnes Slater of Sompting, 1606 (WSRO: STC I/15/238r-v) and Agnes Deyntie of Horsham, 1608 (WSRO: STC I/15/274v).
127 Beverly Lemire, *Dress, Culture and Commerce: The English Clothing Trade before the Factory, 1660–1800* (Basingstoke: Palgrave Macmillan, 1997): pp. 9–41. See also Spufford and Mee, *Clothing of the Common Sort*, pp. 37–41.
128 Lemire, *Dress, Culture and Commerce*, p. 57.
129 Cantaloon and shag are both types of worsted.
130 TNA: PROB 32/67/129; PROB 32/67/145. See Lemire, *Dress, Culture and Commerce*, pp. 47–48.
131 For a transcript of Wood's inventory see Spufford, *Great Reclothing*, pp. 214–217.
132 See for example port books for Rye, TNA: E190/773/12 (1675); E190/783/16 (1686), which record stocks of bodices, stockings and waistcoats.
133 WSRO: EP I/29/106/165.
134 WSRO: EP I/29/188/83.
135 ESRO: PAR 465/6/1.
136 WSRO: Par 516/31/1, nos. 50, 62 67.
137 WSRO: EP I/29/106/215.
138 WSRO: EP I/29/541/34.
139 WSRO: EP I/29/8/15; QR/W60, f. 97.
140 WSRO: EP I/29/106/130. See also probate inventories of Samuel Walter of Arundel, 1649 (WSRO: EP I/29/8/88) and Leonard Pope of Arundel, 1688 (WSRO: EP I/29/8/189).

141 See Jon Stobart, 'Making the Global Local? Overseas Goods in English Rural Shops, c. 1600–1760', *Business History* 59:7 (2017), pp. 1136–1153, for an analysis of imported commodities found in provincial shops in this period.

Chapter 4

1 Peacham, *The Art of Living in London*, pp. 1–2.
2 Peter Borsay, 'The London Connection: Cultural Diffusion and the Eighteenth-Century Provincial Town', *The London Journal* 19:1 (1994): pp. 21–35.
3 Nicholas Barbon, *An Apology for the Builder* (London, 1685): p. 30, quoted in Paul Slack, 'Perceptions of the Metropolis in Seventeenth-Century England', *in* Peter Burke, Brian Harrison and Paul Slack (eds.), *Civil Histories: Essays Presented to Sir Keith Thomas* (Oxford: Oxford University Press, 2000): p. 161.
4 Slack, 'Perceptions of the Metropolis', pp. 161–180.
5 Slack, 'Perceptions of the Metropolis', pp. 161, 168–169. Its closest competitor in terms of size was Paris but after 1700 foreign visitors generally accepted that London was the larger of the two cities in terms of population, if not geographical area.
6 Peter Guillery, 'Houses in London's Suburbs' *in* Matthew Davies, Catherine Ferguson, Vanessa Harding, Elizabeth Parkinson and Andrew Wareham (eds.), *London and Middlesex 1666 Hearth Tax*, part 1 (London: British Record Society, 2014): p. 140; Lawrence Stone, 'The Residential Development of the West End of London in the Seventeenth Century' *in* Barbara C. Malament (ed.), *After the Reformation: Essays in Honour of J. H. Hexter* (Manchester: Manchester University Press, 1980): pp. 167–212.
7 Anna Bryson, *From Courtesy to Civility: Changing Codes of Conduct in Early Modern England* (Oxford: Clarendon Press, 1998): pp. 129–131.
8 For his background and political career see A. Davison, 'Thomas, Pelham (1597–1654), of Laughton and Halland, East Hoathley, Suss' *in* Thrush and Ferris (eds.), *History of Parliament: the House of Commons* [http://www.historyofparliamentonline.org/volume/1604-1629/member/pelham-thomas-1597-1654 (accessed 9 October 2017)].
9 BL: Add MS 33145.
10 Fletcher, *Sussex*, p. 43.
11 Vanessa Harding, 'London and Middlesex in the 1660s' *in* Davies *et al* (eds.), *London and Middlesex 1666 Hearth Tax*, part 1, p. 57.
12 Brian Dietz, 'Overseas Trade and Metropolitan Growth' *in* A. L. Beier and Roger Finlay (eds.), *London 1500–1700: The Making of the Metropolis* (Harlow: Prentice Hall Press, 1986): pp. 123–129.

13 Kirti N. Chaudhuri, *The Trading World of Asia and the English East India Company 1660-1760* (Cambridge: Cambridge University Press, 1978): pp. 277–330; 343–358.

14 Nuala Zahedieh, *The Capital and the Colonies: London and the Atlantic Economy 1660–1700* (Cambridge: Cambridge University Press, 2010): pp. 7, 10.

15 Peter Earle, *The Making of the English Middle Class: Business, Society and Family Life in London 1660–1730* (London: Methuen, 1989): pp. 18–34.

16 John Styles, 'Product Innovation in Early Modern London', *Past and Present* 168 (2000): pp. 124–169.

17 Clare Haru Crowston, *Fabricating Women: The Seamstresses of Old Regime France* (Durham and London: Duke University Press, 2001): p. 50.

18 Ibid., pp. 50, 134.

19 Smith, *Consumption and the Making of Respectability*, pp. 51–53 [quote from p. 52].

20 Chaudhuri, *The Trading World of Asia*, pp. 281–282. See also Douglas, 'Cotton Textiles in England', pp. 28–43.

21 *The Spectator*, No. 129, 28 July 1711.

22 John L. Nevinson, 'Origin and Early History of the Fashion Print', *Smithsonian Institution United States National Museum Bulletin* 250 (1969): pp. 65–92; Alice Dolan, 'An Adorned Print: Print Culture, Female Leisure and the Dissemination of Fashion in France and England, around 1660–1779', *V&A Online Journal*, 3 (2011) [http://www.vam.ac.uk/content/journals/research-journal/issue-03/an-adorned-print-print-culture,-female-leisure-and-the-dissemination-of-fashion-in-france-and-england,-c.-1660-1779 (accessed 19 May 2015)]; Elizabeth Davis, '"Habit de Qualité": Seventeenth-Century French Fashion Prints as Sources for Dress History', *Dress* 40:2 (2014): pp. 117–143.

23 Paul Griffiths, 'Politics made Visible: Order, Residence and Uniformity in Cheapside, 1600–1645' *in* Paul Griffiths and Mark S. R. Jenner (eds.), *Londinopolis: Essays in the Cultural and Social History of Early Modern London* (Manchester: Manchester University Press, 2000): pp. 176–196.

24 Vanessa Harding, 'Shops, Markets and Retailers in London's Cheapside, c1500–1700' *in* Blondé et al (eds.), *Retail Circuits and Practices*, p. 160. See also Patrick Wallis, 'Consumption, Retailing, and Medicine in Early-Modern London', *Economic History Review* 61:1 (2008): 26–53.

25 Market traders sold white meats and dairy products, as well as vegetables, fruit and flowers. Market days and hours were not clearly defined (Harding, 'Shops, Markets and Retailers', pp. 160–161).

26 The market was moved to a new location on the site formerly occupied by two churches (Harding, 'Shops, Markets and Retailers', p. 167).

27 For an account of the rebuilding of the hall after the Great Fire see Joan Imray, *The Mercers' Hall* (London: London Topographical Society, 1991): pp. 23–68.

28 Strype, *Survey of London* (1720) [online] (hriOnline, Sheffield). Available from: [https://www.hrionline.ac.uk/strype/ (accessed 16 January 2017)].

29 In addition to the Royal and New Exchanges discussed here, there was the Exeter Exchange, built in 1676 on the site of Exeter House, and the short-lived Middle Exchange built in 1671–1672 partly within Great Salisbury House, both located on the Strand (see Walsh, 'Social Meaning and Social Space' *in* Benson and Ugolini (eds.), *A Nation of Shopkeepers*, p. 53).

30 Ann Saunders, 'The Organisation of the Exchange' *in* Ann Saunders (ed.), *The Royal Exchange* (London: London Topographical Society, 1997): pp. 87–90. The word 'pawn' derives from the Dutch 'pandt' or the German 'bahn' meaning a street or passageway, presumably referring to the gallery or corridor which led around the rectangle (Saunders, p. 89).

31 Diana de Marly, 'Fashionable Suppliers 1660–1700: Leading Tailors and Clothing Tradesmen of the Restoration Period', *The Antiquaries Journal* 58:2 (1978): p. 335.

32 Levy Peck, *Consuming Splendor*, pp. 46–61.

33 Walsh, 'Social meaning and Social Space', p. 63. Quote from Saunders, 'Organisation of the Exchange', p. 88.

34 Walsh, 'Social meaning and Social Space', pp. 62–72' Levy Peck, *Consuming Splendor*, pp. 52–53.

35 Daniel Defoe, *Moll Flanders* ([1722] Ware: Wordsworth Editions Limited, 1993): p. 252.

36 In June 1668 Pepys was told by a shopkeeper at the New Exchange, forced out of the Royal Exchange by the Fire, that trade there was better than it had been in the city and that he, and other shopkeepers, probably would not return (Robert Latham (ed.), *The Diary of Samuel Pepys: A Selection* (London: Penguin Books, 2003): p. 931).

37 Ann Saunders, 'The Second Exchange', *in* Saunders (ed.), *Royal Exchange*, pp. 121–135.

38 SHC: LM/COR/7/58.

39 De Marly, 'Fashionable Suppliers', pp. 340–341.

40 Anon., *Character of the Beaux*, pp. 27–29.

41 Earle, *The Making of the English Middle Class*, pp. 45–46. For his will see TNA: PROB 11/362/314 (26 February 1680).

42 'Journal', pp. 119, 127, 130, 131, 134, 136, 151, 152.

43 BM: D, 2.1699.

44 See for example *The London Gazette*, no. 3519 (Monday 31 July to Thursday 3 August 1699) for an advert for 'rich China damasks' being sold by the piece at the Royal Exchange.

45 *The Spectator*, no. 24, 28 March 1711; no. 116, 13 July 1711; no. 240, 5 December 1711.

46 John Farrant, 'Growth of Communications' in Kim Leslie and Brian Short (eds.), *An Historical Atlas of Sussex* (Chichester: Phillimore, 1999): pp. 78–79.
47 Thomas de Laune, *The Present State of London* (London, 1681): pp. 385–435.
48 There are regular payments for coach hire in Pelham's account book (BL: Add MS 33145), see for example ff. 47v, 55v, 56r, 158v, 74v, 85v, 102v, 107v), although it is not usually clear whether this is for a coach he hired whilst in London or one he used for his trips to and from London (but see f. 102v 'paid John Vine for the coach that brought us down').
49 'Journal', pp. 250, 251, 284, 291–292.
50 *Diary*, pp. 173, 184.
51 *Diary*, p. 169.
52 Anon., *Grand Concern*, p. 36. As we saw in Chapter Two, the author of *The Grand Concern* disliked stage coaches because it made it easier for people to get to London.
53 ESRO: FRE 5337.
54 Fletcher, *Sussex*, p. 43.
55 BL: Add MS 33145, ff. 16v, 18r, 30r, 40r, 55r.
56 'Journal', p. 280.
57 Elizabeth Bonnick was Jeake the elder's sister. Nathaniel died in 1670 after which she married Southwark glazier, Christopher Dighton (d. 1686) (Smart, 'Biographical Sketch', pp. 78–79).
58 Elizabeth Mackley was the daughter of Rye Mariner, William Key, Samuel Jeake the elder's brother-in-law, who died in 1666. She married John Mackley in 1674. They lived in Tooley Street in Southwark. Mary Jaye was also the daughter of William Key. She married John Jaye in 1681. They lived at the Golden Lion in Fenchurch Street (RCM: RYEYT N39.6.1).
59 *Diary*, pp. 33, 164; ESRO: FRE 5309, 5351. Miller moved from Rye to London in 1682 to avoid religious persecution
60 SHC: LM/COR/7/62.
61 SHC: LM/COR/7/69.
62 Stone, 'Residential Development of the West End', pp. 178–179.
63 ESRO: FRE 5301, 5308, 5309, 5310, 5311, 5358.
64 De Laune, *Present State of London*, pp. 385–435.
65 'Journal', pp. 305–310.
66 *Diary*, pp. 193, 194.
67 ESRO: FRE 520, ff. 17r, 36v.
68 'Journal', p. 280.
69 'Journal', pp. 284–285. Moore was subpoenaed to appear before Chief Justice Keling (Chief Justice of the King's Bench) 'about Thomas Winchester's business'. Why he had been subpoenaed or what the case was about is not explained.
70 'Journal', pp. 70, 282, 284.

71 'Journal', p. 146.
72 'Journal', p. 281.
73 'Journal', p. 290.
74 'Journal', pp. 284, 292–293, 78. The way that Martha's clothes are recorded (i.e. as complete garments rather than separate components) suggests that they may have been ready-made.
75 'Journal', p. 126.
76 'Journal', p. 145.
77 'Journal', p. 119.
78 'Journal', p. 136.
79 'Journal', pp. 150–152.
80 'Journal', pp. 27, 151, 153, 155, 156, 186.
81 'Journal', pp. 192, 199.
82 'Journal', pp. 30, 340.
83 'Journal', p. 128. As Moore notes, he gave away his periwig to John Wood 'without ever wearing it'.
84 'Journal', p. 152.
85 'Journal', pp. 283, 284.
86 'Journal', pp. 151, 188, 202.
87 'Journal', p. 191. Samuel Rolle, *Shlohavot, The Burning of London* (London, 1667); Thomas Vincent, *God's Terrible Voice in the City* (London, 1667); Anon., *A True and Faithful Account of the Several Informations Exhibited to the Honourable Committee appointed the Parliament to Inquire into the Late Dreadful Burning of the City of London* (London, 1667).
88 'Journal', pp. 331, 345.
89 SHC: LM/COR/7/61.
90 SHC: LM/COR/7/90.
91 SHC: LM/COR/7/61.
92 I would like to thank Vanessa Harding for identifying 'Alderman Gurnett' as Richard Gurney or Gurnard. See Keith Lindley, 'Gurney, Sir Richard, Baronet (*bap.* 1578, d. 1647), *Oxford Dictionary of National Biography*, Oxford University Press, 2004 [https://doi.org/10.1093/ref:odnb/11772, accessed 7 August 2018].
93 SHC: LM/COR/7/58.
94 SHC: LM/COR/7/57.
95 SHC: LM/COR/7/51.
96 SHC: LM/COR/7/53.
97 SHC: LM/COR/7/52.
98 SHC: LM/COR/7/70.
99 ESRO: DUN 50/6/52, 54, 62, 65, 81, 84, 86, 97; DUN 51/15.

100 ESRO: DUN 51/15.
101 ESRO: DUN 50/6/62.
102 ESRO: DUN 50/6/104. My assumption here is that the coat was for Walter Roberts senior since the bill is addressed to him.
103 ESRO: DUN 50/6/38. Three of Butler's bills survive dating from 1666, 1669 and 1670 (ESRO: DUN 50/6/15, 50/6/19, 50/6/20). I have been unable to find out where he was based but the fact that his bills do not include the cost of boxes or carriage suggests that he was probably local.
104 ESRO: DUN 37/9, DUN 52/13.
105 *Diary*, pp. 98–99.
106 *Diary*, pp. 100, 102; ESRO: FRE 4816–4838.
107 *Diary*, pp. 120, 159; ESRO: FRE 5301–5315.
108 *Diary*, pp. 165–169.
109 *Diary*, pp. 210, 221.
110 The case, concerning a farm in Wadhurst, had been brought against her by William Benge (see *Diary*, pp. 253–258; TNA: C5/225/47). For her letters sent during this period see ESRO: FRE 5337–5358.
111 *Diary*, p. 222.
112 ESRO: FRE 5241, 5242, 5330, 5318, 5349; *Diary*, pp. 193, 194.
113 ESRO: FRE 5317.
114 ESRO: FRE 5306; 5327.
115 ESRO: FRE 5341.
116 ESRO: FRE 5344.
117 This is a point made by Jane Whittle and Elizabeth Griffiths in relation to the Le Strange household, where Alice Le Strange went to London much less often than her husband, Hamon (Whittle and Griffiths, *Consumption and Gender*, pp. 55–64). See also Bridget Clarke, 'Clothing the Family of an MP in the 1690s: An Analysis of the Day Book of Edward Clarke of Chipley, Somerset', *Costume* 43 (2009), p. 41, for Mary Clarke's dependence on her husband to shop for her in London.

Chapter 5

1 Peacham, *Complete Gentleman*, pp. 220, 221.
2 Ibid., pp. 9, 10.
3 Ibid., p. 12.
4 'Journal', p. 181; Hunter *et al*, *A Radical's Books*, p. 182.
5 Stobart, 'Who were the Urban Gentry?', pp. 89–91; Henry French, '"Ingenious and Learned Gentlemen": Social Perceptions and Self-Fashioning among Parish Elites in Essex, 1680–1740', *Social History* 25:1 (2000): pp. 44–49.

6   This is in contrast to his father, Samuel Jeake the elder, who is always referred to as 'gentleman' presumably because he was a lawyer.
7   See above pp. 9–15.
8   See above pp. 15–17.
9   ESRO: HIC 1166.
10 John Bulwer, *Anthrometamorphosis: Man Transformed or the Artificial Changeling* (London, 1650): p. 259.
11 Evelyn, *Tyrannus*, p. 25.
12 In a diary entry for 6 April 1661 Pepys records how Mr Townsend told him 'of his mistake the other day to put both his legs through one of his knees of his breeches, and went so all day' (Latham (ed.), *Diary of Samuel Pepys*, p. 126).
13 C. Willett Cunnington and Phillis E. Cunnington, *Handbook of English Costume in the Seventeenth-Century* (London: Faber and Faber Limited, 1972): pp. 20–24, 26–31; 34–38; 129–133; 145–154; Ribeiro, *Fashion and Fiction*, pp. 202, 224–225; 232.
14 See above p. 56.
15 See for example 'Journal', pp. 14–16.
16 For leather linings see 'Journal', pp. 126, 128; for 'million' fustian see pp. 127, 135.
17 Robert Latham and William Matthews (eds.), *The Diary of Samuel Pepys: A New and Complete Transcription*, vol. 7 (London: Bell, 1972): p. 315 (8 October 1666).
18 David Kuchta, *The Three-Piece Suit and Modern Masculinity, England 1550–1850* (California: University of California Press, 2002): pp. 81–82. For a discussion of the origins of the 'three-piece suit' (and a critique of Kuchta's analysis of its relationship to changing ideals of 'masculinity') see Ribeiro, *Fashion and Fiction*, pp. 236–238. See also Hayward, '"We Have Better Materials for Clothes, They, Better Taylors"', pp. 64–66, for a discussion of the new-style suit and its relation to French fashion.
19 Latham and Matthews (eds.), *Diary of Samuel Pepys*, vol. 7, p. 353.
20 Anon., *England's Vanity*, pp. 124–125.
21 Kuchta, *The Three-Piece Suit*, p. 87. See illustration of the new-style suit drawn by the earl of Sandwich in 1666, reproduced in Kuchta, p. 83, also the portrait of Sir Edward Turnour, 1672, reproduced in Ribeiro, *Fashion and Fiction*, p. 233 (and detail p. 235).
22 Cunnington and Cunnington, *Handbook*, pp. 136, 147.
23 Thomas Hall, *The Loathsomeness of Long Hair* (London, 1654), pp. 15, 22, 23.
24 Latham (ed.), *Diary of Samuel Pepys*, p. 317.
25 Lynne M. Festa, 'Personal Effects: Wigs and Possessive Individualism in the Long Eighteenth Century', *Eighteenth-Century Life* 29:2 (2005): p. 59.
26 Ribeiro, *Fashion and Fiction*, p. 239.
27 Cunnington and Cunnington, *Handbook*, pp. 129–154; 152–154.
28 Ribeiro, *Fashion and Fiction*, pp. 306–307.
29 Cunnington and Cunnington, *Handbook*, pp. 147–148.

30 Edmund Gosse (ed.), *Restoration Plays* (London: Dent, 1932): p. 474.
31 Smith, *Consumption and the Making of Respectability*, p. 35.
32 Ewart Oakeshott, *European Weapons and Armour from the Renaissance to the Industrial Revolution* (Woodbridge: Boydell & Brewer, 2012), p. 236. See Pepys's account of a Captain Oakeshott walking through Westminster in January 1660 'whose sword got hold of many people in walking' (Latham (ed.), *Diary of Samuel Pepys*, p. 5).
33 Latham (ed.), *Diary of Samuel Pepys*, p. 1015.
34 Barbon, *Discourse of Trade*, p. 65; see above p. 38.
35 See above p. 79.
36 Crowne, *The Country Wit*, p. 4.
37 Anon., *Character of the Beaux*, p. 23.
38 Shadwell, *Epsom Wells*, pp. 54–55.
39 Crowne, *The Country Wit*, pp. 4, 72.
40 *The Spectator*, no. 129, 28 July 1711.
41 See Lee Clatworthy, 'The Quintessential Englishman? Henry Temple's Town and Country Dress, *Costume* 43 (2009), pp. 55–65, for a discussion of the 'town' and 'country' clothing of Henry Temple, first Viscount Palmerston (1676–1757).
42 British School (Temple Newsam House, Leeds Museums and Galleries).
43 In addition to Peacham's *Complete Gentleman* Moore also owned a copy of Edward Waterhouse's *The Gentleman's Monitor* (London, 1665), a study of the rise and fall of great families addressed to the 'nobles and gentry of England'.
44 On 19 October 1676 Moore married his two household servants, Henry Plaw and Mary Holden, but noted with disgust that 'the whore' had given birth to a daughter a mere fifteen weeks and five days later ('Journal', p. 353).
45 'Journal', pp. 124, 125, 132.
46 [http://www.anglican.net/doctrines/1604-canon-law/ (accessed 26 August 2013)]. The relevant canons are 58 and 74.
47 'Journal', pp. 121, 122, 124, 127, 128, 130, 131, 133.
48 'Journal', pp. 125, 126, 128, 130, 144, 145.
49 'Journal', pp. 130, 131, 134, 136, 149.
50 'Journal', pp. 127, 128, 130, 134, 154–156.
51 [http://www.anglican.net/doctrines/1604-canon-law/ (accessed 26 August 2013)], canon 74.
52 Valerie Cumming, C. W. Cunnington and P. E. Cunnington, *The Dictionary of Fashion History* (Oxford: Berg, 2010): p. 158.
53 Anon., *Coma Berenices*, pp. 8–10.
54 'Journal', pp. 123, 132, 147.
55 'Journal', pp. 125, 147.

56 'Journal', pp. 123, 133. In 1669 the nightgown was made up by local tailor, Mr Hull, who had accompanied Moore to London; in 1676 the nightgown was made up by Courtney.
57 Ribeiro, *Fashion and Fiction*, pp. 281–282.
58 'Journal', pp. 14, 124–125, 128.
59 'Journal', pp. 119, 124.
60 'Journal', p. 130.
61 'Journal', pp. 126, 127, 128.
62 'Journal', p. 133.
63 'Journal', p. 151.
64 'Journal', pp. 268, 269.
65 'Summer' shoes were bought in late winter or early spring; 'winter' shoes were bought in the autumn or early winter ('Journal', pp. 268, 269).
66 'Journal', pp. 269–273.
67 'Journal', p. 270.
68 'Journal', pp. 269–273.
69 'Journal', p. 272.
70 'Journal', p. 272.
71 'Journal', p. 273. In June and September 1678 the cost of a pair of Stone's shoes had fallen again to 4s (p. 273). A 'dicker' is a package of ten hides or skins.
72 Hall, *Loathsomeness*, p. 2.
73 Anon., *Coma Berenices*, pp. 8–9.
74 'Journal', p. 128.
75 ESRO: DUN 50/6/52, 54, 62, 65, 81, 84, 86, 97, 104; DUN 51/15.
76 From 1682 these included the cost of keeping one male servant (see ESRO: DUN 50/6/77-80); by the first half of 1684 May had two male servants (ESRO: DUN 50/6/99).
77 ESRO: DUN 50/6/99.
78 ESRO: DUN 50/6/62.
79 ESRO: DUN 50/6/84. The top part of this bill with its date is missing. Heath received payment on 28 April 1682. *Drap de Berry* was produced in the French town of Berry.
80 ESRO: FRE 5057.
81 ESRO: DUN 50/6/86. The top part of this bill with its date is missing. Heath received payment on 20 June 1682. For Moses Sicklemore's will of 1695 see TNA: PROB 11/424/331.
82 ESRO: DUN 50/6/52. The bill does not say who the suit was made for and it is my assumption that it was for Walter senior. The total cost of the taffeta was 19s suggesting that only a small amount was used.
83 ESRO: DUN 51/15, DUN 50/6/62.

84 The bill is dated 27 September 1677 (ESRO: DUN 50/6/54). For the indenture see ESRO: DUN 52/13.
85 ESRO: DUN 50/6/104.
86 For a discussion of mourning clothing see Vincent, *Dressing the Elite*, pp. 61–71.
87 ESRO: DUN 50/6/97. There is no record of whose funerals the Roberts men were attending.
88 ESRO: DUN 50/6/38.
89 ESRO: DUN 50/6/129, 50/7/22, 50/7/26. The first two of these are damaged.
90 ESRO: DUN 50/6/129. This bill is damaged so the date is missing but it preceded the subsequent bill of April 1694. The 'silver cuffs' were probably some kind of braid trim. They may have been designed to turn back over the coat-sleeve cuffs.
91 ESRO: DUN 50/7/26.
92 ESRO: DUN 50/6/81.
93 ESRO: DUN 37/9.
94 The discussion of Samuel Jeake's clothes draws on my previously published article, '"They Tell Me They Were in Fashion Last Year": Samuel and Elizabeth Jeake and Clothing Fashions in Late Seventeenth-Century London and Rye', *Costume* 50:1 (2016): pp. 20–41. Permission to reuse some of the content of this article here and elsewhere in this book has been given by Edinburgh University Press.
95 *Diary*, pp. 117–118. Jeake had the smallpox when he was fourteen (*Diary*, p. 89).
96 RCM: RYEYT N39.56.2.
97 *Diary*, pp. 89–90. In 1676 Jeake paid 3s for a pair of 'convex' spectacles (RCM: RYEYT N39.40).
98 RCM: RYEYT N39.40.
99 Buskins are calf-high or knee-high leather boots. Jeake's 'drawers' are likely to have been worn under his breeches, like the leather 'loynings' worn by Giles Moore. A 'frock' is a loose protective over-garment usually worn by working men.
100 Graham Mayhew, *Tudor Rye* (Hove: Delta Press, 1987): p. 14.
101 The buttons are described as 'glass buttons in silver ouches'. 'Colbertine' lace is a kind of open lace with a square ground, named after Louis XIV's Minister of Finance, Jean-Baptiste Colbert.
102 *Diary*, pp. 36–37, 149–154.
103 *Diary*, pp. 150, 155.
104 Wightman married Jeake's cousin, Anne Key, in 1674 (RCM: RYEYT N39.6.1); they lived 'over against the Salutation Tavern' in Lombard Street in the parish of St Nicholas Acon (ESRO: FRE 5240). He was a member of the Clockmakers' Company, gaining his freedom in 1671. See Brian Loomes, *Clockmakers of Britain, 1286–1700* (Ashbourne: Mayfield Books, 2014), p. 523.
105 ESRO: FRE 4992.

106 His claim was contested by Robert Hooke who said that he had come up with the idea first. The dispute between the two men became a cause célèbre in scientific circles over the next few years. The fact that the balance spring was so successful in improving timekeeping meant that it was rapidly incorporated into watch design. For a discussion of the Hooke/Huygens controversy see Lisa Jardine, *The Curious Life of Robert Hooke: The Man who Measured London* (New York: Harper Perennial, 2004), pp. 197–206. I would like to thank Sir George White, Bt, Consultant Keeper of the Clockmakers' Museum, for his advice on Jeake's watch and Laura Turner, Curator of Horological Collections at the British Museum, for advice on James Wightman.
107 ESRO: FRE 5003.
108 The date is suggested by the sequence of other letters from Wightman to Jeake between April and June 1681 (see ESRO: FRE 5002, 5003, 5009, 5011, 5014, 5017).
109 ESRO: FRE 5047.
110 ESRO: FRE 5047.
111 The bill Wightman sent Jeake recorded '8 dozen of buttons at 3s 6d per dozen' and '4 dozen and ½ of breast buttons' (ESRO: FRE 5011).
112 David Corner, 'The Tyranny of Fashion: The Case of the Felt-Hatting Trade in the Late Seventeenth and Eighteenth centuries', *Textile History* 22:2 (1991): pp. 153–178.
113 ESRO: FRE 5011.
114 ESRO: FRE 5011.
115 ESRO: FRE 5014.
116 Jeake sold a 'silver-hilted rapier' – presumably the one he bought in 1676 – in 1685 for £1 12s (ESRO: RYE 145/11).
117 RCM: RYEYT N39.40; *Diary*, p. 156. The fall also squashed his copper tobacco box flat.
118 Hunter *et al* (eds.), *A Radical's Books*, pp. 116, 182.
119 ESRO: RYE 145/11.
120 ESRO: HIC 1166, p. 113.
121 ESRO: HIC 1166, p. 15. Calamanco is a type of woollen cloth.
122 ESRO: HIC 1166, p. 47. Bays is a coarse woollen cloth with a long nap.
123 'Journal', p. 133.
124 ESRO: HIC 1166, pp. 31, 44, 66, 137.
125 ESRO: HIC 1166, pp. 13, 96. It is not clear whether the stag's skin was to line the breeches or to make the breeches out of.
126 ESRO: HIC 1166, p. 53. Stapley paid Matthew an additional 10s for the cane so the total cost was £1.
127 ESRO: HIC 1166, pp. 78, 139.
128 ESRO: HIC 1166, pp. 134, 175, 176.

129 ESRO: HIC 1166, p. 9. I would like to thank Laura Turner, Curator of Horological Collections at the British Museum, for advice on Benjamin Hill's watches.
130 ESRO: HIC 1166, pp. 44, 122, 175.
131 ESRO: HIC 1166, p. 29.
132 ESRO: HIC 1166, p. 135. It is not clear whether these were the same wigs purchased in 1697; there is no other reference to the purchase of a wig in the intervening period.
133 As Henry French has noted, whilst the ideal of gentility was a widely recognised status stereotype it was constantly being contested and in reality multiple 'gentilities' existed (French, *Middling Sort of People*, p. 205).

Chapter 6

1 Braithwaite, *The English Gentlewoman*, pp. 6, 9.
2 Francis Mayhew is mentioned in Giles Moore's will but his status is not given (TNA: PROB 11/361/89). Moore left Mayhew's three other children, Mary, Martin and Susan, substantial cash bequests (£40, £50 and £30 respectively). He also paid £5 to bind Martin out as an apprentice in 1677 ('Journal', p. 345), suggesting perhaps that his parents were unable to raise this sum.
3 For a discussion of Judith's background and her marriage to William Morley see above pp. 7–9.
4 Widows might continue to wear mourning for three or four years after their husbands' deaths. See Phillis Cunnington and Catherine Lucas, *Costume for Births, Marriages and Deaths* (London: Adam & Charles Black, 1972): p. 264.
5 Cumming *et al*, *Dictionary*, p. 24. 'Bodies' were made in two sections, tied at the sides and fastening down the front or back.
6 Latham and Matthews (eds.), *Diary of Samuel Pepys*, vol. 4, p. 140; Latham (ed.), *Diary of Samuel Pepys*, p. 907. Martha Mayhew does not appear to have been provided with any drawers during the years she lived with her uncle. Overseers of the poor sometimes provided drawers for their male paupers but not for their female paupers (see for example the parish of Ticehurst, ESRO PAR 492/31/1/2 and PAR 492/31/1/21). See Ribeiro, *Dress and Morality*, pp. 120–121, for a discussion of the controversies surrounding women's drawers in the early nineteenth century.
7 Bulwer, *Anthrometamorphosis*, pp. 193–194.
8 Hall, *Loathsomeness of Long Hair*, pp. 107–110.
9 Cunnington and Cunnington, *Handbook,* pp. 80–97; Ribeiro, *Fashion and Fiction*, pp. 203–207, 244–246.
10 Valerie Cumming, *A Visual History of Costume: The Seventeenth Century* (London: B. T. Batsford, 1984): pp. 88, 91, 92, 94, 95; Ribeiro, *Fashion and Fiction*, pp. 244–245.

11 Holme, *Academy of Armory*, Book III, Ch. III, p. 94.
12 Cumming *et al*, *Dictionary*, p. 141; Cunnington and Cunnington, *Handbook*, p. 92; Ribeiro, *Fashion and Fiction*, pp. 208–209; 246; Latham (ed.), *Diary of Samuel Pepys*, p. 993.
13 Holme, *Academy of Armory*, Book III, Ch. III, p. 95.
14 Cumming *et al*, *Dictionary*, p. 127; Ribeiro, *Fashion and Fiction*, pp. 246–248, 309; Cunnington and Cunnington, *Handbook*, pp. 176–177; Cumming, *Visual History of Costume*, p. 122.
15 Cunnington and Cunnington, *Handbook*, pp. 101–105, 177; Holme records that the whisk was 'called of most a gorget or a falling whisk because it falls about the shoulders' (*Academy of Armory*, Book III, Ch. II, p. 17). However, Cunnington and Cunnington point out that the 'gorget' and the 'whisk' could be worn together, suggesting that they were not identical (see p. 177). Valerie Cumming has suggested that the gorget may have been stiffer and flatter than the whisk (pers. comm. 16 June 2018).
16 Cunnington and Cunnington, *Handbook*, pp. 177–178; see above p. 104.
17 Ribeiro, *Fashion and Fiction*, p. 249; Cunnington and Cunnington, *Handbook*, pp. 112–117.
18 'Top knot' described the highest ribbon bow on a woman's head but became a generic term for this type of textile-based headdress; Angela McShane and Clare Backhouse, 'Top Knots and Lower Sorts: Print and Promiscuous Consumption in the 1690s' *in* Michael Hunter (ed.), *Printed Images in Early Modern Britain: Essays in Interpretation* (Farnham: Routledge, 2010): pp. 337–357; see also Backhouse, *Fashion and Popular Print*, pp. 179–185.
19 'Advice to the Maidens of London to Forsake their Fantastical Top Knots' (MC: Pepys IV 365, 1685–1688); 'The Farmer's Wife's Complaint against the Ladies' Commodes and Top Knots' (MC: Pepys V 412, *c*. 1687–1691).
20 There is a copy of the ballad (undated) in the collection of the Folger Shakespeare Library, New York. 'Cat' was slang for a prostitute; owls were considered foolish; apes vain, undiscriminating and licentious [http://data.fitzmuseum.cam.ac.uk/id/object/72012 (accessed 24 July 2018)].
21 For a longer discussion of this, see Tankard '"They Tell Me They Were in Fashion Last Year"', p. 36; 'jessamy' (or 'jasmine') can refer to a pale yellow colour or to a jasmine scent, or perhaps to both.
22 ESRO: FRE 4892.
23 ESRO: FRE 5240.
24 ESRO: FRE 4948. See also FRE 4945.
25 See Ribeiro, *Fashion and Fiction*, pp. 172, 209, 332 and *idem*, *Facing Beauty: Painted Women and Cosmetic Art* (New Haven and London: Yale University Press, 2011): pp. 118–126.

26 Ribeiro, *Facing Beauty*, p. 122. Cochineal is made from the dried and ground bodies of the cochineal insect, *coccus cacti*.
27 SHC: LM/COR/7/53.
28 Plat, *Delights for Ladies* (1635 edition, unpaginated). Sublimate of mercury or mercuric chloride is a toxic crystalline powder ('sublimate, n.' *OED Online*. Oxford University Press, March 2017. Web. 11 May 2017).
29 Mary Evelyn [attributed], *Mundus Muliebris, or the Ladies Dressing Room Unlocked* (London, 1690): p. 19.
30 Hannah Woolley [sometimes spelt 'Wolley'], *The Gentlewoman's Companion* (London, 1673), p. 59. *The Gentlewoman's Companion* is an unauthorised work based on Woolley's earlier books (J. Considine, 'Wolley, Hannah (*b.*1622?, *d.* in or after 1674)', *Oxford Dictionary of National Biography*, Oxford University Press, 2004 [http://www.oxforddnb.com/view/article/29957 (accessed 10 May 2017)].
31 Plat, *Delights for Ladies* (1635 edition, unpaginated).
32 Ribeiro, *Facing Beauty*, pp. 124–125.
33 Ribeiro, *Fashion and Fiction*, p. 249; *Facing Beauty*, pp. 98, 124.
34 Plat, *Delights for Ladies* (1635 edition, unpaginated).
35 Evelyn [attributed], *Mundus Muliebris*, pp. 5, 9.
36 Evelyn [attributed], *Mundus Muliebris*, p. 11.
37 SHC: LM/COR/7/53.
38 Thomas Tuke, *A Discourse against Painting and Tincturing of Women* (London, 1616): p. 30.
39 Thomas Hall, *Against Painting, Spots, Naked Backs, Breast, Arms etc* (London, 1654): p. 100 (this is an appendix to Hall's *Loathsomeness of Long Hair*).
40 Ribeiro, *Facing Beauty*, pp. 107–108.
41 John Gauden (attributed), *Several Letters between two Ladies Wherein the Lawfulness and Unlawfulness of Artificial Beauty in Point of Conscience are Nicely Debated* (London, 1701): p. 118.
42 Anon., *The Law's Resolutions of Women's Rights: Or the Law's Provision for Women* (London, 1632): pp. 129, 130.
43 Amy L. Erickson, *Women and Property in Early Modern England* (London: Routledge, 1995): pp. 24–26, 103–104; J. H. Baker, *An Introduction to English Legal History* (London: Butterworths, 1990): pp. 551–557. Marriage settlements were governed by equity laws which means that disputes were heard in the Court of Chancery.
44 William Gouge, *Of Domestical Duties* (London, 1622): p. 291.
45 Gouge, *Domestical Duties*, p. 281. See Amanda Flather, *Gender and Space in Early Modern England* (Woodbridge: The Boydell Press, 2007), p. 28, for further discussion of this point.
46 See above p. 8.

47 Latham (ed.), *Diary of Samuel Pepys*, p. 696.
48 Latham (ed.), *Diary of Samuel Pepys*, p. 977.
49 In October 1663 Pepys spent £55 on his own clothes and £12 on his wife's clothes (Latham (ed), *Diary of Samuel Pepys*, p. 316).
50 Latham (ed), *Diary of Samuel Pepys*, p. 950.
51 *The Spectator*, no. 129, 28 July 1711.
52 Gosse (ed.), *Restoration Plays*, p. 453.
53 *The Spectator*, no. 129, 28 July 1711.
54 Ribeiro, *Fashion and Fiction*, pp. 329–330; Erin Mackie, *Market à la Mode: Fashion, Commodity and Gender in The Tatler and The Spectator* (Baltimore and London: Johns Hopkins University Press, 1997): pp. 104–143; *The Spectator*, no. 127, 26 July 1711.
55 Anon., *Grand Concern*, p. 30.
56 SHC: LM/1087/6/431, 436.
57 SHC: LM/COR/7/57, 58, 61.
58 SHC: LM/COR/7/52.
59 SHC: LM/COR/7/61.
60 Cunnington and Cunnington, *Handbook*, pp. 94, 96–97.
61 SHC: LM/COR/7/52.
62 SHC: LM/1087/6/436.
63 SHC: LM/1087/6/431.
64 Cunnington and Cunnington, *Handbook*, p. 111.
65 SHC: LM/COR/7/78. On this occasion he also bought her orris powder (dried and ground iris root used on its own as a perfume or as an ingredient in perfumed powders as well as in flavoured syrups) and two pairs of gloves.
66 See above p. 28.
67 SHC: LM/COR/7/69.
68 SHC: LM/COR/7/60.
69 SHC: LM/COR/7/59.
70 SHC: LM/COR/7/57.
71 Cunnington and Cunnington, *Handbook*, p. 117.
72 SHC: LM/COR/7/56. Gresham makes the same point again in a letter dated 7 February 1641 (SHC: LM/COR/7/70).
73 SHC: LM/COR/7/78.
74 See above pp. 7–8.
75 See for example SHC: LM/COR/7/68.
76 SHC: LM/COR/7/61.
77 SHC: LM/COR/7/58. See above p. 90.
78 SHC: LM/COR/7/56.
79 SHC: LM/COR/7/68, 84.
80 'Journal', p. ix.

81 Whittle and Griffiths, *Consumption and Gender*, pp. 28–33.
82 See for example BL: Add MS 33145, f. 63r, 'paid my wife her books at Michaelmas 1633 for the house and made even with her'; 'paid her for her quarterages for herself and children and made even at Michaelmas 1633'.
83 'Journal', pp. 127, 151–152, 321, 342.
84 3s in 1656 and 5s in 1661 ('Journal', pp. 313, 322).
85 See above p. 85.
86 See family tree in 'Journal'.
87 'Journal', p. 79.
88 'Journal', pp. 284, 302.
89 'Journal', p. 116; Allestree [attributed], *Ladies Calling*, p. 144. See above p. 29.
90 Allestree [attributed], *Ladies Calling*, p. 150.
91 Ibid., pp. 151–153.
92 Ibid., pp. 154, 155.
93 Ibid., pp. 165–177.
94 Ibid., pp. 177–179.
95 Ibid., pp. 183–209.
96 'Journal', p. 72.
97 Moore notes in his book that he gave Martha 1s 6d in December 1669 'in payment of her spinning' ('Journal', p. 74).
98 'Journal', pp. 73–77.
99 In July 1669 Moore noted that he had spent the sum of 3s 9d on a quarter of an ounce of fine thread, coarse thread, seven and a half yards of French tape, 'rowle' and wire, three yards of blue inkle, a pair of scissors, needles and paper and a lace pattern. In September he spent another 2s on paper and needles, thread, gimp and tape. In December 1672 Moore noted that he had given Martha 2s to buy yarn so that she could knit herself a pair of stockings ('Journal', pp. 74, 77, 79).
100 'Journal', pp. 76–77.
101 'Journal', p. 74.
102 'Journal', p. 75.
103 'Journal', p. 79.
104 'Journal', pp. 78, 284, 291.
105 'Journal', pp. 70–71. There is no information about what he bought.
106 'Journal', pp. 70–71. Paragon is a type of camlet. Penistone is a coarse woollen cloth produced in Yorkshire.
107 'Journal', p. 71.
108 'Journal', pp. 72–73.
109 Like Moore's, her stockings were knitted by Widow Vinall ('Journal', p. 71); for blue linen aprons see 'Journal', pp. 72, 74, 75, 79; Moore records the purchase of one pair of pattens in September 1669 ('Journal', p. 74).

110 This change in clothing as girls reached adolescence is also noted by Spufford and Mee (*Clothing of the Common Sort*, pp. 176–177).
111 'Journal', pp. 73, 284.
112 Ribeiro, *Fashion and Fiction*, pp. 262–264.
113 'Journal', pp. 75–77. Druggett is fine woollen or woollen and silk mix cloth.
114 'Journal', p. 78.
115 'Journal', p. 80. There are no details about its appearance.
116 It is, however, likely that Martha's coifs were being made for her at home. The purchase of two 'forehead cloths' in 1669 ('Journal', p. 73) – triangular-shaped linen bands to which the coif was pinned – indicates that she was still wearing them.
117 'Journal', pp. 72, 78. Both hoods were bought at Lindfield Fair.
118 In May 1671 Martha bought a cambric 'neck handkerchief' at Lindfield Fair ('Journal', p. 77); for whisks see 'Journal', pp. 72, 78.
119 ESRO PAR 465/6/2. The amount the Rotherfield overseers spent on girls' shoes varied from 1s 8d to 2s 8d.
120 'Journal', pp. 71, 75. The white shoes cost 2s 6d, the same price as several of Martha's other pairs.
121 John Citizen was ordained in 1661, becoming rector of Streat in 1663. The average age at ordination was 23 years which would mean that he was 35 in 1673. He died in 1721. ('John Citizen (CCEd Person ID 62855)', *The Clergy of the Church of England Database 1540–1835* [http://www.theclergydatabase.org.uk (accessed 9 August 2016)].
122 'Journal', p. 80.
123 *Diary*, p. 162.
124 *Diary*, pp. 39, 168, 194, 205–206.
125 ESRO: FRE 5340, 5343, 5350.
126 See above p. 13.
127 This section draws on my previously published article, '"They Tell Me They Were in Fashion Last Year"'.
128 Cunnington and Cunnington, *Handbook*, pp. 172–177.
129 Cunnington and Cunnington, *Handbook*, pp. 177, 178, 181–185.
130 ESRO: FRE 5329.
131 It is not clear what style of mantua Elizabeth was having made, but possibly a loose wrap-around robe, like that worn by fashion doll 'Lady Clapham'.
132 There is no record of where the silk was being painted, possibly in Spitalfields which by the 1690s was already a well-established silk-production district (see Earle, *Making of the English Middle Class*, pp. 19–20).
133 Anterine is a type of worsted with a silk warp and a wool weft.
134 ESRO: FRE 5330.
135 ESRO: FRE 5335.

136 ESRO: FRE 5340.
137 TNA: PROB 11/678/209. The ring had been her grandmother's.
138 For Elizabeth's letters sent during this period see ESRO: FRE 5337–5358.
139 ESRO: FRE 5356.
140 ESRO: FRE 5348.
141 ESRO: FRE 5349. According to *The Dictionary of Fashion History* a dust gown is an 'upper garment worn by women, commonly called a safeguard'; in other words, a garment used to protect underclothing from dirt (Cumming *et al.*, p. 72). However, Elizabeth's dust gown was clearly quite fine, made from silk and decorated with ribbons suggesting that it may have been worn as an informal gown like a nightgown.
142 ESRO: FRE 5340.
143 ESRO: FRE 5341.
144 ESRO: FRE 5430.
145 Jeake owned a copy of the 1617 edition (Hunter *et al.* (eds.), *A Radical's Books*, p. 182).
146 Plat, *Delights for Ladies* (1635 edition, unpaginated); ESRO: FRE 5240.
147 Hall, *Loathsomeness of Long Hair*, p. 102; Hunter *et al* .(eds.), *A Radical's Books*, p. 116.

Chapter 7

1 Hindle, *On the Parish*, p.4. Note that Tom Arkell gives a higher figure of households enduring material hardship in the later seventeenth century of between 35 per cent and 50 per cent (Tom Arkell, 'The Incidence of Poverty in England in the Later 17th Century', *Social History* 12 (1987): pp. 23–47).
2 See Craig Muldrew, *Food, Energy and the Creation of Industriousness: Work and Material Culture in Agrarian England, 1550–1780* (Cambridge: Cambridge University Press, 2011), pp. 19–24, for a discussion of the relationship between the occupational designation 'labourer' and poverty.
3 This is my own assessment based on my work on a range of documentary sources but in particular the records of the Sussex courts of quarter sessions. However, it is corroborated by Alexandra Shepard's analysis of 'statements of worth' in church court depositions which shows that nearly 70 per cent of husbandmen appearing in the church courts of the diocese of Chichester stated they lived by their labour compared to 50 per cent in the diocese of Salisbury and over 30 per cent in the diocese of Canterbury. See Alexandra Shepard, 'Poverty, Labour and the Language of Social Description in Early Modern England', *Past and Present* 201 (2008): pp. 64–65 and *idem*, *Accounting for Oneself: Worth, Status and the Social Order in Early Modern England* (Oxford: Oxford University Press, 2015): pp. 162–163.

4   In comparative terms, those encompassed within the definition of the 'poorer' sort in this chapter are covered by Spufford and Mee in *The Clothing of the Common Sort* in their Chapter 3 ('Clothing the Poorest: Evidence from Poor Relief Records') and Chapter 4 ('Clothing the Families of Labourers, and of Husbandmen and their Peer Groups, Leaving Goods Worth up to £100').
5   For a discussion of the poor's own perception of their social status and material worth see Shepard, 'Poverty, Labour and the Language of Social Description' and *idem*, *Accounting for Oneself*, pp. 114–145.
6   See above pp. 41–45.
7   I have dealt with the subject of the clothing of the rural poor previously in '"A Pair of Grass-Green Woollen Stockings"' and '"I Think Myself Honestly Decked"'.
8   Steve Hindle, 'Civility, Honesty and the Identification of the Deserving Poor in Seventeenth-Century England', *in* Henry French and Jonathan Barry (eds.), *Identity and Agency in England, 1500–1800* (Basingstoke: Palgrave, 2004), pp. 38–59 and *idem*, *On the Parish*, pp. 379–398.
9   A. L. Beier, *Masterless Men: The Vagrancy Problem in England 1560–1640* (London and New York: Methuen, 1985): pp. 3–13.
10 39 Elizabeth I, c.4 (1598) (*Statutes of the Realm* 4:2, 1819)
11 Counterfeit, adj. and n. *OED Online*. Oxford University Press, June 2017, accessed 23 June 2017.
12 Richard Haines, *Provision for the Poor* (London, 1678): p. 5; Peter Laslett, 'Natural and Political Observations on the Population of Late Seventeenth-Century England: Reflections on the Work of Gregory King and John Graunt' *in* Kevin Schurer and Tom Arkell (eds.), *Surveying the People: The Interpretation and the Use of Document Sources for the Study of Population in the Late Seventeenth Century* (Oxford: Leopard's Head Press, 1992): pp. 12–13; Beier, *Masterless Men*, pp. 14–15; David Hitchcock, *Vagrancy in English Culture and Society 1650–1750* (London: Bloomsbury Academic, 2016): pp. 41–42.
13 See Fletcher, *Sussex*, pp. 165–170 for a discussion of vagrancy in Sussex in the first half of the seventeenth century.
14 Beier, *Masterless Men*, p. 15.
15 Beier, *Masterless Men*, pp. 23–25; R. C. Richardson, *Household Servants in Early Modern England* (Manchester: Manchester University Press, 2010): p. 196.
16 R. W. Blencowe, 'Extracts from the Journal and Account Book of Timothy Burrell, Esquire, Barrister-at-Law', *SAC* 3 (1850): p. 133.
17 WSRO: Ep I/33/1611.
18 Redwood (ed.), 'Quarter Sessions Order Book', p. 201.
19 This was based on the earlier rogue taxonomies of John Awdely and Thomas Harman (Awdely, *Fraternity of Vagabonds* (London, 1561), Harman, *Caveat or Warning for Common Cursitors* (London, 1566)). For a brief discussion of rogue

literature see Beier, *Masterless Men*, pp. 7–8, 123–126; for more extended discussion see the essays in Craig Dionne and Steve Mentz (eds.), *Rogues and Early Modern English Culture* (Ann Arbor: University of Michigan Press, 2004) and Hitchcock, *Vagrancy in English Culture and Society*, pp. 55–89.
20 'Gallyslops' or 'gally hose' were full-waisted breeches that narrowed downwards and were shaped to button or tie below the knee (Cunnington and Cunnington, *Handbook*, p. 47).
21 Male beggar.
22 Female beggar and the palliard's pretended wife.
23 Thomas Dekker, *The Bellman of London* (London, 1608): ff. C4r–D1v.
24 Ibid., f. C2v.
25 Thomas Dekker, *Lantern and Candlelight: or the Bellman's Second Night Walk* (London, 1608): ff. G5r-v.
26 Ibid., f. G4v; see David Cressy, 'Trouble with Gypsies in Early Modern England', *The Historical Journal* 59:1 (2016): pp. 45–70.
27 See above p. 67. For other examples see WSRO: QR/W17, f. 19/85, QR/W19, f. 14/80, 14/83, QR/W56, f. 42/57.
28 There were, however, reports of vagrant gangs up to twenty strong congregating at Freshfield forge in Horsted Keynes and Sheffield forge in Fletching in the 1630s (ESRO: QR/E33, f. 2; quoted in Brent, 'Rural Employment and Population in Sussex, (part 2)', p. 46).
29 Beier, *Masterless Men*, p. 144.
30 Alan McGowan, *The Winchester Confessions, 1615–1616: Depositions of Travellers, Gypsies, Fraudsters and Makers of Counterfeit Documents, Including a Vocabulary of the Romany language* (South Chailey: Romany and Traveller Family History Society, 1996). They did, however, speak a distinctive language: Hindes listed over 100 words and phrases which they used amongst themselves. Linguists have identified these as Anglo-Romani, deriving from Hindi (see Cressy, 'Trouble with Gypsies', pp. 66–67).
31 Hunnisett (ed.), *Sussex Coroners' Inquests*, no. 306; for the will of Katherine Aynscombe see TNA: PROB 11/164/274 (1633).
32 WSRO: QR/W92, f. 68.
33 WSRO: EP I/29/47/5. 'Cypress' is a name of several textile fabrics originally imported through Cyprus.
34 For example in 1632, twenty-six-year-old spinster, Elizabeth Cavey of Angmering, told the court that she '[lived] by her labour and in service and is worth nothing but her clothes to her back' (WSRO: EP I/11/15, f. 35v). For a discussion of household servants' relative poverty as revealed by the statements of worth they gave in court see Shepard, *Accounting for Oneself*, p. 131.
35 WSRO: Par 416/37/2. See above pp. 66–67.

36 WSRO: Par 8/31/1 (unpaginated). Mary Jones was buried on 27 May 1681 (WSRO: Parish Register Transcript: Arundel). For a discussion of the provision of garments described as 'mantuas' to female paupers see Spufford and Mee, *Clothing of the Common Sort*, pp. 61–64. In the 1690s the overseers of the parish of Cowfold in Sussex were providing mantuas for some of their pauper girls (see WSRO: Par 59/31/1, ff. 1/48, 1/62).
37 Mary Jones had not been in receipt of a parish pension but she was buried at the parish's expense. She left a four-year-old son, John (WSRO: Par 8/31/1).
38 Hunnisett (ed), *Sussex Coroners' Inquests*, no. 56.
39 Discussed in Chapter Three, pp. 48–49.
40 See above p. 48.
41 For an explanation of 'homemade' see above pp. 48–49; 'cotton' here refers to a type of woollen cloth that has been 'cottoned' – the nap has been raised up and then shorn. For other types of coarse woollen cloth stocked by Sussex mercers see for example probate inventories of Anthony Mutton, 1632 (WSRO: EP I/29/163/6) and Walter Deane, 1661 (WSRO: EP I/29/160/50). See also Spufford and Mee, *Clothing of the Common Sort*, pp. 72–73, 104–108 for a discussion of the types of woollen cloth worn by those in their lowest charge band (goods worth up to £100).
42 For fustian garments see for example wills of Edward Fist of Slinfold, 1600 (WSRO: STC I/15/93r) and William Hogis of Lodsworth, 1600 (WSRO: STC I/15/135v).
43 For leather garments see for example will of William Hogis of Lodsworth, 1600 (WSRO: STC I/15/135v) and Robert Hillier of Mid Lavant, 1602 (WSRO: STC I/15/147v). See above p. 71 for the shop stock of Horsham glover, Henry Lintott, which included nine pairs of leather breeches.
44 There are innumerable references to red petticoats in seventeenth-century wills but see for example wills of Elizabeth Owlder of Findon, 1604 (WSRO: STC I/15/45r) and Joanne Hayne of Washington, 1675 (WSRO: STC I/26/102r-v); for 'grass-green' stockings see WSRO: QR/W64, f. 79.
45 Spufford, *Great Reclothing*, p. 99.
46 WSRO: QR/W92, f. 66.
47 For silver pins see the wills of Joanne Ede of Wisborough Green, 1608 (WSRO: STC I/15/278r-v) and Alice Hill of Thakeham, 1637 (WSRO: STC I/19/83v-84r).
48 WSRO: QR/W8, ff. 6/52, 6/53. For a limited discussion of the colours and trimmings of clothes worn by those in their lowest charge band (goods worth up to £100) see Spufford and Mee, *Clothing of the Common Sort*, pp. 108–114.
49 See above p. 68.
50 WSRO: STC I/15/238r-v.
51 For 'best' and 'worst' red petticoats see wills of Thomasine Varnden of Woodmancote, 1603 (WSRO: STC I/15/167r) and Joanne Gratwick of West Angmering, 1609 (WSRO: STC I/15/301r).

52 Dominique Cardon, *Natural Dyes: Sources, Tradition, Technology and Science* (London: Archetype Publications, 2007): pp. 107–118; 169–176; 345–347.
53 ESRO: QR/E168, ff. 63, 66. In her defence Burgess claimed that the petticoat had been given to her by her mother 'thirteen years since' (see above p. 68).
54 WSRO: QR/W33, f. 30/61.
55 WSRO: QR/W16, f. 18/44.
56 WSRO: QR/W34, f. 35/65.
57 WSRO: QR/W2, f. 2/34.
58 ESRO: QR/E29, ff, 65–66.
59 WSRO: QR/W56, ff. 42/57. See above p. 1.
60 Fletcher, *Sussex*, pp. 156–159. See Hindle, *On the Parish*, pp. 227–299, for an extended analysis of the spread of poor relief across five counties.
61 See above p. 157, citing Hindle, *On the Parish*, p. 4.
62 This is a rough figure derived from the number of communicants (400) included for Arundel in the Compton Census of 1676, inflated by 40 per cent to take account of those under sixteen. See J. H. Cooper, 'A Religious Census of Sussex in 1676', *SAC* 45 (1902), p. 146, for the census figures and Tom Arkell, 'A Method for Estimating Population Totals for the Compton Census Returns' *in* Schurer and Arkell (eds.), *Surveying the People*, pp. 97–116.
63 WSRO: Par 8/31/1. The volume is unpaginated. Some entries are clearly dated; others are only dated by the year of accounting. Some of those receiving weekly pensions had dependents, which means the total number was higher.
64 A. P. Baggs and H. M. Warne, 'Arundel', *in* T. P. Hudson (ed), *A History of the County of Sussex: Volume 5 Part 1, Arundel Rape: South-Western Part, Including Arundel* (Oxford: Oxford University Press, 1997): pp. 10–101. *British History Online* [http://www.british-history.ac.uk/vch/sussex/vol5/pt1/pp10-101 (accessed 13 June 2017)]; The diocesan survey of 1724 records that at that time there were 'many' benefactions to the poor, 'as appears by an old table (now scarcely legible) hanging up in the church, from the poor book and other information amounting to £19 18s 9d but the present parish officers say they receive or can make no more than £19' (Ford (ed.), 'Chichester Diocesan Surveys', p. 59). Some of these are listed in the vestry minute book (WSRO: Par 8/12/2).
65 His father, John Wareham, had died in 1676. His mother, Elizabeth, died in February 1679 and was buried at the parish's expense (WSRO: Parish Register Transcripts: Arundel; Par 8/31/1). In December 1679 'Goody Cock' was being paid 2s a week for Luke's board.
66 The other boy was 'Randall', probably Thomas Randall, the son of Thomas and Elizabeth Randall, who was born in 1667 (WSRO: Parish Register Transcripts: Arundel).
67 WSRO: Par 8/31/1.
68 WSRO: Par 8/31/1.

69 WSRO: Par 8/31/1. This was probably the first half of the apprenticeship fee, which typically cost the overseers between £6 and £7.
70 WSRO: Par 8/31/1. He was buried on 2 June 1680 (WSRO: Parish Register Transcripts: Arundel).
71 Thomas was baptised on 16 July 1672 and Joan on 12 June 1678 (WSRO: Parish Register Transcripts: Arundel). Joan is named Ann in the parish register but is referred to as Joan in the overseers' accounts.
72 The total amount lent to him over this period was £1 8s 6d.
73 There is no record of his burial in the parish register.
74 My assumption is that these items were for the child rather than the mother.
75 There is no record of her burial in the parish register.
76 WSRO: Par 8/31/1.
77 In some months he received a higher pension of 5s or 6s.
78 The suit was made of kersey.
79 His coat and breeches were made of kersey, his waistcoat was made of cotton (here probably meaning a woollen cloth).
80 ESRO: PAR 492/31/1/2 (unpaginated).
81 Straightforward comparisons are obviously difficult and account needs to be taken of the fact that Gynt was receiving his parish pension in the early to mid-1660s whilst Selden was receiving his in 1681. Nevertheless, Arundel does appear to have been more generous than Ticehurst in its cash pensions but less generous in its clothing provision.
82 Peter D. Jones, "'I Cannot Keep My Place Without Being Decent": Pauper Letters, Parish Clothing and Pragmatism in the South of England, 1750–1830', *Rural History* 20:1 (2009): 31–49.
83 In 1664 the Lindfield overseers sold a pair of bodies owned by one of their recently deceased paupers for 3s 2d (WSRO: Par 416/37/2/2). The price of bodices varied considerably: in 1672 Giles Moore spent 4s 6d on a new bodice for Martha, then aged about sixteen or seventeen ('Journal', p. 78); in 1693 the overseers for the parish of Worth paid 3s for a bodice for Widow Rigg (WSRO: Par 516/31/1).
84 Jones, "'I Cannot Keep My Place Without Being Decent"', pp. 38–45. See also *idem* 'Clothing the Poor in Early-Nineteenth-Century England', *Textile History* 37:1 (2006): pp. 17–37.
85 He was paid 6s in both February and March so may still have been unable to work due to illness (ESRO: PAR 492/31/1/2).
86 In 1664 the overseers spent 6d on a 'warrant for poor people to give account of their work' (ESRO: PAR 492/31/1/2).
87 Jones, 'Clothing the Poor', pp. 27–29; *idem*, "'I Cannot Keep My Place Without Being Decent"', p. 39.
88 WSRO: Par 59/31/1, f. 1/9.

89 Jonathan Mote, the son of Stephen and Anne Mote, was baptised on 18 April 1636. His mother was buried on 19 February 1642; his younger brother, Thomas, was buried on 27 July 1642 (WSRO: Parish Register Transcript: Cowfold).
90 Hindle, *On the Parish*, pp. 209–211.
91 Styles, *Dress of the People*, p. 269.
92 'Cotton' here probably refers to a type of woollen cloth.
93 For a discussion of the provision of shoes to the parish poor see Spufford and Mee, *Clothing of the Common Sort*, pp. 56–58.
94 ESRO: PAR 465/6/1; PAR 492/31/1/2.
95 'Journal', 71–80; pp. 268–273. See above pp. 112–113, 149.
96 There are odd references to second-hand clothes in the Rotherfield overseers accounts, for example in 1659 they spent 8d 'for making of Thomas Martin a coat of his father's old coat' and in 1664 they spent 1s on 'an old pair of shoes for French's wife', but these are exceptions (ESRO: PAR 465/6/1).
97 Basil Lubbock (ed.), *Barlow's Journal of his Life at Sea in King's Ships, East and West Indiamen and Other Merchantmen from 1659 to 1703* (London: Hurst and Blackett, 1934): pp. 15–16.
98 Patricia Fumerton, *Unsettled: The Culture of Mobility and the Working Poor in Early Modern England* (Chicago: University of Chicago Press, 2006): pp. 66–68. Barlow was going to Manchester as a trial apprentice to a 'whitester' or bleacher.
99 Lubbock (ed.), *Barlow's Journal*, p. 16.
100 Lubbock (ed), *Barlow's Journal*, pp. 20–21.
101 See above pp. 43–45.
102 BL: Roxburghe 2.117; Roxburghe 1.352–353.
103 Shepard, *Accounting for Oneself*, p. 122.
104 Grevett had allegedly called Mercy Lock a whore and her husband a cuckold 'with a mind and purpose to disgrace, defame and abuse them' (WSRO: Ep I/11/12, ff. 141r-v).
105 WSRO: Ep I/11/12, ff. 73v–74r.
106 WSRO: Ep I/11/12, ff. 72r.
107 WSRO: Ep I/11/12, ff. 75r-v.
108 WSRO: Ep I/11/12, ff. 72v–75v.
109 Shepard, 'Poverty, Labour and the Language of Social Description', pp. 66–68; *idem*, *Accounting for Oneself*, pp. 125–126.
110 Shepard, 'Poverty, Labour and the Language of Social Description', pp. 52, 58; *idem*, *Accounting for Oneself*, p. 126.
111 There are no surviving overseers' accounts for the parish of Easebourne where Alice Hayward lived that would allow us to check whether she was receiving poor relief.
112 WSRO: Ep I/11/13, ff. 183v–185v (Atwood v Puttock).
113 WSRO: Ep I/11/14, ff. 199r-v.
114 ESRO: QR/EW35, f. 86.

Conclusion

1. SHC: LM/COR/7/25.
2. SHC: LM/COR/7/65.
3. SHC: LM/1083/83. For her legal will see SHC: LM/1083/57.
4. For the tomb see [https://www.dorney-history-group.org.uk/the-garrard-monument-st-james-the-less-dorney/ (accessed 2 October 2017)].
5. Barbon, *Apology for the Builder*, p. 30. See above p. 73.
6. SHC: LM/COR/7/52. See above p. 91.
7. ESRO: DUN 50/6/38. See above pp. 93–95.
8. See above pp. 51–53, 58–61, 84–88.
9. WSRO: EP I/29/106/165. See above pp. 68–70.
10. See above pp. 63–65.
11. WSRO: QR/W92, f.66, EP I/29/47/5. The 1678 probate inventory of Harting mercer, Thomas Vallor, recorded 133 individual debtors (WSRO: EP I/29/98/95). See above p. 58.
12. We know from mercers' bills that survive for the period 1636 to 1649 that James typically wore cloth suits in relatively muted colours, such as the 'sad-coloured cloth suit' made for him in 1645 (SHC: LM/1087/8/949). For other mercers' bills see SHC: LM/1087/6/424, 428, LM/1087/8/951, 954, 956, 957, 958, 959. Some of his suits were more flamboyant, for example the 'finger satin' suit lined with taffeta, made for him in 1638 (SHC: LM/1087/8/956).
13. Anon., *England's Vanity*, p. 31. See above p. 25.
14. See above pp. 107–109, 138–139.
15. Anon., *Coma Berenices*, p. 9. See above p. 111.
16. Latham (ed.), *Diary of Samuel Pepys*, p. 696. See above p. 138.
17. SHC: LM/COR/7/53. See above p. 135.
18. See above pp. 163–165.
19. ESRO: QR/E29, ff. 65–66. See above p. 167.
20. The figure of 25 per cent includes 5 per cent estimated to be in receipt of parish relief and 20 per cent estimated to be 'in need' (see above p. 157).
21. Lubbock (ed.), *Barlow's Journal*, pp. 15–16. See above p. 173.
22. WSRO: Par 8/31/1. See above pp. 169–170.
23. For private pews in St Mary's, Ticehurst, see ESRO: PAR 492/9/1/1; Ford (ed.), 'Chichester Diocesan Surveys', p. 49.
24. 'The Contention Between a Countryman and a Citizen for a Beauteous London Lass', c. 1685–1688 (MC: Pepys III 255); The Country Lass, c. 1628 (BL: Roxburghe I 52, 53). See above pp. 43–45.

Bibliography

Manuscript Sources

The British Library (BL)

Add 33145: Accounts of disbursements by Sir Thomas Pelham, 1626–1649.

East Sussex Record Office (ESRO)
Parish Records

PAR 465/6/1: Rotherfield Overseers' Account Book, 1658–1665.
PAR 465/6/2: Rotherfield Overseers' Account Book, 1666–1678.
PAR 492/9/1/1: Ticehurst Churchwardens' Accounts, 1685–1733.
PAR 492/31/1/2: Ticehurst Overseers' Disbursements, 1665–1676.
PAR 492/31/1/21: Ticehurst Paupers' Ledger, 1655.

Transcripts of Parish Registers

LIB/500866: Ticehurst baptisms (1559–1727).
LIB/500874: Ticehurst burials (1559–1953).

Quarter Sessions Rolls (Eastern Sussex)

QR/E9: April 1609
QR/E11: July 1614
QR/E19: January 1618
QR/E29: January 1627
QR/E33: January 1633
QR/EW35: July 1636
QR/E44: January 1639
QR/E63: January 1644
QR/E85: October 1649
QR/E91: April 1651
QR/E117: October 1657
QR/E123: April 1659
QR/E168: January 1671

DUNN: *Archive of the Roberts Family and the Dunn Family*

DUN 1-14: Title Deeds: Roberts family, 1335–1841.
DUN 37: General Accounts, 1563–1823.
DUN 49: Testamentary Papers, 1494–1746.
DUN 50/6: Vouchers to Account, 1657–1689.
DUN 50/7: Vouchers to Account 1655–1700.
DUN 51: Correspondence of the Roberts family, the Temple family, the Busbridge family, the Farnden family and other correspondence, 1626.
DUN 52: Personal Papers of the Roberts Family, 1538–c.1830.

FREWEN: *Archive of the Frewen family*

FRE 520: Account and Memoranda Book of John Everenden of Sedlescombe, 1586–1678.
FRE 612: Book of Costumes.
FRE 4814–5249: Letters to Samuel Jeake the Younger, 1664–1686.
FRE 5301–5333: Letters from Samuel Jeake the Younger to his Wife, Elizabeth Jeake, 1696–1699.
FRE 5334–5336: Letters to Elizabeth Jeake, 1693.
FRE 5337–5358: Letters from Elizabeth Jeake, Widow, to her Mother, Barbara Hartshorne, 1701.

HICKSTEAD: *Archive of the Stapley, Wood and Davidson families*

HIC 467: Account Book, 1642–1823.
HIC 472: Account Book, 1730–1756.
HIC 1105, 1106: Case and Opinion, with an Inventory of Richard Stapley III's Goods, 1724.
HIC 1166: Diary of Richard Stapley III, 1682–1724.

RYE: *Archive of Rye Corporation*

RYE 145/11: General Ledger of Samuel Jeake the Younger, 1680–1688.

Rye Castle Museum (RCM)

RYEYT INV 17.71: Samuel Jeake the Younger's Horoscopes of 182 People, mostly of Rye.
RYEYT N39.6.1: Samuel Jeake the Elder's Inventory, Notes and Accounts Relating to the Estate of his Brother-in-Law, William Key, Mariner, 1666–1679.
RYEYT N39.40: Samuel Jeake the Younger's Personal Expense Accounts, January 1674–January 1680.
RYEYT N39.56.2: Scrap of Paper with Notes by Samuel Jeake the Younger Concerning the Astrological Circumstances of Haircuts he had in 1672.

Surrey History Centre (SHC)

The Loseley Manuscripts

LM/COR/7/: Gresham Family Personal Correspondence.
LM/1083/: Gresham Family Estates, Chiefly in Lincolnshire.
LM/1087/6/box2: 17th and 18th Century Bills and Receipts Relating to, *inter alia*, the Gresham Family, the Hendley family, the More family.
LM/1087/8/box1: 17th and 18th Century Bills and Receipts Relating to, *inter alia*, the Gresham Family.
LM/1228-1232: Gresham Family Estates, Chiefly in Lincolnshire.

The National Archives (TNA)

Port Books

E190/772/12: Meeching with Lewes Coastal, 1675.
E190/773/9: Rye Overseas, 1675.
E190/773/12: Rye Coastal, 1675.
E190/775/12: Chichester Coastal, 1678.
E190/783/16: Rye Coastal, 1686.

Prerogative Court of Canterbury

Probate Accounts

PROB 32/67/145: Samuel Dalling, Southwark, 1699.

Probate Inventories

PROB 4/18013: Giles Moore, Horsted Keynes, 1679.
PROB 4/9733: John Godfrey, Chichester, 1683.
PROB 4/12601: Walter Roberts, Ticehurst, 1700.
PROB 32/67/129: Samuel Dalling, Southwark, 1699.

Wills

PROB 11/164/274: Katherine Aynscombe, Mayfield, 1633.
PROB 11/171/483: Anthony May, Ticehurst, 1636.
PROB 11/184/257: John Bishop, Midhurst, 1640.
PROB 11/325/393: Anthony Stapley, Hickstead, 1667.
PROB 11/344/553: Thomas May, Ticehurst, 1674.
PROB 11/361/89: Giles Moore, Horsted Keynes, 1679.
PROB 11/362/314: Joseph Floyd, London, 1680.
PROB 11/372/186: John Godfrey, Chichester, 1683.
PROB 11/383/199: Edward May, Ticehurst, 1686.

PROB 11/395/383: James Gresham, Haslemere, 1689.
PROB 11/399/318: Walter Roberts, Ticehurst, 1690.
PROB 11/424/331: Moses Sicklemore, London, 1695.
PROB 11/483//349: Anna Farnden, Ticehurst, 1705.
PROB 11/662/135: Joseph Tucker, Rye, 1733.
PROB 11/678/209: Elizabeth Tucker, Rye, 1736.

Miscellaneous

AO 3/370: Hawkers, Pedlars and Petty Chapmen Register of Licences, 1697–1698.
C5/632/33: Stapley versus Stapley, 1670.
C5/225/47: Benge versus Jeake, 1700.
C231/7: Chancery and Lord Commissioners' Office: Crown Office, Docket Books, 1660–1678.
E134/35&36Chas2/Hil6: Hind versus Stapley and Stapley, 1683–5.
E134/36Chas2/East6: Hind versus Stapley and Stapley, 1684–5.

West Sussex Record Office (WSRO)

Chichester City Archives

Chicity/AH/11: Indenture, Clothworkers', Dyers', Weavers' and Fustian Weavers' Guild, 1616.
Chicity/AH/12: Indenture, Mercers' Guild, 1622.

Parish Records

Par 8/12/2: Arundel Vestry Book, 1646–1842.
Par 8/31/1: Arundel Overseers' Accounts, 1678–1704.
Par 59/31/1: Cowfold Overseers' Accounts, Rates and Bills, 1635–1699.
Par 384/6/1: Horsted Keynes, Journal of Giles Moore, 1656–1679.
Par 416/37/2: Lindfield Overseers' Miscellaneous: Inventories, 1656–1799.
Par 516/31/1: Worth Overseers' Receipts and Disbursements, 1621–1698.

Transcripts of Parish Registers

Arundel: Baptism and Burial Registers.
Cowfold: Baptism and Burial Registers.

Diocese and Archdeaconry of Chichester

Deposition Books

EP I/11/12: November 1611–January 1618.
EP I/11/13: January 1617–March 1626.

EP I/11/14: March 1626–March 1631.
EP I/11/15: May 1631–December 1636.

Probate Accounts

EP I/33/1611: Richard Barker, Arundel, 1611.
EP I/33/1648: Thomas Kewell, Lyminster, 1648.
EP I/33/1682: George Mersher, Birdham, 1682.

Probate Inventories

EP I/29/47/5: Jane Smith, Chidham, 1619.
EP I/29/8/15: Thomas Moore, Arundel, 1621.
EP I/29/541/34: Edward Napper, Chichester, 1623.
EP I/29/163/6: Anthony Mutton, Rusper, 1632.
EP I/29/205/21: Richard Hamper, Washington, 1639.
EP I/29/176/21: Thomas Puttock, Slinfold, 1639.
EP I/29/138/47: Thomas Fielding, Midhurst, 1647.
EP I/29/8/88: Samuel Walter, Arundel, 1649.
EP I/29/160/50: Walter Deane, Rudgwick, 1661.
EP I/29/106/130: Henry Lintott, Horsham, 1670.
EP I/29/206/162: William Silverlock, Westbourne, 1678.
EP I/29/98/95: Thomas Vallor, Harting, 1678.
EP I/29/106/165: Michael Woodgate, Horsham, 1679.
EP I/29/106/215: John Waller, Horsham, 1687.
EP I/29/8/189: Leonard Pope, Arundel, 1688.
EP I/29/188/83: John Penfold, Storrington, 1691.
EP I/29/149/224: Thomas Allen, Petworth, 1692.

Wills

STC I//15/93r: Edward Fist, Slinfold, 1600.
STC I/15/135v: William Hogis, Lodsworth, 1600.
STC I/15/147v: Robert Hillier, Mid Lavant, 1602.
STC I/15/150r: Eme Smyth, Harting, 1602.
STC I/15/153r: Alice Pettit, Oving, 1602.
STC I/15/167r: Thomasine Varnden, Woodmancote, 1603.
STC I/15/45r: Elizabeth Owlder, Findon, 1604.
STC I/15/233r-v: Alice Bartholomew, Treyford, 1605.
STC I/15/238r-v: Agnes Slater, Sompting, 1606.
STC I/15/274v: Agnes Deyntie, Horsham, 1608.
STC I/15/278r: Alice Burt, Binsted, 1608.
STC I/15/278r-v: Joanne Ede, Wisborough Green, 1608.
STC I/15/301r: Joanne Gratwick, West Angmering, 1609.

STC I/15/321v: William Napper, Wisborough Green, 1609.
STC I/19/83v-84r: Alice Hill, Thakeham, 1637.
STC I/26/102r-v: Joanne Hayne of Washington, 1675.

Archdeaconry of Lewes
Ep II/17/192: Horsted Keynes, Church Terrier, 1675.

Shillinglee Archive
Shillinglee MSS 454-476: Letters from Thomas Godfrey to Sir Edward Turnour (Norfolk Estates and Lighthouses), 1682–1695.

Quarter Sessions Rolls (Western Sussex)
QR/W2: September 1605
QR/W8: January 1615
QR/W13: January 1618
QR/W16: July 1625
QR/W17: October 1625
QR/W19: 1626/1627
QR/W33: January 1638
QR/W34: April 1638
QR/W53: April 1645
QR/W56: April 1646
QR/W60: October 1647
QR/W64: January 1649
QR/W82: April 1655
QR/W90: January 1658
QR/W92: October 1658
QR/W110: April 1664
QR/W122: March 1668
QR/W156: October 1679
QR/W213: January 1696

Printed primary sources

Allestree, Richard [attributed], *The Ladies Calling in Two Parts by the Author of the Whole Duty of Man* (Oxford, 1673).
Ames, Richard, *The Folly of Love, or, An Essay upon Satire against Women* (London, 1691).
Anon., *The Law's Resolutions of Women's Rights: Or the Law's Provision for Women* (London, 1632).

Anon., *New Additions to Youth's Behaviour* (London, 1663).
Anon., *A True and Faithful Account of the Several Informations Exhibited to the Honourable Committee appointed to the Parliament to Inquire into the Late Dreadful Burning of the City of London* (London, 1667).
Anon., *Grand Concern of England Explained* (London, 1673).
Anon., *Coma Berenices or the Hairy Comet* (London, 1676).
Anon., *The Character of the Town Miss* (London, 1680).
Anon., *England's Vanity or the Voice of God against the Monstrous Sin of Pride in Dress and Apparel* (London, 1683).
Anon., *A Satire against the French* (London, 1691).
Anon., *The Character of the Beaux* (London, 1696).
Anon., *The English Chapman's and Traveller's Almanac* (London, 1697).
Awdely, John, *Fraternity of Vagabonds* (London, 1561).
Barbon, Nicholas, *Discourse showing the Great Advantages that New Buildings and the Enlarging of Towns and Cities Do Bring to a Nation* (London, 1678).
Barbon, Nicholas, *An Apology for the Builder* (London, 1685).
Barbon, Nicholas, *Discourse of Trade* (London, 1690).
Bertelli, Pietro, *Diversarum Nationum Habitus*, 3 volumes (Padua, 1589, 1594, 1596).
Bird, Ruth (ed.), 'The Journal of Giles Moore', *Sussex Record Society* 68 (1971).
Blencowe, Robert Willis, 'Extracts from the Journal and Account Book of Timothy Burrell, Esquire, Barrister-at-Law, 1683–1714', *Sussex Archaeological Collections* 3 (1850): pp. 117–172.
Boorde, Andrew, *Introduction to Knowledge* (London, 1542).
Boyle, Francis, *Several Discourses and Characters Addressed to the Ladies of the Age* (London, 1689).
Boyle, Francis, *Discourses Useful for the Vain Modish Ladies and their Gallants* (London, 1696).
Braithwaite, Richard, *The English Gentlewoman* (London, 1631).
Braithwaite, Richard, *The English Gentleman* (London, 1631).
Bulwer, John, *Anthrometamorphosis: Man Transformed or the Artificial Changeling* (London, 1650).
Cooper, J. H., 'A Religious Census of Sussex in 1676', *Sussex Archaeological Collections* 45 (1902): pp. 142–148.
Crowne, Thomas, *The Country Wit* (London, 1675).
Defoe, Daniel, *Moll Flanders* (London, 1722).
Defoe, Daniel, *A Tour through the Whole Island of Great Britain* (London, 1724).
Dekker, Thomas, *The Seven Deadly Sins* (London, 1606).
Dekker, Thomas, *The Bellman of London* (London, 1608)
Dekker, Thomas, *Lantern and Candlelight: or the Bellman's Second Night Walk* (London, 1608).
Evelyn, John, *Tyrannus, or, the Mode in a Discourse of Sumptuary Laws* (London, 1661).

Evelyn, Mary (attributed), *Mundus Muliebris, or the Ladies Dressing Room Unlocked* (London, 1690).
Ford, Wyn K. (ed.), 'Chichester Diocesan Surveys 1686 and 1724', *Sussex Record Society* 78 (1992): p. 155.
Fryer, Jonathan (ed.), *George Fox and the Children of Light* (London: Kyle Cathie, 1991).
Gauden, John (attributed), *Several Letters between Two Ladies Wherein the Lawfulness and Unlawfulness of Artificial Beauty in Point of Conscience are Nicely Debated* (London, 1701).
Gilbert, Samuel, *An Almanac for Six Years* (London, 1697).
Gosse, Edmund (ed.), *Restoration Plays* (London: Dent, 1932).
Gouge, William, *Of Domestical Duties* (London, 1622).
Haines, Richard, *Provision for the Poor* (London, 1678).
Hall, Thomas, *The Loathsomeness of Long Hair, with an Appendix Against Painting, Spots, Naked Backs, Breast, Arms etc* (London, 1654).
Harman, Thomas, *Caveat or Warning for Common Cursitors* (London, 1566).
Holme, Randle, *Academy of Armory* (Chester, 1688).
Houghton, John, *England's Great Happiness, or a Dialogue between Content and Complaint* (London, 1677).
Hunnisett, R. F. (ed.), *Sussex Coroners' Inquests 1603–1688* (Kew: PRO Publications, 1998).
Hunter, Michael and Gregory, Annabel (eds.), *An Astrological Diary of the Seventeenth Century: Samuel Jeake of Rye 1652–1699* (Oxford: Clarendon Press, 1988).
Hunter, Michael, Mandelbrote, Giles, Ovenden, Richard and Smith, Nigel (eds.), *A Radical's Books: The Library Catalogue of Samuel Jeake of Rye, 1623–1690* (Woodbridge: D. S. Brewer, 1999).
Langley, William, *The Death of Charles the First Lamented* (London, 1660).
Latham, Robert and Matthews, William (eds.), The *Diary of Samuel Pepys: A New and Complete Transcription*, 11 volumes (London: Bell/ Bell and Hyman, 1970–1983).
Latham, Robert (ed.), *The Diary of Samuel Pepys: A Selection* (London: Penguin Books, 2003).
Laune, Thomas de, *The Present State of London* (London, 1681).
Leveson Gower, Granville, *Genealogy of the Family of Gresham* (London: Mitchell and Hughes, 1883).
Lubbock, Basil (ed.), *Barlow's Journal of his Life at Sea in the King's Ships, East and West Indiamen and other Merchantmen from 1659–1703* (London: Hurst and Blackett, 1934).
Markham, Gervase, *The English Housewife*, ed. Michael R. Best (Montreal: McGill-Queen's University Press, 1986).
McGowan, Alan, *The Winchester Confessions, 1615–1616: depositions of travellers, gypsies, fraudsters and makers of counterfeit documents, including a vocabulary of Romany language* (South Chailey: Romany and Traveller Family History Society, 1996).
Millard, Peter (ed.), *Notes of Me: The Autobiography of Roger North* (Toronto: University of Toronto Press, 2000).
Morley, Henry (ed.), *A Survey of London Written in the Year 1598 by John Stow* (Stroud: Alan Sutton Publishing, 1994).

Morris, Christopher (ed.), *The Illustrated Journeys of Celia Fiennes, 1685–c1712* (London: Macdonald & Co, 1982).
Mun, Thomas, *England's Treasure by Foreign Trade* (London, 1664).
Murphy, Anne L. (ed.), *The Worlds of the Jeake Family of Rye, 1640–1736* (Oxford: Oxford University Press, 2018).
Ogilby, John, *Britannia, or, The Kingdom of England and Dominions of Wales Actually Surveyed* (London, 1675).
Peacham, Henry, *The Complete Gentleman* (London, 1634).
Peacham, Henry, *The Art of Living in London* (London, 1642).
Plat, Hugh, *Delights for Ladies. To Adorn their Persons, Tables, Closets and Distillatories* (London, 1617).
Redwood, B. C. (ed.), 'Quarter Sessions Order Book, 1642–1649', *Sussex Record Society* 54 (1954).
Rolle, Samuel, *Shlohavot, The Burning of London* (London, 1667).
Shadwell, Thomas, *Epsom Wells* (London, 1673).
Strype, John, *Lessons Moral and Christian for Youth and Old Age* (London, 1699).
Thirsk, Joan and Cooper, J. P. (eds.), *Seventeenth-Century Economic Documents* (Oxford: Oxford University Press, 1972).
Tittler, Robert (ed.), 'Accounts of the Roberts Family of Boarzell, Sussex c1568–1582', *Sussex Record Society* 71 (1977–1979).
Tuke, Thomas, *A Discourse against Painting and Tincturing of Women* (London, 1616).
Turner, Edward, 'Extracts from the Diary of Richard Stapley, Gent, of Hickstead Place in Twineham, from 1682 to 1724', *Sussex Archaeological Collections* 2 (1849), pp. 102–119.
Turner, Edward, 'The Stapley Diary', *Sussex Archaeological Collections* 18 (1866), pp. 151–162.
Vaisey, David (ed.), *The Diary of Thomas Turner 1754–1765* (Oxford: Oxford University Press, 1985).
Vanbrugh, John, *The Relapse or Virtue in Danger* (London, 1697).
Vaughan, William, *Directions for Health, Natural and Artificial* (London, 1626).
Vincent, Thomas, *God's Terrible Voice in the City* (London, 1667).
Waterhouse, Edward, *The Gentleman's Monitor* (London, 1665).
Wood, Lambert, *The Life and Reign of King Charles From his Birth to his Death* (London, 1659).
Woolley, Hannah, *The Gentlewoman's Companion* (London, 1673).

Ballads (accessed through the online UCSB English Broadside Ballad Archive)

'A New Song called Jack Dove's Resolution' (*c.* 1602–1646), BL: Roxburghe 1.160–161.
'The Country Lass' (*c.* 1628), MC: Pepys 1.268.
'Ragged Torn and True, or the Poor Man's Resolution' (1628–1629), BL: Roxburghe 1.352–353.

'The Fantastic Age or the Anatomy of England's Vanity in Wearing the Fashions of Several Nations' (*c.* 1633–1669), BL: Roxburghe 1.476–477.
'The Milkmaid's Life' (*c.* 1633–1669), BL: Roxburghe 1.244–245.
'The Map of Mock-Beggar's Hall with his Situation in the Spacious Country called Anywhere' (*c.* 1640), BL: Roxburghe 1.252–253.
'Mock-beggars Hall, with his Situation in the Spacious Country called Anywhere' (*c.* 1640), BL: Roxburghe 3.218–219.
'News from Hyde Park' (*c.* 1682), BL: Roxburghe 2.379.
'The Virgin's Vindication, or, the Conceited Fashion-Mongers Fairly Exposed' (*c.* 1664–1703), MC: Pepys 5.432.
'A Description of Old England, or a True Declaration of the Times' (*c.* 1674–1679), NLS: Crawford 1244.
'God Speed the Plough, and Bless the Corn Mow' (1684–1686), MC: Pepys 4.272.
'True Blue Ploughman' (1685), BL: Roxburghe 2.471.
'Downright Dick of the West' (1685–1688), BL: Roxburghe 2.117.
'The Invincible Pride of Women' (*c.* 1675–1696), MC: Pepys 4.153.
'The London Ladies' Vindication of Top-Knots' (*c.* 1675–1696), MC: Pepys 4.363.
'The Countryman's Delight' (1681–1684), MC: Pepys 4.349.
'The Country Gentleman, or, the Happy Life' (*c.* 1684–1686), NLS: Crawford 549.
'The Contention between a Countryman and a Citizen for a Beauteous London Lass' (1685–1688), MC: Pepys 3.255.
'Advice to the Maidens of London to Forsake their Fantastical Top Knots' (1685–1688), MC: Pepys 4.365.
'The Innocent Country Maids' Delight' (1685–1688), BL: Roxburghe 2.230.
'The Farmer's Wife's Complaint against the Ladies' Commodes and Top Knots' (c.1687–1691), MC: Pepys 5.412.
'The Young Men's Advice to Proud Ladies' (1692), NLS: Crawford 744.
'A Cheat in All Trades' (c.1700–1720), NLS: Crawford 458.

Newspapers

The London Gazette, no. 3519 (Monday 31 July to Thursday 3 August 1699).
The Spectator, no. 24 (28 March 1711), no. 116 (13 July 1711), no. 127 (26 July 1711), no. 129 (28 July 1711), no. 240 (5 December 1711).

Secondary Works

Andrews, J. H., 'The Port of Chichester and the Grain Trade', *Sussex Archaeological Collections* 92 (1954): pp. 93–105.
Arkell, Tom, 'The Incidence of Poverty in England in the Late 17th Century', *Social History* 12 (1987): pp. 23–47.

Arkell, Tom, 'A Method for Estimating Population Totals for the Compton Census Returns' *in* Kevin Schurer and Tom Arkell, eds. *Surveying the People: The Interpretation and the Use of Document Sources for the Study of Population in the Late Seventeenth Century* (Oxford: Leopard's Head Press, 1992): pp. 97–116.

Arkell, Tom, 'The Probate Process' *in* Tom Arkell, Nesta Evans and Nigel Goose, eds. *When Death Do Us Part: Understanding and Interpreting the Probate Records of Early Modern England* (Oxford: Leopard's Head Press, 2000): pp. 3–13.

Backhouse, Clare, *Fashion and Popular Print in Early Modern England* (London: I. B. Tauris, 2017).

Baker, J. H., *An Introduction to English Legal History* (London: Butterworths, 1990).

Barry, Jonathan, 'Introduction' *in* Jonathan Barry and Christopher Brooks, eds. *The Middling Sort of People: Culture, Society and Politics in England, 1550–1800* (Basingstoke: Macmillan, 1994): pp. 1–27.

Beier, A. L., *Masterless Men: The Vagrancy Problem in England 1560–1640* (London and New York: Methuen, 1985).

Borsay, Peter, 'The London Connection: Cultural Diffusion and the Eighteenth-Century Provincial Town', *The London Journal* 19:1 (1994): pp. 21–35.

Brent, Colin, 'Rural Employment and Population in Sussex between 1550 and 1640 (part one)', *Sussex Archaeological Collections* 114 (1976): pp. 27–48.

Brent, Colin, 'Rural Employment and Population in Sussex between 1550 and 1640 (part two)', *Sussex Archaeological Collections* 116 (1978): pp. 41–55.

Brent, Colin, *Pre-Georgian Lewes c890–1714: The Emergence of a County Town* (King's Lynn: Colin Brent Books, 2004).

Bryson, Anna, *From Courtesy to Civility: Changing Codes of Conduct in Early Modern England* (Oxford: Clarendon Press, 1998).

Buck, Anne, *Dress in Eighteenth-Century England* (London: B. T. Batsford, 1979).

Buck, Anne, 'Clothing and Textiles in Bedfordshire Inventories, 1617–1620', *Costume* 34 (2000): pp. 26–38.

Cardon, Dominique, *Natural Dyes: Sources, Traditions, Technology and Science* (London: Archetype Publications, 2007).

Carter, Philip, 'Men about Town: Representations of Foppery and Masculinity in Early Eighteenth-century Urban Society' *in* Helen Barker and Elaine Chalus, eds. *Gender in Eighteenth-Century England: Roles, Representations and Responsibilities* (Harlow: Routledge, 1997): pp. 31–57.

Carter, Philip, *Men and the Emergence of Polite Society, 1660–1800* (Abingdon: Routledge, 2014).

Chaudhuri, Kirti N., *The Trading World of Asia and the English East India Company 1660–1760* (Cambridge: Cambridge University Press, 1978).

Clarke, Bridget, 'Clothing the Family of an MP in the 1690s: An Analysis of the Day Book of Edward Clarke of Chipley, Somerset', *Costume* 43 (2009): pp. 38–54.

Clatworthy, Lee, 'The Quintessential Englishman? Henry Temple's Town and Country Dress', *Costume* 43 (2009): pp. 55–65.

Cliffe, Trevor, *Puritan Gentry Besieged, 1650–1700* (London: Routledge, 1993).

Coleman, Donald C., 'An Innovation and its Diffusion: The "New Draperies"', *Economic History Review* 22:3 (1969): pp. 417–429.

Corner, David, 'The Tyranny of Fashion: The Case of the Felt-hatting Trade in the Late Seventeenth and Eighteenth Centuries', *Textile History* 22:2 (1991): pp. 153–178.

Cox, Nancy, *The Complete Tradesman: A Study of Retailing, 1550–1820* (Aldershot: Routledge, 2000).

Cox, Nancy, '"Beggary of the Nation": Moral, Economic and Political Attitudes to the Retail Sector in the Early Modern Period' *in* John Benson and Laura Ugolini, eds. *A Nation of Shopkeepers: Five Centuries of British Retailing* (London: I. B. Tauris, 2003): pp. 26–51.

Cox, Nancy and Dannehl, Karin, *Perceptions of Retailing in Early Modern England* (Aldershot: Routledge, 2007).

Cressy, David, 'Trouble with Gypsies in Early Modern England', *The Historical Journal* 59:1 (2016): pp. 45–70.

Crowston, Clare H., *Fabricating Women: The Seamstresses of Old Regime France* (Durham and London: Duke University Press, 2001).

Cunnington, Phillis and Lucas, Catherine, *Costume for Births, Marriages and Deaths* (London: Adam & Charles Black, 1972).

Davis, Elizabeth, '"Habit de Qualité": Seventeenth-century French Fashion Prints as Sources for Dress History', *Dress* 40:2 (2014): pp. 117–143.

Dawson, Mark, *Gentility and the Comic Theatre in Late Stuart London* (Cambridge: Cambridge University Press, 2005).

Dietz, Brian, 'Overseas Trade and Metropolitan Growth' *in* A. L. Beier and Roger Finlay, eds. *London 1500–1700: The Making of a Metropolis* (Harlow: Prentice Hall Press, 1986): pp. 115–140.

Dionne, Craig and Mentz, Steve (eds.), *Rogues and Early Modern English Culture* (Ann Arbor: University of Michigan Press, 2004).

Dolan, Alice, 'An Adorned Print: Print Culture, Female Leisure and the Dissemination of Fashion in France and England around 1660–1779', *V&A Online Journal* 3 (2011).

Douglas, Audrey W., 'Cotton Textiles in England: The East India Company's Attempt to Exploit the Developments in Fashion, 1660–1721', *Journal of British Studies* 8:2 (1969): pp. 28–43.

Earle, Peter, *The Making of the English Middle Class: Business, Society and Family Life in London 1660–1730* (London: Methuen, 1989).

Erickson, Amy, *Women and Property in Early Modern England* (London: Routledge, 1995).

Erickson, Amy, 'Using Probate Accounts' *in* Tom Arkell, Nesta Evans and Nigel Goose, eds. *When Death do us Part: Understanding and Interpreting the Probate Records of Early Modern England* (Oxford: Leopard's Head Press, 2000): pp. 103–119.

Everitt, Alan, 'Social Mobility in Early Modern England', *Past and Present* 33 (1966): pp. 56–73.

Everitt, Alan, 'The Marketing of Agricultural Produce' *in* Joan Thirsk, ed. *The Agrarian History of England and Wales: Vol IV 1500–1640* (Cambridge: Cambridge University Press, 1967): pp. 466–592.

Farrant, John, 'Growth of Communications' *in* Kim Leslie and Brian Short, eds. *An Historical Atlas of Sussex* (Chichester: Phillimore, 1999): pp. 78–79.

Festa, Lynn M., 'Personal Effects: Wigs and Possessive Individualism in the Long Eighteenth Century', *Eighteenth-Century Life* 29:2 (2005): pp. 47–90.

Flather, Amanda, *Gender and Space in Early Modern England* (Woodbridge: The Boydell Press, 2007).

Fletcher, Anthony, *Sussex 1600–1660: A Community in Peace and War* (Chichester: Phillimore, 1975).

French, Henry, '"Ingenious and Learned Gentlemen": Social Perceptions and Self-Fashioning among Parish Elites in Essex, 1680–1740', *Social History* 25:1 (2000): pp. 44–66.

French, Henry, *The Middle Sort of People in Provincial England 1600–1750* (Oxford: Oxford University Press, 2007).

Fumerton, Patricia, *Unsettled: The Culture of Mobility and the Working Poor in Early Modern England* (Chicago: University of Chicago Press, 2006).

Griffiths, Paul, 'Politics made Visible: Order, Residence and Uniformity in Cheapside, 1600–1645' *in* Paul Griffiths and Mark S. R. Jenner, eds. *Londinopolis: Essays in the Cultural and Social History of Early Modern London* (Manchester: Manchester University Press, 2000): pp. 176–196.

Guillery, Peter, 'Houses in London's Suburbs' *in* Matthew Davies *et al*, eds. *London and Middlesex 1666 Hearth Tax*, part 1 (London: British Record Society, 2014): pp. 140–153.

Harding, Vanessa, 'Shops, Markets and Retailers in London's Cheapside, c1500–1700' *in* Bruno Blondé, Peter Stabel, Jon Stobart and Ilja Van Damme, eds. *Retail Circuits and Practices in Medieval and Early Modern Europe* (Turnhout: Brepols, 2006): pp. 155–170.

Harding, Vanessa, 'London and Middlesex in the 1660s' *in* Matthew Davies *et al*, eds. *London and Middlesex 1666 Heath Tax*, part 1 (London: British Record Society): pp. 25–57.

Harte, Negley B., 'State Control of Dress and Social Change in Pre-Industrial England' *in* Donald C. Coleman and A. H. John, eds., *Trade, Government and Economy in Pre-Industrial England* (London: Littlehampton Book Services, 1976): pp. 132–165.

Harte, Negley B, 'The Economics of Clothing in the Late Seventeenth Century', *Textile History* 22:2 (1991): pp. 277–296.

Hayward, Maria, '"We have Better Materials for Clothes, They, Better Taylors": The Influence of La Mode on the Clothes of Charles II and James II' *in* Tony Clayton and Charles-Edouard Levillain, eds. *Louis XIV Outside In: Images of the Sun King Beyond France, 1661–1715* (Abingdon: Routledge, 2015): pp. 57–75.

Hentschell, Ruth, 'A Question of Nation: Foreign Clothes on the English Subject' *in* Catherine Richardson, ed. *Clothing Culture, 1350–1650* (Aldershot: Ashgate, 2004): pp. 49–62.

Herrup, Cynthia, *The Common Peace: Participants and the Criminal Law in Seventeenth-Century England* (Cambridge: Cambridge University Press, 1987).

Hindle, Steve, *On the Parish? The Micro-Politics of Poor Relief in Rural England, c1550–1750* (Oxford: Oxford University Press, 2004).

Hindle, Steve, 'Civility, Honesty and the Identification of the Deserving Poor in Seventeenth-century England' *in* Henry French and Jonathan Barry, eds. *Identity and Agency in England, 1500–1800* (Basingstoke: Palgrave, 2004): pp. 38–59.

Hitchcock, David, *Vagrancy in English Culture and Society 1650–1750* (London: Bloomsbury Academic, 2016).

Huggett, Jane E., 'Rural Costume in Elizabethan Essex: A Study Based on the Evidence from Wills', *Costume* 33 (1999): pp. 74–88.

Imray, Joan, *The Mercers' Hall* (London: London Topographical Society, 1991).

Jardine, Lisa, *The Curious Life of Robert Hooke: The Man who Measured London* (New York: Harper Perennial, 2004).

Jones, Ann R. and Stallybrass, Peter, *Renaissance Clothing and the Materials of Memory* (Cambridge: Cambridge University Press, 2000).

Jones, Peter, 'Clothing the Poor in Early Nineteenth-century England', *Textile History* 37:1 (2006): pp. 17–37.

Jones, Peter, '"I Cannot Keep My Place Without Being Decent": Pauper Letters, Parish Clothing and Pragmatism in the South of England, 1750–1830', *Rural History* 20:1 (2009): pp. 31–49.

King, Steven, 'Reclothing the English Poor, 1750–1840', *Textile History* 33:1 (2002): pp. 37–47.

Kuchta, David, *The Three-Piece Suit and Modern Masculinity, England 1550–1850* (California: University of California Press, 2002).

Laslett, Peter, 'Natural and Political Observations on the Population of Late Seventeenth-Century England: Reflections on the work of Gregory King and John Graunt' *in* Kevin Schurer and Tom Arkell, eds. *Surveying the People: The Interpretation and the Use of Document Sources for the Study of Population in the Late Seventeenth Century* (Oxford: Leopard's Head Press, 1992): pp. 6–30.

Lemire, Beverly, 'Consumerism in Preindustrial and Early Industrial England: The Trade in Secondhand Clothes', *Journal of British Studies* 27:1 (1988): pp. 1–24.

Lemire, Beverly, *Dress, Culture and Commerce: The English Clothing Trade before the Factory, 1660–1800* (Basingstoke: Palgrave Macmillan, 1997).

Lemire, Beverly, 'Shifting Currency: The Culture and Economy of the Second Hand Trade in England, c. 1600–1850' *in* Alexandra Palmer and Hazel Clark, eds. *Old Clothes, New Clothes: Second Hand Fashion* (Oxford: Berg, 2005): pp. 29–47.

Mackie, Erin, *Market à la Mode: Fashion, Commodity and Gender in The Tatler and The Spectator* (Baltimore and London: Johns Hopkins University Press, 1997).

Marly, Diana de, 'Fashionable Suppliers 1600–1700: Leading Tailors and Clothing Tradesmen of the Restoration Period', *The Antiquaries Journal* 58:2 (1978): pp. 333–351.

Mayhew, Graham, *Tudor Rye* (Hove: Delta Press, 1987).

McKellar, Elizabeth, *The Birth of Modern London: The Development and Design of the City 1660–1720* (Manchester: Manchester University Press, 1999).

McKendrick, Neil, 'The Consumer Revolution of Eighteenth-century England' *in* Neil McKendrick, John Brewer and John H. Plumb, *The Birth of a Consumer Society: The Commercialization of Eighteenth-century England* (London: Europa Publications, 1982): pp. 9–33.

McShane, Angela and Backhouse, Clare, 'Top Knots and Lower Sorts: Print and Promiscuous Consumption in the 1690s' *in* Michael Hunter, ed. *Printed Images in Early Modern Britain: Essays in Interpretation* (Farnham: Routledge, 2010): pp. 337–357.

Morgan, Roy, *Chichester: A Documentary History* (Chichester: Phillimore, 1992).

Muldrew, Craig, *Food, Energy and the Creation of Industriousness: Work and Material Culture in Agrarian England, 1550–1780* (Cambridge: Cambridge University Press, 2011).

Muldrew, Craig, '"Th'Ancient Distaff" and "Whirling Spindle": Measuring the Contribution of Spinning to Household Earnings and the National Economy in England, 1550–1770', *Economic History Review* 65:2 (2012): pp. 498–526.

Murphy, Anne L., '"You Do Manage It So Well that I Cannot do Better": The Working Life of Elizabeth Jeake of Rye (1667–1736)', *Women's History Review* 27:7 (2018): pp. 1190–1208.

Nevinson, John L., 'Origin and Early History of the Fashion Print', *Smithsonian Institution United States National Museum Bulletin* 250 (1969): pp. 65–92.

North, Susan, '"Galloon, Incle and Points": Fashionable Dress and Accessories in Rural England, 1552–1665', *in* Richard Jones and Christopher Dyer, eds. *Farmers, Consumers, Innovators: The World of Joan Thirsk* (Hatfield: University of Hertfordshire Press, 2016): pp. 104–123.

Oakeshott, Ewart, *European Weapons and Armour from the Renaissance to the Industrial Revolution* (Woodbridge: Boydell and Brewer, 2012).

Overton, Mark, Whittle, Jane, Dean, Darron and Hann, Andrew, *Production and Consumption in English Households, 1600–1750* (Abingdon: Routledge, 2004).

Peck, Linda Levy, *Consuming Splendor: Society and Culture in Seventeenth-Century England* (Cambridge: Cambridge University Press, 2005).

Priestley, Margaret, 'Anglo-French Trade and the "Unfavourable Balance" Controversy, 1660–1685', *Economic History Review* 4:1 (1951): pp. 37–52.

Reinke-Williams, Tim, 'Women's Clothes and Female Honour in Early Modern London', *Continuity and Change* 26:1 (2011): pp. 69–88.

Ribeiro, Aileen, *Dress and Morality* (London: B. T. Batsford, 1986).

Ribeiro, Aileen, *Fashion and Fiction: Dress in Art and Literature in Stuart England* (New Haven and London: Yale University Press, 2005).

Ribeiro, Aileen, *Facing Beauty: Painted Women and Cosmetic Art* (New Haven and London: Yale University Press, 2011).

Richardson, R.C., *Household Servants in Early Modern England* (Manchester: Manchester University Press, 2010).

Roche, Daniel, *The Culture of Clothing: Dress and Fashion in the Ancien Regime* (Cambridge: Cambridge University Press, 1996).

Rublack, Ulinka, *Dressing Up: Cultural Identity in Renaissance Europe* (Oxford: Oxford University Press, 2010).

Saunders, Ann, 'The Organisation of the Exchange' *in* Ann Saunders, ed. *The Royal Exchange* (London: London Topographical Society, 1997): pp. 85–98.

Saunders, Ann, 'The Second Exchange', *in* Ann Saunders, ed. *The Royal Exchange* (London: London Topographical Society, 1997): pp. 121–135.

Saunders, Anne S., 'Provision of Apparel for the Poor in London, 1630–1680', *Costume* 40 (2006): pp. 21–27.

Shepard, Alexandra, *Meanings of Manhood in Early Modern England* (Oxford: Oxford University Press, 2003).

Shepard, Alexandra, 'Poverty, Labour and the Language of Social Description in Early Modern England', *Past and Present* 201 (2008): pp. 51–95.

Shepard, Alexandra, *Accounting for Oneself: Worth, Status and the Social Order in Early Modern England* (Oxford: Oxford University Press, 2015).

Slack, Paul, 'Perceptions of the Metropolis in Seventeenth-century England' *in* Peter Burke, Brian Harrison and Paul Slack, eds. *Civil Histories: Essays Presented to Sir Keith Thomas* (Oxford: Oxford University Press, 2000): pp. 161–180.

Slack, Paul, 'The Politics of Consumption and England's Happiness in the Later Seventeenth Century', *English Historical Review* 122:497 (2007): pp. 609–631.

Smart, T. W. W., 'A Biographical Sketch of Samuel Jeake Senior of Rye', *Sussex Archaeological Collections*, 13 (1861): pp. 57–79.

Smith, Woodruff D., *Consumption and the Making of Respectability* (London: Routledge, 2002).

Smyth, Adam, 'Almanacs, Annotators and Life-writing in Early Modern England', *English Literary Renaissance* 38:2 (2008): pp. 200–244.

Spufford, Margaret, *The Great Reclothing of Rural England: Petty Chapmen and their Wares in the Seventeenth Century* (London: The Hambledon Press, 1984).

Spufford, Margaret, 'The Cost of Apparel in Seventeenth-century England, and the Accuracy of Gregory King', *Economic History Review* 53:4 (2000): pp. 677–705.

Spufford, Margaret, 'Fabric for Seventeenth-century Children and Adolescents' Clothes', *Textile History* 34:1 (2003): pp. 47–63.

Spufford, Margaret and Mee, Susan, *The Clothing of the Common Sort, 1570–1700* (Oxford: Oxford University Press, 2017).

Spurr, John, 'From Puritanism to Dissent, 1660–1700' *in* Christopher Durston and Jacqueline Eales, eds. *The Culture of English Puritanism, 1560–1700* (Basingstoke: Palgrave Macmillan, 1996): pp. 234–265.

Stedman, Gesa, *Cultural Exchange in Seventeenth-Century France and England* (Farnham: Routledge, 2013).
Stobart, Jon, 'Who were the Urban Gentry? Social Elites in an English Provincial Town, c. 1680–1760' *Continuity and Change* 26:1 (2011): pp. 89–112.
Stobart, Jon, *Sugar and Spice: Grocers and Groceries in Provincial England, 1650–1830* (Oxford: Oxford University Press, 2013).
Stobart, Jon, 'The Village Shop, 1660–1760: Innovation and Tradition' *in* Richard Jones and Christopher Dyer, eds. *Farmers, Consumers, Innovators: The World of Joan Thirsk* (Hatfield: University of Hertfordshire Press, 2016): pp. 89–102.
Stobart, Jon, 'Making the Global Local? Overseas Goods in English Rural Shops, c. 1600–1760', *Business History* 59:7 (2017): pp. 1136–1153.
Stone, Lawrence, 'The Residential Development of the West End of London in the Seventeenth Century' *in* Barbara C. Malament, ed. *After the Reformation: Essays in Honour of J. H. Hexter* (Manchester: Manchester University Press, 1980): pp. 167–212.
Styles, John, 'Product Innovation in Early Modern London', *Past and Present* 168 (2000): pp. 124–169.
Styles, John, *The Dress of the People: Everyday Fashion in Eighteenth-Century England* (New Haven and London: Yale University Press, 2007).
Tankard, Danae, '"A Pair of Grass-green Woollen Stockings": The Clothing of the Rural Poor in Seventeenth-century Sussex', *Textile History* 43:1 (2012): pp. 5–22.
Tankard, Danae, '"I Think Myself Honestly Decked": Attitudes to the Clothing of the Rural Poor in Seventeenth-century England', *Rural History* 26:1 (2015): pp. 17–33.
Tankard, Danae, 'Giles Moore's Clothes: The Clothing of a Sussex Rector, 1656–1679', *Costume* 49:1 (2015): pp. 32–54.
Tankard, Danae, '"They Tell Me They Were in Fashion Last Year": Samuel and Elizabeth Jeake and Clothing Fashions in Late Seventeenth-century London and Rye', *Costume* 50:1 (2016): pp. 20–41.
Tankard, Danae, '"Buttons no Bigger than Nutmegs": The Clothing of Country Gentlemen, c1660–1715', *Cultural and Social History* 14:1 (2017): pp. 1–16.
Thirsk, Joan, 'The Farming Regions of England', in Joan Thirsk, ed. *The Agrarian History of England and Wales: Vol IV 1500–1640* (Cambridge: Cambridge University Press, 1967): pp. 1–112.
Thirsk, Joan, *Economic Policy and Projects: The Development of a Consumer Society in Early Modern England* (Oxford: Clarendon Press, 1978).
Thomas-Stanford, Charles, *Sussex in the Great War and Interregnum* (London: Chiswick Press, 1910).
Veblen, Thornstein, *The Theory of the Leisure Class: An Economic Study of Institutions* ([1889] London: Penguin Books, 1994).
Vincent, Susan, *Dressing the Elite: Clothes in Early Modern England* (Oxford: Berg, 2003).

Vincent, Susan, *The Anatomy of Fashion: Dressing the Body from the Renaissance to Today* (Oxford: Berg, 2009).

Wallis, Patrick, 'Consumption, Retailing, and Medicine in Early-Modern London', *Economic History Review* 61:1 (2008): 26–53.

Walsh, Claire, 'Social Meaning and Social Space in the Shopping Galleries of Early Modern London' *in* John Benson and Laura Ugolini, eds. *A Nation of Shopkeepers: Five Centuries of British Retailing* (London: I. B. Tauris, 2003): pp. 2–79.

Warneke, Sara, 'A Taste for Newfangledness: The Destructive Potential of Novelty in Early Modern England', *The Sixteenth Century Journal* 26:4 (1995): pp. 881–896.

Weatherill, Lorna, *Consumer Behaviour and Material Culture in Britain 1660–1760* (London: Routledge, 1996).

Wear, Andrew, *Knowledge and Practice in English Medicine, 1550–1680* (Cambridge: Cambridge University Press, 2000).

Welch, Evelyn, *Shopping in the Renaissance: Consumer Culture in Italy 1400–1600* (New Haven and London: Yale University Press, 2005).

Whittle, Jane and Griffiths, Emma, *Consumption and Gender in the Early Seventeenth-Century Household* (Oxford: Oxford University Press, 2012).

Wrightson, Keith, '"Sorts of People" in Tudor and Stuart England' *in* Jonathan Barry and Christopher Brooks, eds. *The Middling Sort of People: Culture, Society and Politics in England, 1550–1800* (Basingstoke: Macmillan, 1994): pp. 28–51.

Wrigley, E. A., 'A Simple Model of London's Importance in Changing English Society and Economy, 1650–1750', *Past and Present* 37:1 (1967): pp. 44–70.

Zahedieh, Nuala, *The Capital and the Colonies: London and the Atlantic Economy 1660–1700* (Cambridge: Cambridge University Press, 2010).

Reference works

Cumming, Valerie, *A Visual History of Costume: The Seventeenth Century* (London: B.T. Batsford, 1984).

Cumming, Valerie, Cunnington, C. W. and Cunnington, P. E., *The Dictionary of Fashion History* (Oxford: Berg, 2010).

Cunnington, C. Willett and Cunnington, Phillis E., *Handbook of English Costume in the Seventeenth Century* (London: Faber and Faber, 1972).

Hudson T. P. (ed.), *A History of the County of Sussex: Volume 5, Part I* (Oxford: Oxford University Press, 1997)

Loomes, Brian, *Clockmakers of Britain, 1286–1700* (Ashbourne: Mayfield Books, 2014).

Salzman, L. F. (ed.), *A History of the County of Sussex: Volume 3* (Oxford: Oxford University Press, 1935).

Salzman, L. F. (ed.), *A History of the County of Sussex: Volume 9* (Oxford: Oxford University Press, 1937).

Salzman, L. F. (ed.), *A History of the County of Sussex: Volume 7* (Oxford: Oxford University Press, 1940)

Wright, R. P. (ed.), *The Standard Cyclopedia of Modern Agriculture and Rural Economy* (London: Gresham, 1910).

Unpublished PhD theses

Mee, Susan, 'The Clothing of the Common Sort, 1570 to 1700: A Study Based on Evidence from Probate Accounts and Poor Relief Records', University of Roehampton, 2005.

Online sources

Anglican [https://www.anglican.net/]
British History Online [http://www.british-history.ac.uk/]
Centre for Metropolitan History, Institute of Historical Research [http://www.history.ac.uk/cmh/main]
Clergy of the Church of England Database [http://theclergydatabase.org.uk/]
Dorney History Group [https://www.dorney-history-group.org.uk/]
Fitzwilliam Museum, Cambridge [https://www.fitzmuseum.cam.ac.uk]
History of Parliament Online [http://www.historyofparliamentonline.org/]
HRI Online, University of Sheffield [https://hridigital.shef.ac.uk/hrionline/]
Oxford Dictionary of National Biography [http://www.oxforddnb.com/]
Oxford English Dictionary Online [http://www.oed.com/]
UCSB English Broadside Ballad Archive [https://ebba.english.ucsb.edu/]
V&A Online Journal [http://www.vam.ac.uk/content/journals/research-journal/]
West Sussex Lieutenancy [http://www.westsussexlieutenancy.org.uk/]

Index

Headings in italics indicate a book or journal. Page numbers in italics refer to illustrations and those followed by n. refer to notes with their number.

accessories 87, 127
   men's 124, 185
   women's 135, 140–2, 144, 154
Adam and Eve 23–4
advertising 79–81, 107
Alcock, Francis 125
Allen, Thomas and James (of London) 85, 87
Allen, Thomas (of Petworth) 56–7, 64
Allestree, Richard 11, 17, 29, 46, 145
almanacs 16, 122–3
apprentices 39, 79, 159, 169
aprons 48, 56, 147, 163–4, 186
Apsley, Anthony 14–15
arcades (Exchanges) 76, 77–9, 213 n.29, 213 n.36
The Art of Living in London (Peacham, 1642) 40
Arundel, Sussex 17, 18, 19, 191 n.19
   parish poor 168–70, 187, 233 n.81
Atwood, John 176

ballads 29, 30–1, 41–5, 132–3, 174, 178
bands (collars) 52, 101, *111*, 112
Barber, John 169
Barbon, Nicholas 34–5, 37–8, 73, 107
Barham, David 57
Barker, Henry 159
Barker, Richard 58
Barlow, Edward 173–4, 177–8, 186–7
Bartholomew, Alice 49
beaux 32, 40–1
beggars 158–61, 175, 230 n.28
Bell, Humphrey 63
The Bellman of London (Dekker, 1608) 159–60
Best, William 51, 53, 61, 147
Bishop, John 48, 71–2

bodices 130–1, 140, 148, 150, 171
bodies 130, 147–8, 170, 171, 222 n.5, 233 n.83
Bonnick, Elizabeth 67, 83, 214 n.57
Booker, Joanne 67–8
boots 60, 112–13, 119, 124, 220 n.99
   See also shoes
Braithwaite, Richard 24, 26, 27, 34, 36, 41, 129
breeches 101, 103–4, *105*, 123, 125, 168
   cloth used 48, 51, 52, 61, 112, 172
   gallyslops 159, 230 n.20
   leather 40, 109, 124
   linings 60, 103, 112, 163, 172
   petticoat breeches 101, *102*
   trousers 112
   working clothes 162, 163
Brooke, Christopher 26, 36
Burgess, Dorothy 165
Burrell, Timothy 159
Burt, Alice 49
Burt, John 167, 179, 186
Burt, Walter 124
Busbridge, Thomas 15, 95, 116
buskins 119, 220 n.99
Button, Francis 159

caps 110, *111*, 124
   children 165
   women's 140, *141*
   See also hats
cassocks 51, 101, 110
Catt, William 69–70
Challoner, Elizabeth 146, 149
chapmen 47, 56–7, 63, 64–5
The Character of the Beaux (1696) 40–1, 79
Charman, Mary 53–4

Chichester, Sussex 8, 17, 18, 84, 191 n.19
  businesses 19–21, 48, 198 n.135
  siege of 8, 20
children 6, 114, 130, 144–7
  paupers 159, 168–9, 171
church courts 6, 21, 66–7, 162, 175–7, 228 n.3
  See also court records
Citizen, John 10, 145, 146, 149, 186, 227 n.121
Civil War 10, 20
clergy
  Giles Moore 10, 100
  style of dress 51, 110–11, 113, 185
  William Sheward 16
cloaks 48, 51, 61, 101, *105*, 110
cloth
  homemade 48–9
  linen 56–7, 207 n.58
  theft of 5, 48–9
  woollen 48–9, 50–1, 52–3, 163, 178, 205 n.13, 231 n.41
clothing
  alterations 91, 93
  bequests of 6, 48, 49, 163, 182
  market 5, 205 n.2
  marking 55, 58
  parish provision 168–73, 178
  ready-made 47, 68–71, 184
  repair 51, 60
  seasonal clothing 89, *106*, 107
  second-hand 47, 65–8, 234 n.96
  and social status 1, 23–6, 45–6, 175–6, 184–5
  theft of 5, 50, 56, 58, 62–3, 67–8, 159, 165, 167
  See also men's clothing; women's clothing; working clothes
coats 60, 103–4, *105*, 114, 116, 172
coifs 63, 132, 147, 148, 227 n.116
Coleman, James 70
collars. *See* bands
Coma Berenices or the Hairy Comet (1676) 24–5, 30, 35, 111, 113
The Complete Gentleman (Peacham, 1622) 11, 99
consumption, excessive 2, 26, 34–8, 41, 46
Copper, John 49
coroners' inquests 5, 162–3

cosmetics 34, 81, 135–6
Cotman, Roger 167
cotton industry 57, 71, 74, 76
Coulstocke, Elizabeth 49–50
The Country Wit (Crowne, 1675) 34, 40
countrymen 43–4, 45
countrywomen 44–5, 147, 149
court records 1, 5, 191 n.19
  See also church courts; theft
Courtney, Hercules 21, 61, 112
Coventry, Lady *141*
Cowfold parish records 171–2
Cowper, William 22
Cox, Nancy 4
cravats 95, 103, 104, 116
  steinkirks 32, 104, 107, 132, 150
Crowne, John 34, 40

Dalling, Samuel 69
Deane, Walter 58
Dekker, Thomas 159–60
Delights for Ladies (Plat, 1602) 135, 155
Diggens, Charles 60
Directions for Health (Vaughan, 1626) 28–9
documentary sources 100–1, 129–30, 161
  contemporary literature 23
  coroners' inquests 5–6
  court records 5, 191 n.19
  overseers' accounts 5, 6–7
  probate records 5, 6
doublets 101, *102*, 112
  cloth used 51, 52, 87
  poor people 162, 163, 165
Douglas, Audrey 57
Downright Dick 43, *44*, 45
drawers 69, 101, 103, 130, 168–9, 220 n.99
Duke, William 162
dust gowns 154, 228 n.141
dyeing (of cloth) 49, 50, 72, 165

East India Company 74, 75–6, 96, 120
economic situation 27, 37–8, 41, 157
  power of London 74–5
Egyptians (gypsies) 160, 230 n.30
elderly people 28, 29–30
England's Great Happiness (Houghton, 1677) 37
England's Vanity (1683) 25, 27, 35, 103, 185

The English Gentlewoman (Braithwaite, 1631) 24, 26, 27, 34, 36, 41, 129
Epsom Wells (Shadwell, 1673) 11, 36, 46, 109
Etherege, George 104, 138–9
Evelyn, John 28, 101
Everenden, John 84
Exchanges 76, 77–9, 213 n.29, 213 n.36
Exeter Exchange 213 n.29

fabric. *See* cloth
fairs 47, 55, 61–5, 69, 71, 144
Farnden, James 162
fashion 29–34, 39–45, 184–6, 185
    country 107–9, 138–9
    foreign 27–8, 36, 37–8, 75–6, 103, 107
    London 37–9, 43, 75–6, 96–8
Fenn, Nathaniel 58
Floyd, Joseph 79
fops 31–2, 33, 104
foreign goods 2, 45
    fashion 27–8, 36, 37–8, 75–6, 79, 103, 107
    See also international trade
France
    fashions 37, 75–6, 79, 103, 107, 134, 140
    imports 13, 19, 37, 57, 134, 195 n.84, 207 n.63
    silk industry 75
frocks 69, 119, 162, 220 n.99
Furlonger, Katharine 164–5

Garrard family 7, 8
gentry 40–1, 99–100, 107–9, 129–30, 138–9
Godden, Margaret 164
Godfrey, John 21
'golden age' 41–5
Goldsmith, Thomas 159
gorgets 132, 140, *141*, 149, 223 n.15
Gorman, Mr 85
gowns 48, 130, 147–8
    dust gowns 154, 228 n.141
    Judith Morley's 89–93, 139–42
Grafton, John 177
The Grand Concern (1673) 39–40, 41
Gratwick, Joanne 48
Great Fire of London (1666) 77, 79, 88, 96, 213 n.36
Gresham, James 7, 8–9, 135, 186, 235 n.12

proxy shopping 79, 83, 89–93, 139–42, 182
Gresham, John 7, 8–9
Gresham family 7–9
Grevett, Margaret 175
guilds 20–1
    See also mercers
Gynt family 170–1, 172–3, 233 n.81
gypsies 160, 230 n.30

haberdashers
    itinerant traders 63, 71
    London 77–8, 85, 87
    Sussex 21, 58, 60–2
hairstyles
    men's styles 113, 122
    men's wigs 103–4, 113, 123, 125
    women's styles 135, 142, *143*, *148*, 154
Hale, William 164
Hall, Richard 176–7, 178
Harland, Richard 51–3, 55, 61
Hartshorne, Barbara 12, 14, 150, 154–5
Haslemere, Surrey 9, 182
hats 70, 87, 120, 122, 124, 132
    See also caps
Hawkins, Joan 163
Hayward, Alice 175–6, 177, 178
Heath, John 15, 94–5, 114, 118, 126
Henslowe, Philip 65
Hill, Benjamin 124–5
Hills, Elizabeth 50, 67
Hindle, Steve 6, 171
Holford, James 51, 55, 58, 60, 85, 110
homemade cloth 48–9, 163, 231 n.41
hoods 132, 148
Horsted Keynes, Sussex 9, 10, 58, 60, 147
Houghton, John 37
Hull, Mr 51, 85
Hunter, Michael 12–13
husbandmen 5, 43–4, 157

Indian cotton 57, 71, 74, 76
Ingram, Arthur 107–8, 109
international trade 13, 71, 74–5
    in cloth 57, 71, 74, 76
    France 19, 134, 195 n.84
    Sussex ports 19–20, 21
    See also foreign goods
itinerant traders 5, 47, 55, 63–5, 71, 164

Jackson, John 80
Jacomb, Thomas 80
Jaye family 83, 214 n.58
Jeake, Betty 14, 154–5
Jeake, Elizabeth (née Hartshorne) 11, 12, 13–14, 119, 149–50, 155
　clothing 129–30, 150, 152–5
　travel to London 82, 96–7, 98
Jeake, Samuel (elder) 14, 67, 210 n.125, 217 n.6
Jeake, Samuel (younger) 11–14, 63, 118–19, 194 n.73
　clothing 119–22, 184–5
　status 99–100, 126
　trade 57, 134
　travel to London 82, 83, 84, 95–7, 98
Joab, Elizabeth 67
Jones, Mary 163
Jones, Samuel 116

Key, Anne 68, 210 n.125
Key, Anne. *See* Wightman, Anne (née Key)

labourers 157, *166*, 167
lace 63, 64, 119, 140, 163–5, 220 n.101
The Ladies Calling (Allestree, 1673) 11, 29, 46, 145
Lady Clapham (fashion doll) 132, *133*
Lantern and Candlelight (Dekker, 1608) 160
laundering 56
leather 71
　breeches/linings 40, 60, 103, 163, 172
　See also boots; shoes
Lee, Edward 167
Lemire, Beverly 65
Lewes, Sussex 17, 18, 21–2, 84, 191 n.19
　shops 52, 53, 60–1, 125
Licensing Hawkers and Pedlars, Act for (1696) 65
Lincolnshire 7–8
linen 52, 178
　cloth 56–7, 207 n.58
　household 54–5
　neckwear 132, 148, 163, 164, 186
linen industry 13, 47, 54–7, 72
linings (of breeches) 60, 103, 112, 163, 172
Lintott, Henry 71

Lintott, James 123, 124
Lock, Mercy 175, 176
London 19, 35, 38–41, 73–4, 211 n.5
　fashion 25, 37–9, 43, 75–6, 96–8, 109
　provincial consumers 81–4
　ready-made clothing 68–71
　sartorial codes 40–1, 45–6
　the Season 74, 109
　second-hand clothing 65
　shopping 84–8, 95–7, 183
　shops 76–81, 98
　tailors 90, 93–5, 98
　textile industry 75
　travel to 81, 83–4
　See also proxy shopping
The London Gazette 81
Lord Clapham (fashion doll) *117*

Mackley, Eizabeth 83, 214 n.58
The Man of Mode (Etherege, 1676) 104, 138–9
mantuas 132, *133*, 150–2, 154
Marden, Joan 48–9
marking (identification)
　cloth 49
　clothing 55, 58
Marshall, William 21, 51, 52, 53, 61
Martin, Henry 63
masks 147
Matthew, James 123, 124
May, Edward 15, 196 n.102
　clothing 94–5, 114–18
　status 100, 126, 185
May family 14–15
Mayhew, Francis 129, 144, 222 n.2
Mayhew, Martha 9, 10
　clothing 51, 62, 129–30, 144–9, 156, 186
　education 146
　travel to London 85, 146, 147, 148
mending. *See* repair of clothes
men's clothing 100–7
　country clothing 40–1, 45–6, 99–100, 107–9
　mourning clothes 116
　nightgowns 112, 123–4
　sartorial choices 28–9, 30, 31–2, 126–7
　shopping 4, 190 n.13
　young men 28–9, 31–2, 42
　See also clothing

mercers 15, 20–1, 47, 50, 54, 164
    clothing repair 60
    fashion 75, 76, 79, 107
    London 73, 93–4, 98
    Mercers' Hall 77
    probate records 59, 69
    ready-made clothing 69–70
    second-hand clothing 67, 69
    silk industry 75
    Sussex 21, 50–2, 55, 56–61, 58, 95, 112, 116, 123–4, 184
merchants 7, 78
    Samuel Jeake 12–13, 100
Le Mercure Galant 76
Michelborne, Elizabeth 164–5
Middle Exchange 213 n.29
Middleton, Edmund 21, 61, *62*
Miller, Elizabeth 97, 98, 150, 152, 154
Miller, Thomas 12–13, 83, 96–7
Moore, Giles 9–11, 46, 51, 100
    clothing 68, 110–13, 126, 183–4, 185
    shopping in London 79–80, 84–8, 112
    shopping in Sussex 21, 49, 51–3, 55, 58–63, 112
    travel to London 82, 83, 84, 98
Moore, Susan 10, 61–2, 98, 130, 144
Moore, Thomas 71
More family 9
Morley, John 84
Morley, Judith 7–9, 129, 137–8, 181–3
    clothing 139–44, 155–6
    proxy shopping 89–93, 130
Morley, William 8, 183
Mote, Jonathan 171–2, 234 n.89
mourning clothes 116, 156, 222 n.4
Mutton, Anthony 60

Napper, Edward 70–1
Napper, William 48
Nash, Thomas 95, 116
neckwear, linen 132, 148, 163, 164, 186
New Additions to Youth's Behaviour (1663) 26–7, 34
New Exchange 76, 78–9, 213 n.36
Newland, Thomas 177
nightgowns 112, 123–4, 132
nonconformists 12–13, 96
Norton, George 60
Le Nouveau Mercure Galant 76

Old (Royal) Exchange 76, 77–8, 79
older people 28, 29–30
outerwear 48
    men's styles 101, *102*, 103–7, *110*
    women's styles 130–2, *151*
overseers' accounts 5, 6–7
    parish clothing provision 50, 54, 56, 69–70, 168–73, 178, 187
    sale of goods 66–7, 162–3

Pankhurst, Francis 56
Paris, France 75, 76, 211 n.5
parish poor 157, 167–8
    clothing provision 6–7, 50–1, 56, 66–7, 69–70, 168–73, 178
Parson, Richard 60
pawnbrokers 58, 67
Peacham, Henry 11, 25–6, 40, 73, 99
pedlars 63, 64–5, 184
    See also itinerant traders
Pelham, Sir Thomas 21, 74, 82–3
Pelham family 15, 144
Pelling, Thomas 51, 53, 147
Penfold, John 69
Pepys, Samuel 213 n.36
    clothing 101, 103, 104, 107
    wife's clothing 130, 132, 138, 186
perfume 81, 123, 135
petticoats 90, 130, 140, 150, 231 n.44
    cloth used 48, 147, 163, 165, 186
    decorative 148, 150, 152
    second-hand 162
Pettit, Alice 48, 49
Phillips, John 177
Phillips, Mary 58
Pierce, Mary 64
Plat, Hugh 135, 155
Pollard, Mr 90, 91, 139
poor people 45, 66–7, 157–8
    clothing 5, 161–7, 173–9, 178
    parish poor 167–73
    use of tailors 53–4
    vagrants 158–61
port sales 65, 66
postal services 83, 182
probate records 5, 162
    chapmen 64
    clothing bequests 6, 48, 49, 68, 163, 182
    Giles Moore 10

Judith Morley 182–3
    mercers 56–8, 69, 184
    salesmen 69
property rights, of women 136–8, 191 n.25
prostitutes 33, 34, 40, 136
proxy shopping 76, 88–9, 97, 186
    James Gresham 7, 79, 83, 89–93,
        139–42, 155, 182
    James Wightman 120
    John Heath 114–15
Punishment of Rogues, Vagabonds and
    Sturdy Beggars Act (1598) 158
purchasing 4
Puttock, Katherine 176

rapiers. *See* swords
ready-made clothing 47, 68–71, 184
The Relapse (Vanbrugh, 1696) 31–2
repair of clothes 51, 60
retailers. *See* shops
ribbons 87
    in men's clothing 94, 101, 103, 114–15
    in top knots 223 n.18
    in women's clothing 147, 150, 163–4,
        179
Rigglesford, William 55
Roberts, John 15, 95, 114, 115–16
Roberts, Walter junior 15, 94, 114
Roberts, Walter senior 14–15, 93–5, 114–18
    status 100
rogues 159–60
    See also vagrants
Royal Exchange 76, 77–8, 79
Royalist support 8, 9, 10, 11, 110
rural life 18
    idealised 41–5
russet cloth 48–9, 163
Rye, Sussex 11, 12, 18, 19, 57, 129

sacs 132
salesmen 69
sartorial choices 2, 184–7
    instability of 25, 26–8, 41–3
    men 28–9, 30, 31–2, 126–7
    older people 29–30
    women 29, 30, 31
sartorial codes 40–1, 45–6, 104, 107
Scotch men 55, 63
    See also itinerant traders

Scrase, Richard 113
seamstresses 47, 56, 71, 72, 78, 184
second-hand clothing 47, 65–8, 234 n.96
Selden family 169–70, 233 n.81
servants 43, 62, 138, 145, 159, 162, 177
    clothing 39, 53, 68, 71, 162
Shadwell, Thomas 11, 36, 46, 109
Shepard, Alexandra 175, 176
Sheward, William 16, 17, 100, 124
shirts 55, 56, 101, 163, 168–9
shoemakers 60, 70–1
shoes 112–13, 149, 172–3, 178, 219 n.65
    See also boots
shopping 4, 184
    gender roles 98, 185–6, 190 n.13
    London 84–8, 95–7, 183
    Sussex 55, 57–65, 123, 183–4
shops 205 n.2
    London 76–81, 98, 213 n.29, 213 n.36
    Sussex 20–1, 56–8
    See also haberdashers; mercers; tailors;
        textile industry
shoulder knots 103, 114–15, 120, 122, 126
silk industry 15, 74–5, 120
    painted silk 152, 154, 227 n.132
skirts 140, 148, 150
Slater, Agnes 165
sleeves
    men's styles 103
    women's styles 130, 131, 140, 147–8, 150
Slowman's Fair 67–8
Smith, Jane 162
Smith, Richard 123
smocks 56, 101, 131, 136, 163
Snatt, Stephen 21, 53, 61
snuff boxes 32
social milieu 2, 100, 129
social status 2, 39, 157, 187
    of clothing 1, 23–6, 45–6, 175–6, 184–5
The Spectator 76, 81, 109, 138–9, 185
spinning 47, 49, 50, 54–5, 206 n.41
Spufford, Margaret 5–6, 63, 65, 163
Stacey, John 140
stagecoaches 39, 81–2, 84
Stapley, Anthony 16–17, 125, 196 n.109
Stapley, Richard 16–17, 100–1, 122–5, 185,
    196 n.109
Steele, Joanne 167
steinkirks 32, 104, 107, 132, 150

stockings 32, 58, 110
   home-knitted 49, 50, 147, 226 n.99
   ready-made 69, 90, 114–15, 147, 168–9
   repair 53
   second-hand 67, 68
stolen items. *See* theft
stomachers 130, 140, 147, 150
Stone, Thomas 60, 113
Styles, John 75, 171
suicides 5, 162, 191 n.21
suits
   men's styles 53, 60, 66, 94, 101, 103–4, 107, 114–16, 119, 120–3, 126, 182, 185
   women's styles 60, 85, 130, 147–8
   working clothes 168–9, 170, 172
sumptuary laws 25, 26, 27, 36
Surrey 8, 9
Sussex 3, 17–18, *19*
   market towns 18
   second-hand clothing 65–8
   shopping 55, 57–65, 123, 183–4
   shops 20–1, 56–8
   transport 18–19, 22
   wool industry 47–51, 198 n.135
Swinpane, Edward 85, 87
swords 94–5, 114, 119
   as accessories 126, *127*
   status 107

tailors 47
   London 90, 93–5, 98
   Sussex 51–4, 61
   trade tokens *52*, *62*
   travel to London 84–5
Taverner, Jane 62
Templar, Thomas 78, 79
Terry, Francis 167
textile industry 47, 184, 205 n.2
   cotton 57, 71, 74, 76
   gender roles 49, 54–5, 72
   linen 13, 47, 54–7
   London 75
   silk 74–5, 152, 154, 198 n.135, 227 n.132
   Sussex 20–1, 47–51
   wool 13, 25, 47–51
   See also shops
textiles. *See* cloth

theft
   cloth 5, 48–9
   clothing 5, 50, 56, 58, 62–3, 67–8, 159, 165, 167
   yarn 49–50
   See also court records
Ticehurst, Sussex 14–15, 170–1, 233 n.81
Tidy, Christopher 176
Tiler, Bartholomew 66
tobacco boxes 115
Toleration Act (1689) 13
top knots 29, 31, 132–3, 150, *151*, 154, 223 n.18
'town miss' 33–4
trade. *See* international trade
trade cards 80
trade tokens *52*, *62*
tradesmen, in London 39
trains 150, 152
transport 18–19
   road 22, 82, 83–4, 93
   by water 18–19, 84
travel
   to London 39, 81–4
   in Sussex 18
trousers 112
Turner, Thomas 60
Turnour, Sir Edward 53
Turnpike Act (1749) 81

undergarments
   men's 101, 103, 168–9, 220 n.99
   women's 130
urban life. *See* London

vagrants 158–61, 175, 230 n.28
Vallor, Thomas 57
Vanbrugh, John 31–2
Vaughan, Alice 167
Vaughan, William 28–9
velvet 90, 124, 139–40, 143–4

waistcoats 48, 51, 123, 172
   men's styles 79, 101, 112, 120
   second-hand 162
   women's styles 90–3, 130, 140
Waller, John 70
Wallis, John 125
Wareham, Luke 168–9

washing. *See* laundering
watches 119–20, 124–5, 221 n.106
Waters, Edward 51, 53, 54, 56, 61, 147
    trade tokens *52*
Watts, Mary 1
weavers 47, 48, 49
West, Francis 60
West, Mary 165
whisks 132, 140, *141*, 149, 223 n.15
White, Alexander 84
Wightman, Anne (née Key) 68, 134, 220 n.104
Wightman, James 119–22, 220 n.104
wigs 103–4, 113, 123, 125
    See also hairstyles
Williams, Katherine 9, 135, 186
wills. *See* probate records
women
    dependent status 4, 98, 130, 136–8, 156, 185–6, 191 n.25
    education 146, 150
    'town miss' 33–4
women's clothing *89*, 130–4, *151*
    country clothing 44–6, 138–9, 149
    mourning clothes 156, 222 n.4
    nightgowns 132
    sartorial choices 29, 30, 31
    See also clothing
Wood, John 69
Woodgate, Michael 56, 58, *59*, 69
wool industry 13, 25, 47–51, 72
woollen cloth 48–9, 178
    types of 50–1, 52–3, 163, 205 n.13, 231 n.41
working clothes 161–70, 172, 173–9, 186–7

yarn 49–50, 226 n.99
Young, Katherine 62–3
young men 28–9, 31–2, 42
    See also men

www.ingramcontent.com/pod-product-compliance
Lightning Source LLC
Chambersburg PA
CBHW070022010526
44117CB00011B/1681